Where did that Regiment Go?

Where Did That Regiment Go?

The Lineage of British Infantry and Cavalry Regiments at a Glance

Gerry Murphy

Gerry Murphy was granted a Fellowship by his industry, has written many published papers and has made major contributions to standard scientific text books. He served in the Royal Marines Reserve. He is often called upon by official bodies to verify regimental titles in documents and on monuments. He has made particular study of regimental amalgamations and saw the need to produce a lineage chart. He was born and educated in Liverpool.

First published in 2009 by Spellmount
This edition published in 2016

The Mill, Brimscombe Port
Stroud, Gloucestershire, GL5 2QG
www.thehistorypress.co.uk

British Library Cataloguing in Publication Data.
A catalogue record for this book is available from the British Library.

ISBN 978 0 7509 6850 8

Typesetting and origination by The History Press
Printed and bound in Great Britain by TJ International Ltd

Contents

NINETEENTH CENTURY

TWENTIETH CENTURY

TWENTY-FIRST CENTURY

CAVALRY – HISTORICAL SUMMARY

SEVENTEENTH CENTURY

EIGHTEENTH CENTURY

NINETEENTH CENTURY

TWENTIETH CENTURY

TWENTY-FIRST CENTURY

APPENDICES

Preface

The publication of the Defence White Paper, July 2004 'Delivering Security in a Changing World' by General Jackson, Chief of the General Staff, has changed the face of the British Army. It led to a major reorganisation of infantry regiments with larger regiments and new titles appearing with the innovation of abbreviated titles. Following this upheaval, this book seeks to provide a complete lineage chart of all the amalgamations for both infantry and cavalry regiments.

Many books have been published on the genealogy of army regiments detailing the amalgamations or origins of regiments up to the time of publication. This work is an attempt to draw up a family tree or lineage chart of all regiments but breaking them down into bite-size pages conveniently set out by divisions, which has been the British Army's formal classification of infantry regiments, such as Guards, Scottish, Queen's, King's, Prince of Wales's and Light Divisions. Regiments not allocated to a division such as the Parachute Regiment and Royal Gurkha Rifles are naturally included.

The cavalry lineage chart is classified in order of precedence. Although the Royal Marines are administered by the Admiralty and are not part of the army structure, a lineage chart has been included to complete the picture of the armed forces. Such charts are long overdue to military enthusiasts, military and even family historical societies, who wish to trace their descendant's regiments, and for other reference sources such as military museums and libraries.

Lineage charts may be available 'in house' within military organisations, but there is a dearth of such charts in the public domain. Tracing regimental amalgamations can be a tedious process. Confucius had it right when he said that one picture is worth a thousand words. The lineage charts attempt to give a visual overview of the amalgamations since Lord Edward Cardwell made the first and significant mergers reducing 110 infantry regiments to sixty-nine two-battalion regiments in 1881. The last 125 years of infantry amalgamations have been comprehensively charted and described. The cavalry regimental organisation was untouched by Cardwell, but 1815 has been taken as a suitable starting point from which all amalgamations of the cavalry have been charted. Additional cavalry charts are included dedicated to the origin of the Life Guards and also the difficult transition from Regiments of Horse to Dragoon Guards and Dragoons.

All of the 110 infantry and thirty-three cavalry regiments on the regular establishment are listed on a 'where are they now?' basis. The infantry and cavalry records of events have been separated as each had its own history and milestones. The infantry history details major conflicts in general chronological order. The cavalry record concentrates mainly on cavalry roles. The transformation of Household Cavalry, Regiments of Horse, Horse Grenadiers, Horse Grenadier Guards, Dragoon Guards, Light Dragoons, Hussars, Lancers and finally the mechanisation into tank regiments are all summarised.

This record of the founding of the British Army from Charles II's bodyguard of a few troops of Mounted and Foot Guards in 1660 through 350 years of transition can only be a brief synopsis to complement the lineage charts. It is not within the scope of this publication to comprehensively detail major battles, conflicts or even regimental history.

Long-established names such as the Light Infantry, Rangers, Dragoons or even Horse Grenadier Guards have long since disappeared from regimental titles so the reintroduction of the title Light Dragoons in 1992 was welcome. The new regimental titles of 'the Duke of Lancaster's Regiment' and 'The Rifles', together with their abbreviated titles of LANCS and RIFLES, have shown that innovation is still around. Territorial titles such as 'the Royal Regiment of Scotland', 'the Yorkshire Regiment', 'the Mercian Regiment' and 'the Royal Welsh Regiment' will now take their place alongside existing regiments in the army's ongoing history into the new millennium.

The Strategic Defence and Security Reviews, 2010–15, were modeled on traditional enemies, but now included world terrorist groups such as Al Qaeda. The government reduced the army to 82,000 Regulars and the Territorial Army (TA) now rebranded as Army Reserve at 30,000. In July 2012, the Defence Secretary specified units being taken out of the order of battle. Such was the concern about cyber attacks and cyber warfare that the Defence Secretary announced a new regiment to be raised as cyber troops effective April 2015 and it was designated 77th Brigade and called Chindits. For 350 years the army had recruited those who met traditional man/women specifications for its regiments, but this changed as cyber skills were required and not normal military skills. In 2014–15, a new enemy appeared, ISIS (Islamic State of Iraq and Syria) or ISIL (Iraqi State of Iraq and the Levant), desecrating holy sites both Muslim and Christian in Iraq and Syria. The government also lifted gender restrictions on front-line combat troops.

The British Army will include for the very first time an Army Reserve in its ARMY 2020 order of battle.

Most conflicts have been briefly summarised for the seventeenth, eighteenth and nineteenth centuries with the corresponding Battle Honours in the appendices. It is fully acknowledged that such a cavalry charge through the history of the British Army cannot hope to be comprehensive; but is hoped that it is of value as a quick reference and that it helps to place the regiments in context. The twentieth- and twenty-first century conflicts have not been summarised as the world wars and recent conflicts are thoroughly covered by other publications and it would of course be absurd to attempt to summarise a world war in a few pages. It is after all the *lineage* of the regiments that we are concerned with here, and those named regiments we know were all created in earlier centuries.

The appendices detail the stewardship, infantry roles and weapons, regimental identification, organisation, rank and insignia, Battle Honours and Colours and other related data of interest.

Acknowledgements

On my first visit to the battlefield at Waterloo, I stood at the monument to the 27th (Inniskilling) Regiment of Foot and paid my respects. The wreath that was placed there was from the Royal Irish Rangers. I was rather taken aback, as they were unknown to me and certainly did not figure in my memory of regiments present at the battle. I later found out from David Ascoli's book that the 27th were an antecedent regiment of the Royal Irish Rangers.

During the research for this book, Ascoli's *Companion to the British Army 1660–1983* was my bible, together with Christopher Chant's *Handbook of British Regiments*. Henry and Catherine Adams's *History of the British Regular Army 1660–1990* is specifically formatted to encompass all regiments raised, disbanded and re-formed in chronological order, which was of particular interest as it includes the many high numbered regiments raised for major eighteenth-century conflicts. I therefore wish to thank Catherine Adams for allowing me to include the references to all the high-numbered regiments during the Seven Years' War, American War of Independence and the French Napoleonic Wars and also details of the dual-numbered regiments (with Marines) during the War of Jenkins's Ear. For reference to uniforms Barthorp and Lawson's publications were of great value.

The regimental headquarters and museums of particular regiments have been most co-operative and I am indebted to Major John Spiers of RHQ RIFLES, Peninsular Barracks Winchester, for putting me right on the formation of the five battalions of The Rifles. Major Colin Gray, RHQ Royal Irish Regiment was most gracious in reading through my draft relating to the Royal Irish Regiment and its relationship to the Ulster Defence Regiment through its formation and disbandment during the Troubles in Northern Ireland and I am grateful for his effort and comments.

Gavin Edgerley-Harris, museum archivist of the Gurkha Museum, Peninsula Barracks, Winchester, cross-checked my data on the arrival of the Gurkhas and furnished me with useful information about the Nepalese War. Thanks to WO1 W.D.G. Mott OBE, Welsh Guards Garrison Sergeant Major, London District, Horse Guards, Whitehall, who was most accommodating about my enquiries regarding the higher Warrant Officer ranks and the duties of a GSM. The Duke of Lancaster's RHQ clarified the amalgamation of the three incoming battalions. The regimental museums were most co-operative in answering my initial queries on amalgamations, especially the Royal Welsh Regiment.

I would like to thank the non-military websites that allowed me to use material: Greenwich Maritime Museum Website, Maritime Art, 'Capture of Havana', Douglas McCarthy, Picture Library Manager, National Maritime Museum Greenwich; British Empire, Stephen Luscombe, www.britishempire.co.uk. Finally a special thanks to my daughter Rachel for her support, suggestions and proofreading, and my grandson Corin Betts for help with indexing this new edition.

This fully updated new edition includes cavalry, regimental and infantry battalion losses, resulting from the recommendations of the Strategic Defence and Security Reviews of 2010–15. The Yorkshire Regiment were unique in deciding to renumber their remaining battalions when the 2nd Battalion was removed from the order of battle. I wish to thank the RHQ, Yorkshire Regiment, who clarified the exchanging of both Queen's and Regimental Colours, and explained Honorary Colours.

I would not have been able to proceed with my addition of the forty-six regimental badges when I listed all regiments in the British Army in their order of precedence together with listing Army Reserve without the help of the MoD copyright department, who allowed us access to high-resolution regimental cap badges, and my son-in-law Paul Doherty, a software engineer who resides in Canada. In addition, Paul's contribution to defining the job specification for cyber troops was most valuable.

Infantry – Historical Summary

SEVENTEENTH CENTURY

The Origins of the British Regular Army

At the time of the Restoration of Charles II in 1660, Parliament had requested the disbandment of the army of the Commonwealth. Charles was only allowed to keep his bodyguard, which consisted of two household horse regiments and his personal guard, His Majesty's Regiment of Guards that had served him in exile and whose loyalty was considered beyond question. His Majesty's Regiment was raised abroad in 1656 as the Royal Regiment of Guards and was augmented by the newly raised King's Own Regiment of Foot Guards. These two guard regiments would merge in 1665 into the Royal Regiment of Foot Guards (later 1st Foot Guards). For security in the country, Parliament put their confidence in the militia under lord-lieutenants, who were controlled by Parliament and had no intention of raising an army. There were, however, some English and Scottish troops serving with the Dutch Republic and a number of Parliamentary troops still left in France at Dunkirk. These troops were not involved in the disbandment. Also free from disbandment were the ex-soldiers who were manning the many forts as garrison troops. The garrison troops soon came into the pay of Charles.

General Monck was a major figure in setting the tone for the monarchy in the vacuum that existed after the last of the Cromwells. Monck took five weeks to march from Coldstream (Scotland) to London in support of the King's restoration. He was the first to greet Charles at Dover on his arrival from Holland on 25 May 1660 and accompanied him into London. To Charles's bodyguard was soon added General Monck's Regiment of Foot. General Monck was made Commander-in-Chief and would become Duke of Albemarle, a name associated with the regiment until his death in 1670, when it became the Coldstream Regiment of Foot Guards (later 2nd Foot Guards).

The disbandment of the army was practically complete by December 1660, except for the King's bodyguard who were last in line for disbandment. A fortuitous riot by the Fifth Monarchists not only halted the final disbandment, but as the security of the monarch was visibly threatened, he was allowed to keep his own bodyguard. General Monck's Regiment of Foot ceremoniously lay down their arms on Tower Hill on St Valentine's Day 1661, according to Parliament's request, but immediately took them up again as the Lord General's Regiment of Foot in support of the King. The Coldstream (Guards) would be the longest serving regiment with unbroken service in the British Army and would continue to wear Monck's Order of the Garter as a cap badge.

The Scots Regiment of Foot Guards was raised as a Royal Regiment on the Scottish establishment. This regiment had had a previous existence as Argyll's Regiment and was re-formed by Charles in 1661. For the defence of his kingdom, Charles brought back from France 'Le Regiment de Douglas' (a regiment raised by Sir John Hepburn in Scotland for service to the French Crown under a warrant issued by Charles I in 1633). Parliament objected and the regiment returned to France. Le Regiment de Douglas (the former Le Regiment d'Hebron) would finally return to the British establishment in 1673, but would maintain its seniority as the Royal Regiment or 1st Foot, as it was raised in 1633. This regiment would be dubbed 'Pontius Pilates' bodyguard' for its longevity.

Charles II married the Portuguese princess Catherine of Braganza, and through this marriage gained Bombay and the port of Tangier. Not being allowed to raise an army in England, Charles could at least raise regiments to garrison his new acquisitions out of his own pocket, which pleased Parliament. The Tangier Horse and the 1st Tangier Regiment (later 2nd Foot) were raised for service in 1661. In Bombay, where trading was established, the first troops were raised to guard the factories and compounds as early as 1652. The East India Company had formalised the raising of a regiment of Europeans as the Bombay Regiment, to garrison Bombay, which was leased by Charles to the Company.

Mindful of Parliament's concerns about raising an army in peacetime, in October 1664 Charles directed that 'twelve hundred land soldiers be forthwith raised to be distributed into his Majesty's Fleets, prepared for sea service'. The regiment was raised as the Duke of York and Albany's Maritime Regiment of Foot and was also known as the Admiral's Regiment to distinguish it from the existing Lord General's Regiment.

The regiment's members were first referred to as Marines at the start of the Third Dutch War, when de Ruyter surprised the British fleet at anchor in Sole Bay. Captain Taylor, Lord Arlington's secretary, wrote, 'those Marines of whom I have oft so wrote you, behaved themselves stoutly'. This regiment was the forerunner of the Royal Marines, today still under the control of the Admiralty. By designating this force as a sea service, Charles had trumped any possible Parliamentary objections. In 1665 Charles recalled from duties in the Dutch Republic a further regiment, the Holland Regiment (later 3rd Foot or Buffs).

The Dutch were a threat to Britain in world trade. They had an ever-expanding navy and the wars were mainly maritime affairs. Parliament had no difficulty agreeing funds for the navy's upkeep. In the Second Dutch War (1665–67) the Duke of York (the future James II) defeated the Dutch fleet off Lowestoft, but the war was not a success for Charles, who had to suffer the indignity of having his flagship towed down the Medway by de Ruyter. At the Treaty of Breda, Britain retained New Amsterdam. The Third Dutch War (1672–74) saw Britain in alliance with France. Charles had to raise his army to 18,000 (twenty-two regiments) to support Louis XIV and at its conclusion in 1674, New Amsterdam became British by the Treaty of Westminster. It was renamed New York and the army was disbanded again.

The growing influence of the House of Orange in Holland and public opinion in Britain in support of William Prince of Orange, who had married Mary, daughter of the Duke of York, forced Charles into an alliance with the Dutch against France and its Catholic monarchy in 1676. This was a cause in which Parliament raised no objections and gave support for the raising of twenty additional regiments. The war did not materialise and again Parliament requested disbandment to pre-1665 levels. In Tangier in 1680, the Moors were restless and the Guards regiments were sent out, together with half a battalion of the Royal Regiment. The situation in Tangier deteriorated and Charles was forced to raise a 2nd Tangier (later 4th Foot) Regiment for its defence. The troops returned home and by the time Charles died in 1685 his standing regular army consisted of the household troops of Life Guards and Royal Regiment of Horse (later Horse Guards), two dragoon regiments, three foot guard regiments and four regiments of foot under the names of their colonels, but later ranked 1st to 4th Foot.

The Monmouth Rebellion

When James II came to the throne a rebellion broke out, led by the Duke of Monmouth who landed at Lyme Regis and raised his standard in the West Country. Monmouth, the illegitimate son of Charles II, was previously Commander-in-Chief of the army and had commanded troops in the Third Dutch War, during which young Marlborough was present. Monmouth was considered a serious Protestant successor to the throne and a real threat to his Catholic uncle. The militia raised 4,000 troops against Monmouth's 1,500, but the Devonshire Militia thought better of it and retired to Exeter. James put down the rebellion with the Tangier veterans at Sedgemoor in July 1685 (where Marlborough was second in command). The country was now in turmoil at this insurrection and it was acknowledged that the militia were unreliable. James took advantage of the rebellion and withdrew further regiments from service in Holland and put two regiments onto the permanent establishment (later the 5th and 6th Regiments of Foot). These two regiments were raised for service in Holland in 1674 against the French and soon returned to Holland until 1688.

The Train of Artillery was raised in 1685 and with it the 7th Regiment of Foot to guard it (see Appendix 2) and were called fusileers, because of their short musket, similar to the French fusil. In 1685 James raised a substantial number of regiments. Six regiments of horse, two dragoons and eight foot regiments were raised, named after their colonels and later ranked 8th Foot to 15th Foot. In Ireland some regiments were formed from existing garrison troops, of which the Earl of Granard's Regiment (later 18th Foot) survived.

At Hounslow in July 1687, James assembled his army, all formed up, dressed and numbered in a direct confrontation with Parliament, and he requested funds for its upkeep. Parliament offered James half the money he has asked for, and to add insult to injury, directed it to be spent on the discredited militia and not the army. James dissolved Parliament and the feud continued. James appointed Catholics to senior positions in the army, leading to the resignation of some colonels. New regiments were raised in 1688 of which the 16th and 17th Foot survived on the establishment. The order of precedence of regiments (and their numbers) was beginning to be introduced.

William III and the Declaration of Rights

When William of Orange arrived (by invitation) at Brixham Torbay, in November 1688, the 4th Foot was the first regiment to welcome him and forever were allowed to wear the lion of England as their cap badge. Deserted by everyone, including his soldiers, James left for France, having disbanded most of his army. The Marines Regiment, now titled Prince George of Denmark's Regiment of Foot (James's son-in-law), was also disbanded because it stayed loyal to James. William brought with him some Dutch troops, notably 2,000 Dutch Guards, known as the 'Third Foot Guards'. These are not to be confused with the Scots Regiment of Foot Guards (later Third Guards) who came onto the British establishment in 1689. Two new regiments were raised in support of the new king, the 19th and 20th Foot.

William III was presented with the Declaration of Rights in 1689, which accepted William and Mary as rulers and the bloodless 'Glorious Revolution' was complete. The Declaration set out the relationship between King, Parliament and the army. 'The raising and keeping of a standing army within the kingdom in time of peace, unless it is with the consent of Parliament, is against the law.' The constitutional principle was now established: Parliament was in control of the army. With the possibility of a rebellion in Ireland and Scotland by James's sympathisers (the Jacobites) and war with France, Parliament decided against the disbandment of the army. When troops were sent to Flanders, the Royal Scots mutinied at Tilbury, as they were still sympathetic to James and had Dutch officers forced upon them, but they soon surrendered. The government was unsure how to punish the offenders. The Articles of War applied to troops during hostilities and the civil law could not apply, as troops officially did not exist in times of peace. This dilemma was overcome by the introduction of the Mutiny Act of 3 April 1689, which applied at any time. This disciplinary code governed all servicemen and was to be reviewed every year.

Ireland and the War of the League of Augsburg

Assisted by France, James made a bid for a return to power; in March 1689 he landed in Ireland and captured Dublin. The Protestants in the north sided with William and sought refuge in Londonderry and Enniskillen. The rest of Ireland was under the control of the Jacobites, and the Protestants in Derry remained under siege from December 1689 for over 100 days until merchant ships arrived in July and broke the blockade to bring food. Three regiments were raised by Protestants for the defence of Enniskillen, two cavalry regiments and the Inniskillings, later the 27th Foot.

William decided to fight James in Ireland and invaded with his army, defeating him at the Battle of the Boyne on 1 July 1690 (Julian calendar, 12 Gregorian). Limerick defied William until finally falling in October 1691. William returned to England and called on the Scottish Highland chiefs to take an oath of allegiance; the MacDonalds did so but not within the allotted time (partly due to the dithering of officials) and were massacred at Glencoe. By concentrating his efforts in Ireland, William neglected the threat from Europe. The War of the League of Augsburg or War of the Grand Alliance (1689–97) was an attempt to block French ascendancy. The alliance consisted of Britain, the Netherlands, and Russia. Louis XIV of France had re-formed his army and expanded his borders, annexing Alsace and the rich wine province of Orange, to which the Dutch held hereditary titles. In 1685 Louis had revoked the Edict of Nantes (1598), which gave Protestants religious freedom, and began persecuting them.

Further British regiments were raised for the war; four cavalry and ten foot regiments came onto the establishment, the largest intake of regiments to date. The Scots Regiment of Foot Guards came onto the English establishment as the Scotch Guards (later Scots Guards) and maintained its precedence from 1661. The 21st Foot was also raised but kept its 1678 precedence (raised in Scotland in 1678). The new Scottish regiments to appear later became the 21st, 25th and 26th Foot. The English regiments later ranked as the 22nd, 24th, 28th, 29th and 30th Foot. The single Welsh regiment later ranked as the 23rd Foot, and the Irish regiment later ranked as the 27th Foot, previously raised in Enniskillen. The 19th Foot, later 1st Yorkshire and the Green Howards, raised a second battalion in 1689 quite quickly after being formed.

The French beat an Anglo-Dutch fleet at Beachy Head, but a threatened invasion from a French army of 30,000 was prevented by the destruction of the French fleet at the Battle of Cap de la Hogue by Admiral Russell. The British under William were defeated at Landen in 1693, the French under the Duke of Luxemburg inflicting heavy casualties. William, who had previously made John Churchill Duke of Marlborough, would not allow him to lead his troops, as he had misgivings about the Duke's previous allegiance to James. Unlike General Monck who changed loyalties and was accepted and honoured by Charles, William not only overlooked his best and experienced general, but even sent him to the Tower in 1692 for covert correspondence with James.

The town of Namur was lost only to be retaken in 1695 (William's only major victory on foreign soil). The Earl of Granard's Regiment was the first regiment to be awarded an honour in battle. For their bravery at the siege of Namur, William III awarded the regiment the 'Royal' title. The Earl of Granard's Regiment was re-designated the Royal Regiment of Ireland, which became the 18th (the Royal Irish Foot in 1751). It was awarded the badge of the Lion of Nassau and the motto *Virtutis Namurcencis Praemium*. To pay for the war, William borrowed £1 million and introduced the first National Debt with the Bank of England to manage it. With the Treaty of Ryswick in 1697 the war with France came to an end and Louis XIV accepted William as ruler of Britain, promising not to give support to James II or his descendants. With the nation bankrupt and the army unpaid, Parliament once again demanded the disbandment of the army. William threatened to abdicate and Parliament compromised on a token army of 7,000 with an additional 12,000 for the security of Ireland. The 28th Foot was disbanded in 1697, the 29th Foot in 1698 and the 30th Foot in 1699. Rather than disband ten regiments altogether, William decided to reduce them to cadres.

EIGHTEENTH CENTURY

Marlborough's Battles: The War of the Spanish Succession

At his death in 1700 Charles II of Spain left his throne to the grandson of King Louis XIV of France, Philip of Anjou. Since Philip was also in the line of succession for the French throne, there was fear in Europe that Spain and France would be united under one monarch, thus destroying the delicate balance of power. The resultant War of the Spanish Succession (1702–15) was fought predominately in the Low Countries, Spain and the Rhine area, and at sea in the Atlantic, West Indies and the Mediterranean.

When King William III died in 1702, his sister-in-law Anne was not recognised as Queen by the French, who supported the claim of James II's son, James Stuart, known as the Old Pretender. The 28th Foot and 29th Foot were re-formed. Six Marine regiments were raised in 1702 together with a further six regiments for sea service. Colonel Field in *Britain's Sea Soldiers* defines the distinction between Marines and regiments for sea service: 'These last regiments were to serve not as Marines but as land forces to make descents or otherwise as occasion requires.'

Marines	Foot
1st Saunderson's	30th 1714
2nd Villiers's	31st 1714
3rd Fox's	32nd 1714
4th Shannon's	disbanded 1713
5th Holt's	disbanded 1713
6th Mordaunt's	disbanded 1713

Sea Service Regiments	Foot
7th Huntingdon's	33rd 1715
8th Lucas's	34th 1715
9th Donegal's (raised 1701)	35th 1715
10th Caulfield's (raised 1701)	36th 1715
11th Meredith's	37th 1715
12th Coote's	39th 1715

Saunderson's, Villiers's and Fox's Marine regiments became the 30th, 31st and 32nd Foot in 1714, and the remaining three Marine regiments disbanded. The Seymour Regiment, already established (later to be the 4th Foot), was converted to a Marines regiment as the Queen's Regiment of Marines or Seymour's Marines and they also returned to the line in 1715. The infantry regiments raised for sea service were converted to line regiments as shown. The 38th Regiment of Foot was also raised, but in 1705. Such was the need for soldiers on board ships that a number of existing army line regiments went to sea as Marines under their colonels's names but later would be numbered 6th Foot, 19th Foot and 20th Foot.

John Churchill, who was a Protestant, had served successfully as a soldier under James II, but transferred his allegiance to William of Orange. His relationship deteriorated with William and especially Mary and he spent some time in the Tower. He was reconciled with the court and finally given command of the army when war seemed likely; William wanted no more repeats of Landen. Churchill as Captain General of the British Army was sent to the continent where he had successes in 1702 at Kaiserworth, Venloo and Liège and he was created Duke of Marlborough. Marlborough's greatest victories were yet to come, at Blenheim (1704), Ramillies (1705), Oudenarde (1709), and Malplaquet (1709).

To fight at Blenheim, Marlborough had to march his army 250 miles from Holland to Germany and his army all arrived, fresh. Marlborough was known to look after his men and had previously laid out stores, food and even campsites en route in advance. Such was his attention to detail, there was even a change of boots at Heidelberg. The Battle of Blenheim established Marlborough as one of the great commanders of history. On his famous march, surrounded by enemies, Marlborough had to resort to subterfuge and outwitted his enemies to arrive at the Danube where he was joined by Eugene. All the crossings were under French control and Marlborough forced a crossing at Donauworth, which was a battle in itself. Marlborough and Prince Eugene of Savoy were up against the French and Bavarians under Marshals Tallard and the Elector of Bavaria. The French never expected Marlborough to attack, as they had 56,000 troops in the fortified towns of Lutzingen, Oberglau, and Blenheim. Marlborough had a collection of British, Austrian, Hanoverians, Danes and Brandenburghers totalling 52,000. The front was 4 miles long with Blenheim next to the Danube.

- Very early in the morning, Marlborough advanced his army to his start line, surprised the French and disturbed their breakfast. In the morning the French opened up a fierce bombardment, countered by the Allies but then they do nothing else and had a late breakfast. Marlborough waits for Eugene to get into position and arranges for pontoon and bridges to allow crossing of the river Nebel, at his centre.
- At lunchtime, Eugene is in position and Marlborough orders General Cutts's division to attack the French fortified in Blenheim. A ferocious battle ensues and the French stay put but are densely packed. Eugene assaults Lutzingen but has no success.

- British reinforcements are brought up, but fail to take Blenheim. The Marquis de Clerambault, the defender, is alarmed at the British assault and draws many battalions from the French centre into Blenheim which is now packed tight like sardines. Tallard is furious. Marlborough seizes on the French tactical blunder and informs Cutts to back off his battalions and just contain the French in Blenheim with a fire fight. The situation around Blenheim deteriorates for the French, when the elite of the French Royal Household cavalry are routed when charged by the small British force of dragoons. The dragoons put the Gendarmerie to flight.
- In the centre at Oberglau, the Allied attack fails and they have to withdraw against the Irish Brigade serving under the French. (Irish regiments sympathetic to the Stuarts were serving in the French army.) Marlborough supports the assault with infantry and artillery which manage to cross the Nebel. General Charles (Marlborough's brother) Churchill now advances in the centre, crosses the Nebel successfully but is soon attacked and in trouble. Eugene comes to their rescue with his cavalry and restores the situation.
- The flanks are now subdued and Marlborough orders a major attack on the centre led by his cavalry followed by his infantry. The assault stalls with the French cavalry counter attacks and a major struggle continues until the cavalry are driven off. It was touch and go and those extra battalions wasted by the Marquis de Clerambault which where bottled up in Blenheim could have won the day for the French. It is no surprise that the Marquis drowned himself on his horse in the Danube in shame. The French put up a fierce resistance and the Blenheim defenders finally gave up when the British set fire to thatched cottages and smoked them out. Colours and standards galore were captured and the French losses were enormous, 34,000 killed or wounded. The Allies lost 13,000.

Gibraltar

At the Treaty of Utrecht 1713, Gibraltar became British, having been captured by 2,300 English and Dutch Marines in 1704. The Marines were descendents from the 1,200 raised by Charles II. The Spanish Army and French Marines tried to recapture it, but resupply and finally reinforcements from the guards and infantry kept it in British hands. In 1827 the Royal Marines would be granted the distinction of a Battle Honour 'Gibraltar' (see Appendix 5). On 1 May 1707 the Act of Union of England and Scotland was enacted and Great Britain was established. The British Army replaced the English and Scottish Armies. Scottish regiments such as the Scots Regiment of Foot Guards, the Royal Regiment (1st Foot), the Royal Scots Dragoons (2nd Dragoons) and Scots Fusiliers (21st Foot) now joined the British establishment with their order of precedence intact.

Jacobite Rebellion 1715

The Jacobites rebelled again in 1715 in support of the Old Pretender (James Edward Stuart, son of James II). This was stimulated by the death of Queen Anne without a direct heir, resentment over the Act of Union and the beginning of the Hanoverian succession of King George I. Quite a number of cavalry regiments were raised and the army was mobilised. The Jacobite support originated in Scotland and Northumberland, but the Jacobites made for Catholic Lancashire and entered Preston. The 26th Foot and Hanoverians arrived as reinforcements for the King's army and the Jacobites were surrounded at the bridge over the River Ribble; after two days they surrendered. After the battle at Sheriffmuir, the rebellion soon petered out and James left for France. The Artillery Regiment became the Royal Artillery in 1716.

The prospect of Britain and France allied in a war against Spain meant that James left France for refuge in Spain. When Spain annexed Sardinia and Sicily the War of the Quadruple Alliance (1718–20) started. The alliance consisted of Austria, France, the Netherlands and Britain. In 1717 the 40th Foot was raised in Nova Scotia, Canada, where they stayed for forty-four years on garrison duty, and the 41st Foot in 1719 from Invalids at Chelsea. James now had Spanish support and a threatened Spanish invasion of Scotland was prevented only by a mighty storm. Those Spanish troops that did arrive were defeated alongside the Highlanders at Glensheil in 1719 and the rebellion finally ended.

War of Jenkins's Ear

During a series of incidents involving Spanish abuse of British seamen in the Americas, a Spanish coastguard sliced off the ear of Captain Robert Jenkins, or so the captain claimed. Jenkins was brought before the House of Commons to exhibit his ear in a bottle. As Winston Churchill wrote, 'whether it was in fact his own ear, or whether he had lost it in a seaport brawl remains uncertain, but the power of this shrivelled object was immense.' (Thompson p.14) It led to Britain declaring war on Spain and France.

The War of Jenkins's Ear (1739–41) became part of a bigger conflict, the War of the Austrian Succession (1740–48). It originated when the King of Austria, Charles VI, died leaving his daughter Maria Theresa as heir. Bavaria and Prussia objected and the ruler of Bavaria proclaimed himself Emperor of Austria. Prussia annexed Silesia (part of Austria). France and Spain supported the German states, but Britain sided with Austria and supported Maria Theresa and went to war.

Six regiments were raised as Marines in 1739 with a further four in 1740 and were later dual-numbered as foot regiments with 1st to 10th Marines dual-numbered 44th to 53rd Regiments of Foot in 1741. The infantry of the line regiments raised were 54th Foot to 60th Foot in 1741 with the 61st, 62nd, 63rd and 64th raised by 1743. After hostilities the Marines went to the Admiralty and the renumbering of remaining line regiments took place in 1748, officially ratified in 1751 (Adams, p.43).

Date	Regiment		Renumber	Date
			54th to 43rd (Monmouthshire)	1751
		Dual Number		
1739	1st Marines (Wolfe)	44th Foot	55th to 44th (East Essex)	1751
1739	2nd Marines (Robinson)	45th Foot	56th to 45th (1st Nottinghamshire)	1751
1739	3rd Marines (Lowther)	46th Foot	57th to 46th (South Devonshire)	1751
1739	4th Marines (Tyrrell)	47th Foot	58th to 47th (Lancashire)	1751
1739	5th Marines (Douglas)	48th Foot	59th to 48th (Northamptonshire)	1751
			60th Disbanded	
			61st Disbanded	
			62nd Dsbanded	
1739	6th Marines (Morton)	49th Foot	63rd to 49th (Hertfordshire)	1751
			64th Disbanded	
1740	7th Marines (Cornwallis)	50th Foot	Disbanded	1748
1740	8th Marines (Hammer)	51st Foot	Disbanded	1748
1740	9th Marines (Powlett)	52nd Foot	Disbanded	1748
1740	10th Marines (Jefferies)	53rd Foot	Disbanded	1748

The 43rd or Black Watch was raised in 1739 in the Highlands from independent companies to police the area, being the first light troops and the oldest highland regiment. In 1749 it was renumbered as the 42nd Foot.

The British, Austrian and Hanoverians as the 'Pragmatic Army' under the Earl of Stair were on the River Main to influence the election of the Archbishop of Mainz, an elector in the Holy Roman Empire and therefore important in the affairs of Hanover. The French, under Marshal de Noailles, were shadowing the Allies and controlled the Rhine. The Allies camped at Aschaffenburg where King George II joined them. The French built bridges and crossed the Main near Dettingen and blocked the Allied advance. The Pragmatic Army had to turn about and in a night march full of confusion, found that the French had crossed the Main again behind them at Aschaffenburg. The Allies had the River Main on their left, the French in front (near Dettingen) and to the rear, and the impassable Spessart Forest to their right.

Trapped, the Allies had to fight their way out and to make matters worse the French began to bombard them from across the river. The Duc de Grammont was ordered to only occupy Dettingen, but this he failed to do and with an excess of zeal, he attacked the Allies. Marshal de Noailles was furious. The initial French assault by guards was repulsed. The French cavalry attack had some success against the Allied infantry but the 3rd Dragoons in their counter-attack first lost their guidon and then regained it.

Cavalry and infantry attacks continued and as the battle drew to a close the British infantry stood their ground well and were more decisive in their fire. The French evacuated Dettingen and the battle was over. George II was the last British monarch to lead his troops into battle. Twenty-six regiments hold Dettingen as a Battle Honour.

At Fontenoy in 1745, the King's second son, Prince William Duke of Cumberland and Captain General, led the British forces against the German-born French Marshal Saxe who intended to capture Tournai in Flanders (Belgium). Cumberland was beaten at Fontenoy, but to his credit he retired in good order and prevented a rout. The infantry had stubbornly resisted the French attack with infantry and cavalry but could not resist the fresh Irish Brigade in French service. At Fontenoy over 1,200 British were killed and Marshal Saxe occupied Tournai. The British Army withdrew to Britain to put down the Jacobites again.

Jacobite Rebellion 1745

The Jacobites aided by Scottish Highlanders under the Young Pretender, Charles Edward Stuart, son of the Old Pretender and known as Bonnie Prince Charlie, invaded England and caused mayhem in the country and panic in London. The army in Belgium was recalled and another fifteen foot regiments were raised, numbered 65th to 79th. The Highlanderss had successes at Prestonpans and Falkirk against the British Army. At Prestonpans, the indignity of the British Army under General Cope being chased by the Highlanderss gave rise to the rhyme 'Hey Johnny Cope are ye waulking yet?' At Falkirk they fared little better under General Hawley.

The Jacobites were finally defeated by Cumberland who used his artillery to great effect at Culloden Moor in 1746. The Scots were routed by the cavalry and Cumberland showed no mercy to the fugitives who were run down and slaughtered, giving rise to his nickname 'Butcher Cumberland'. While in Scotland, Cumberland destroyed the last vestiges of the Jacobite uprisings. The hastily raised 65th to 79th Foot were disbanded after Culloden. Returning to Belgium, Cumberland came up again against Saxe at Lauffield in 1747 and again lost the encounter. In 1747/8, the 60th, 61st, 62nd and 64th were disbanded. The Marines went onto the Admiralty establishment in 1747 and the foot regiments numbered 44th to 49th remained vacant. Finally the Treaty of Aix-la-Chapelle ended the war in 1748, with Maria Theresa confirmed on the Austrian throne. In 1751 the 54th to 59th and the 63rd Foot were consecutively renumbered 44th Foot to 49th Foot.

The Regimental System: The Reforms of George II

George II, concerned at the diversity of uniforms, titles and the autocracy of the colonels who commanded his regiments, decided to introduce reforms. Influenced by Frederick of Prussia and having been present at Oudenarde and Dettingen, he felt himself qualified for the task. Marlborough had previously argued for a rationalisation of uniforms. Formally, both cavalry and infantry regiments were named after their colonel, each regiment adopting its own Colours, uniforms, and badges. When the colonel changed, so did the name of the regiment and also the uniform, which was confusing. The first clothing regulation appeared in 1742 and was enforced by a number of Royal Warrants.

1st Royal Warrant 1743

Infantry regiments were to have two Colours or flags: the King's Colour and the Regimental Colour of the facings of the regiment; blue for a Royal Regiment, other regiments using Colours such as buff, green, or white. Guards regiments were excluded as they had a sovereign's colour and a regimental colour for each battalion. The artillery was also excluded as they carried no Colour – their guns represented the Colours. Household cavalry regiments carried standards and dragoons carried guidons.

2nd Royal Warrant 1747

Uniforms were to be standard, except for facings, and regimental numbers replaced colonels's names. The regimental numbers were to be consecutive and ranked from the oldest regiment and were to be put on the Colours.

3rd Royal Warrant 1751

This warrant was really to clarify the second warrant; no colonel was to put his arms, crest, device or livery on any part of the appointments of his regiment. There were, however, some exceptions: thirteen regiments were permitted to wear Royal devices and ancient badges on their caps, Colours and appointments. These were the seven Royal Regiments of the 1st, 2nd, 4th, 7th, 18th, 21st, and 23rd and the 'Six Old Corps' of the 3rd, 5th, 6th, 8th, 27th, and 41st. The schedule of the 1751 Warrant listed the ancient badges traditionally carried on the Colours of the 'Six Old Corps' as opposed to those regiments who carried their colonel's crest on their Colours. The ancient badges were as follows:

1st Royal Regiment (later Royal Scots): King's cipher, within a circle of St Andrew and a crown over it.
2nd the Queen's Royal Regiment: crowned garter, encircling Queen's cipher on a red background.
3rd Regiment of Foot or 'The Buffs': green dragon.
4th the King's Own Royal Regiment: crowned garter, encircling the King's cipher on a red background.
5th Regiment of Foot (later Northumberland): St George killing the Dragon.
6th Regiment of Foot (later 1st Warwickshire): an antelope.
7th Royal Fusiliers: crowned garter encircling a rose.
8th (The King's Regiment): crowned garter encircling the White Horse of Hanover on a red background.

18th Royal Irish Regiment: crowned harp on a blue background.
21st Royal North British Fusiliers (later Royal Scots Fusiliers): crowned thistle within a circle of St Andrew.
23rd Royal Welch Fusiliers: Prince of Wales's feathers out of a coronet.
27th the Inniskilling Regiment of Foot: castle with three turrets, St George's Colours flying and all on a blue background, the name Inniskilling over it.
41st the Invalids (later the Welsh): crowned garter, encircling a rose and thistle.
These badges would continue with most of the regiments.

Both the infantry and the cavalry were redesignated with their new numbers based on seniority. The cavalry have retained those numbers up to the present time, but for a few regiments, while the infantry have completely lost regimental numbers in the recent amalgamations. The Army List of 1754 defined the regiment by its ranking number and dropped the colonel's name. Old habits died hard, however, with the regiments holding on to their colonels's names until 1760.

The Seven Years' War

The Seven Years' War (1756–63) pitted Britain, Prussia and Hanover against France, Austria, Poland, Russia, Sweden, Saxony, and later Spain. It amounted to a fight for the existence of Prussia. Overseas, it was a duel in which France and Britain fought for supremacy in Canada, the West Indies and India. Initially twelve regiments were re-formed, the 50th to 62nd Foot. The 50th and 51st Foot were lost in battle in Canada in 1756 and the regiments were renumbered consecutively 50th to 60th Foot (Adams, p.45). The 61st Foot was re-formed in 1756 with the 62nd to 64th Foot in 1757. Established regiments, such as the 3rd, 4th, 8th, 11th, 12th, 19th, 20th, 23rd, 24th, 31st, 32nd, 33rd, 34th, 36th and 37th, were allowed to form second battalions. These new second battalions were converted to new regiments in 1758 and numbered 61st Foot to 75th Foot. As a result of this formation of regiments, the newly re-formed 61st to 64th Foot were renumbered 76th to 79th Foot.

Date Re-formed	Foot		Foot and Established Title	Date
1754	50th	Lost in battle		
1754	51st	Lost in battle		
1755	52nd	Renumbered	50th (West Kent)	1756
1755	53rd	Renumbered	51st (2nd Yorkshire WR)	1756
1755	54th	Renumbered	52nd (Oxfordshire)	1756
1755	55th	Renumbered	53rd (Shropshire)	1756
1755	56th	Renumbered	54th (Norfolk)	1756

1755	57th	Renumbered	55th (Westmorland)	1756
1755	58th	Renumbered	56th (West Essex)	1756
1755	59th	Renumbered	57th (West Middlesex)	1756
1755	60th	Renumbered	58th (Rutlandshire)	1756
1755	61st	Renumbered	59th (2nd Nottingham)	1756
1755	62nd	Renumbered	60th (King's Royal Rifle Corps)	1756
			61st	1756
			62nd	1757
			63rd	1757
			64th	1757

In 1758 second battalions of established regiments were re-formed into new foot regiments e.g. the 2nd Battalion 3rd Foot became the 61st Foot and in 1782 were called the South Gloucestershire.

Raised	Foot		
1756	2/3rd	Re-formed as	61st (South Gloucestershire)
1756	2/4th	Re-formed as	62nd (Wiltshire)
1756	2/8th	Re-formed as	63rd (West Suffolk)
1756	2/11th	Re-formed as	64th (2nd Staffordshire)
1756	2/12th	Re-formed as	65th (2nd Yorkshire NR)
1756	2/19th	Re-formed as	66th (Berkshire)
1756	2/20th	Re-formed as	67th (South Hampshire)
1756	2/23rd	Re-formed as	68th (Durham)
1756	2/24th	Re-formed as	69th (South Lincolnshire)
1756	2/31st	Re-formed as	70th (Surrey)
1756	2/32nd	Re-formed as	71st Disbanded 1763
1756	2/33rd	Re-formed as	72nd Disbanded 1763
1756	2/34th	Re-formed as	73rd Disbanded 1763
1756	2/36th	Re-formed as	74th Disbanded 1763
1756	2/37th	Re-formed as	75th Disbanded 1763
1756	61st	Renumbered	76th Disbanded 1763
1757	62nd	Renumbered	77th Disbanded 1763
1757	63rd	Renumbered	78th Disbanded 1767
1757	64th	Renumbered	79th Disbanded 1763

The regiments 71st to 79th Foot have no connection with modern regiments. The 80th to 84th Foot were raised in 1758, the 85th to 91st in 1759, the 92nd to 97th in 1760, the 98th and 119th in 1761 and the 120th to 124th in 1762 (Adams, p.50). The army was brought up to a strength of 85,000. The British Army was fighting on four fronts in the Seven Years' War, in India, Canada, the West Indies and Europe. The conflict can be broken down into the following five sectors.

War in India 1756–63

British interest in India began with the formation of the East India Company in 1600 through a charter from Queen Elizabeth with the first trading stations (known as factories) at Surat, north of Bombay, in 1608 and Fort St George, Madras, in 1639. Bombay was gained by Charles II on his marriage, but was leased to the Company by Charles in 1668 because he could not afford to maintain his dowry. Bombay replaced Surat as the Company's headquarters. Stations at Hooghly in Calcutta (Bengal) and Fort St David south of Madras were set up in 1690. The Company had its own army, augmented by British troops when required. The Dutch, Portuguese and French all had their commercial interests in India. The Mogul Empire was breaking up and in the chaos that followed France took Madras and was preparing to extend its influence. Robert Clive, who joined the East India Company as a clerk at 19, volunteered as a soldier and took charge of the Company's army of 200 Europeans and 300 sepoys and seized the city of Arcot in 1751. Arcot was soon under siege and Clive, when just 26 and with only eighty Europeans and 120 sepoys left, withstood the fifty-day siege and repelled a dawn attack by 10,000 soldiers. 12,000 rounds were fired in less than an hour by the efficient teams loading and unloading in the rear and passing the muskets to the soldiers on the ramparts.

Arcot was an eighteenth-century mixture of Rorke's Drift and the Alamo and helped to establish British interest in the Carnatic (Madras area). Clive returned to England but went back to India in 1756 as Governor and marched into Calcutta, which was under siege and defeated the Nawab of Bengal (Suraj-ud-Dowlah) who had destroyed British trading stations and supposedly suffocated 120 of his prisoners in the 'Black Hole of Calcutta', although the supposed atrocity has since been questioned by some historians as propaganda.

With 1,000 Europeans and 2,000 sepoys Clive went on to defeat the Nawab's 50,000-strong army at Plassey in 1757. Although the 1st Madras Europeans received the first Indian Battle Honour for Arcot, they were an East India Company regiment (which became the Royal Dublin Fusiliers after the Indian Mutiny). It was the Dorset Regiment that was allowed to have '*Primus in Indis*' on their Battle Honour for Plassey.

The newly promoted Lieutenant Colonel Eyre Coote took over command of British forces in Madras after Clive left for England. His army of Indian troops and the 84th Foot defeated the French and their Indian allies at Wandiwash in 1760, and when they took refuge in Pondicherry they surrendered after a four-month siege. The captured French General de Lally was allowed to return to France to defend himself for losing India. The French – looking for a scapegoat – found him guilty and condemned him to death and he was executed in 1766; in Voltaire's phrase '*pour encourager les autres*' (Keegan and Wheatcroft, p.179). The British were in control of Bengal and now had influence in the south-east and the French were losing their influence on the subcontinent. The British Army captured Pondicherry twice more, in 1778 and 1793. Pondicherry had been given back to the French after the Treaty of Paris (1763) and again in 1814 after the French Revolutionary Wars.

Canada: The French and Indian War (1754–63)

During this period France had a strong foothold in North America and Canada in particular, and was competing with Britain's many trading stations and forts. If any problems arose the British could call on support from the colonists in America, and indeed, hostilities were taking place between France and Britain before the major conflict of the Seven Years' War.

Major General Braddock was sent out from Virginia in 1755 with 2,000 British and colonists to assault Fort Duquesne. They were ambushed by the French and Indian allies, losing over 400 killed including Braddock. A general uprising against the British occurred, with many settlers being killed. The British captured Nova Scotia and deported the French to New Orleans. In 1757 the French General Montcalm arrived in Canada and took Fort Ticonderoga as his base and fortified it with 5,700 troops, including 3,000 French regulars.

Ticonderoga is a triangular wedge of land at the Y junction of the rivers into Lake Champlain and quite a formidable obstacle. Commander-in-Chief Canada, Major General James Abercromby, with 15,000 men including 6,000 regulars, failed to capture the fort in 1758, losing twenty-three officers and 570 men in the process. This was the time when the British realised that their formal tactics did not work in close ground such as forests. Major Rogers (an American national) was requested to devise tactics more suitable to the conditions. Rogers's brief was to harass the French and their allies using field craft. He raised his 'Rogers's Rangers', the first units to use what would later become light infantry tactics, and could possibly be termed the first commando.

The new Commander-in-Chief North America, Lieutenant General Amherst, arrived from England with three brigades of 11,600 men, including Brigadier Wolfe, with the aim of capturing the French Fort of Louisbourg. Wolfe's brigade took the high ground and after a bombardment, the French surrendered in July 1758, losing 240 guns and 5,600 prisoners. The French were now isolated and their position critical. The British success encouraged Prime Minister Pitt to extend operations with an attack on Quebec.

For Wolfe's success at Louisburg, he was made acting Major General and he was given his own command to take Quebec. Admiral Saunders and Wolfe travelled the 400-mile length of the St Lawrence waterway in thirty-five ships of the line with eleven additional warships and 10,000 soldiers. The first assault failed when Wolfe attacked the French fortifications. Wolfe's army climbed the precipitous Heights of

Abraham and lined up at dawn in a long line. The French were taken by surprise and attacked the British who rose from the ground to meet them. Both Wolfe and the French commander, Montcalm, were killed.

Special mention at the Battle of Quebec goes to the sailor James Cooke, who would become one of the greatest explorers of his or any age. When the invading fleet went down the St Lawrence River, a tricky passage indeed, the invading fleet were fortunate to have this very competent young man on HMS *Pembroke* to navigate as pilot. Cooke drew up an Admiralty chart for the St Lawrence River. He would later explore the southern hemisphere on his voyage of discovery circumnavigating New Zealand and charting Australia. Without his detailed knowledge of the river, the surprise attack would not have been possible. After Quebec the French attempted to retake it, but failed. Fort Ticonderoga finally fell to Amherst, Montreal fell to the British in 1760. French influence in North America was at an end.

The West Indies 1756–63

In the Caribbean, Guadeloupe was the first island to be captured, in 1759, and the 63rd Foot (West Suffolk and later the Manchester Regiment) gained its first Battle Honour and adopted the French fleur-de-lys as its cap badge. Guadeloupe Day would be commemorated by the regiment and its successors. In 1762 Admiral Rodney and the Earl of Albemarle with seventeen regiments and 11,000 men captured Martinique, a rich sugar island and France's last possession in the West Indies, together with St Lucia, Grenada, St Vincent and Dominica. When Spain joined the war in 1762, Cuba was invaded, with Havana withstanding a two-month siege before falling to the 4th, 34th and 40th Foot. Three members of the Keppel family were at Havana. George, as Earl Albemarle and Commander-in-Chief Augustus, as Commodore and 2 I/C Navy and the Honourable William who stormed Moro Castle where the 56th Foot (later the Essex regiment) would be awarded a Battle Honour. Disease was rife in Havana: 694 died from disease while only 342 were killed in action.

War in Europe (1756–63)

The Duke of Cumberland, hero and monster of Culloden, was put in command of the Allied forces of Britain, Hanover and Brunswick and was sent to defend Hanover with 50,000 men. He lost the Battle of Hastenbeck (26 July 1757) to the French and had to evacuate the city under the terms of the Convention of Klosterzeveyen. Cumberland was disgraced, and his father King George II declared that he had 'ruined his country and his army'.

George II now put the Allied armies in Europe under the assured leadership of Duke Ferdinand of Brunswick. The Battle of Minden was unique in that the British infantry successfully charged 10,000 French cavalry, a very rare event. The brigades of Major General Waldegrave – 23rd, 37th and 12th Foot together with Major General Kingsley's 25th, 51st, and 20th Foot and Hanoverians – defended against three waves of cavalry when only in line, not square. Wearing roses on Minden Day is part of the annual celebration by the regiments who took part or their successors. Indeed, the officers of the Royal Regiment of Fusiliers, following the Lancashire Fusiliers tradition, go so far as to consume a rose floating in a traditional silver goblet of wine (champagne of course) in recognition of the wild roses growing in abundance at Minden.

Infantry successes were also achieved at Warburg (1760), Belle Isle (1761), and Wilhelmstahl (1762). Such were the successes at Quebec, Guadeloupe, Minden, Lagos and Quiberon Bay (where Admiral Hawke destroyed the French invasion fleet off the coast of France) that 1759 was declared 'The year of Victories' or *Annus Mirabilis*, and a happy Walpole said, 'one is forced to ask every morning what victory there is for fear of missing one.'

Pontiac's Conspiracy (1763–64)

Although French influence had gone from Canada, Indian resistance continued with the ever-advancing settlers wanting territory. Matters were made worse by a Governor general whose policy towards the Indians was far from satisfactory. Chief of the Ottawa Indians from 1755, Pontiac, resenting the continued colonisation, formed a federation and united the tribes against the British. In 1763 they rose and captured eight out of the twelve British forts west of the Niagara, killing 2,000 settlers. General Amherst had no answer to the insurrection, apart from giving the Canadian Indians attacking Fort Pitt blankets infected with smallpox. Eventually a peace treaty was agreed with firm boundaries established. At the Treaty of Paris in February 1763, Canada was ceded to Britain who would now be custodians of North America, India and the West Indies, although Pondicherry was to be handed back to the French.

The new regiments above 71st Foot were all disbanded in 1763. The 78th Foot was abroad in 1763 and finally disbanded in 1767 (Adams, p.50).

India: Campaigns against the Nawab of Bengal and Rohilla (First and Second) Wars

Although the French political influence in India had disappeared after the Seven Years' War, the French military were still advising and holding cities. Campaigns in India continued with Sir Hector Munro's defeat of Mir Kasim – the deposed Nawab of Bengal – in 1764 at Buxar. The defeat of the Nawab's Allied armies strengthened Britain's influence in East India.

Colonel Champion led a force from the Bengal East India Company and defeated the Mahrattas at Bareilly in 1774 in support of the loyal Nawab of Oudh. Lord Cornwallis put down a rebellion in Rohilcund in 1794 in the First and Second Rohilla War.

India: The Mysore Wars

The First Mysore War (1766–69) revolved around Hyder Ali, a Muslim who had seized the Hindu state of Mysore and came to the attention of the Presidency in Bombay. They were becoming concerned about the expansion of Mysore under Ali with the influence of the French, who were training Ali's army. The East India Company joined forces with the Nizam of Hyderabad to defeat Ali's army, but Ali soon gave up and peace was arranged.

A severe famine raged through Bengal in 1769/70 killing thousands and bankrupting the East India Company. The Regulating Act of 1773 transformed the private East India Company into a British administrative agency with the first British Governor General, Warren Hastings, appointed from London to administer Bengal. The East India Company continued to appoint a director and his staff to manage its commercial interests.

Hyder Ali was defeated in the Second Mysore War (1780–84) at Sholinghur by Sir Eyre Coote's force, even though it was heavily outnumbered. At the port of Mangalore, 1,800 British and Indian troops were besieged by 69,000 troops belonging to Tippoo Sultan, son of Hyder Ali. The siege lasted from 9 May 1783 to 30 January 1784 and in the end the British had to surrender. Further reverses took place and it took the peace between France and Britain to end the war with the Treaty of Mangalore.

In the Third Mysore War (1790–92) Lord Cornwallis laid siege to the impregnable fortress at Nundy Droog. Tippoo Sultan had to cede part of his territory. During the Fourth Mysore War (1799) Lieutenant General Stuart with his Bombay army invaded Mysore from the Malabar Coast and had a success at Seedaseer, while Lieutenant General Harris invaded from the Madras area with the newly arrived Colonel Wellesley and his 33rd Foot. Having picked up reinforcements from the Nizam of Hyderabad, Harris and Wellesley now had 20,000 troops and moved onto Malavelly where they defeated Tippoo's army, who retreated into Seringapatam.

Tippoo finally met his demise at his last stand as 'Tiger of Mysore' at Seringapatam when it was stormed by Wellesley's troops in 1799. The state of Mysore was split between the Nizam of Hyderabad and the Company. By the end of the Mysore Wars, Britain had extended its influence inland and controlled the bottom tip of India.

The American War of Independence

After the Seven Years' War, Britain was a significant world power, but massively in debt. Parliament decided to introduce a series of taxes and duties, and for them to apply to the colonists in America as to native Britons. Britain considered that the colonists should contribute towards the cost of the upkeep of the army and navy that defended them. The Stamp Act of 1765 – a tax on documents and newspapers – was rejected by the colonists who took exception to this with the eminently reasonable objection: 'No Taxation without Representation'. The Act was duly repealed on 18 March 1766.

In 1767 Parliament introduced another revenue act and ordered the colonists to pay duty on imported tea and other products. Ugly scenes followed in Boston in 1770, when British troops were goaded by colonists, resulting in loss of control and the killing of five colonists.

In 1773, some colonists dressed as Mohawk Indians showed their displeasure at British regulations by opening and finally throwing 340 bales of tea from the ships of the East India Company into Boston harbour, hence the 'Boston Tea Party'. The colonists refused all demands to pay for the loss of the tea and the port was closed. The colonists were also aggravated when the British put restrictions on their expansion westwards, which disturbed Indian homelands. The Stamp Act problem had brought down the government and the situation in America was causing concern. The colonists were boycotting British goods. The colonists's reaction to all this intervention was to introduce the First Continental Congress, held at Philadelphia on 5 September 1774. Its first motion repealed all recent British legislation. Britain thought the Congress was an illegal administration and many, including the King, thought it would lead to war.

In April 1775, British troops from Charlestown under Colonel Smith were sent to Concord to seize hidden military stores in the hands of the rebel colonists. Paul Revere (who was at the Boston Tea Party) made his famous ride from Charlestown to Lexington, to warn the militia. At Lexington, the first casualties occurred when the advance guard of the British troops encountered militia who ran off after the initial firing of shots. At Concord, the militia – who were made of sterner stuff – stood their ground, the order to fire was given mistakenly and a fire fight took place. The British withdrew and were harassed all the way back to Charlestown until a British brigade under Colonel Lord Percy came to their rescue. The British casualties were seventy-three dead and 200 wounded out of 700. The American War of Independence (1775–83) had started.

Britain sent out Sir William Howe who brought with him two divisional commanders, Major General Burgoyne and Major General Clinton. The militia descended on Boston and dug in above Charlestown, half a mile away from Boston across Boston harbour. Behind Charlestown are the heights of Bunker Hill and Breeds Hill and both were fortified by 10,000 militia. General Gage – the Loyalist British Military Governor of Massachusetts and effectively Commander-in-Chief – wanted to shift them, although he had only 4,000 troops. In addition to his two brigades, he had two battalions of Marines. On 17 June 1775 the British attacked across the river, supported by the Royal Navy. After two assaults the colonists were finally chased off by the 1st Marines and 47th Foot. The Battle of Bunker Hill saw 226 British killed and 828 wounded (Thompson, p.22).

The Second Continental Congress at Philadelphia in June 1775 appointed George Washington as Commander-in-Chief of the new Continental Army. General Washington sent 2,000 troops under General Benedict Arnold in September 1775 to capture Montreal and Quebec with the view to rallying French Canadians to his cause, but was unsuccessful. Montreal was captured and Quebec was under siege from the beginning of December. Quebec held firm against assault, but was iced-in and relief came with the thaw. Captain Douglas, of the *Isis* in England, was told to get relief to Quebec at all costs before they starved, and that the fate of Canada was in his hands. He did exactly that, ploughing his ship through nearly 200 miles of ice field in the Gulf of St Lawrence. It took him three weeks to batter his way through, and finally arrived at dawn on 6 May (Hibbert, p.95).

The Montreal garrison now withdrew and Washington's efforts in Canada ended. In September 1775, Gage was replaced by Sir William Howe. General Clinton travelled south to meet reinforcements from Britain. Boston was blockaded and when it became untenable the British evacuated it in March 1776 and sailed for Halifax, Nova Scotia. Lord Cornwallis brought reinforcements from Britain, which arrived in April and May 1776 at Charleston, South Carolina, with Commodore Sir Peter Parker attempting a sea and land operation. Parker bombarded the fortifications protecting the harbour in June, but his ships could not get in close enough and General Clinton's proposed attack was abandoned. The local Loyalists were defeated at Widow Moore's Creek and expected local support evaporated, putting an end to the campaign in the south.

The representatives of the thirteen original colonies signed the Declaration of Independence in Philadelphia in July/August 1776. New York was soon occupied by the colonists and General Howe was determined to recapture it. With Clinton's reinforcements, Howe had 20,000 men and he attacked Long Island in August and then Manhattan Island, where Washington withdrew to Harlem Heights. The British entered New York to a welcoming crowd. Howe pushed Washington onto White Plains where there was a major engagement, and then Washington withdrew to North Castle. Washington, followed by Cornwallis, was forced to withdraw to the Delaware River for winter. Washington seized the initiative, when he famously crossed the Delaware to achieve a victory at the Battle of Trenton on 26 December 1776. When Barack Obama was inaugurated as President of the United States on 20 January 2009, in his speech he quoted words from Thomas Paine's essay *The Crisis*, which Washington ordered to be read out to inspire his troops before the crossing. 'Let it be told to the future world that in the depth of winter, when nothing but hope and virtue could survive, that the city and the country, alarmed at one common danger, came forth to meet it.'

Howe sent Lord Cornwallis and 5,000 troops to the well-defended position at Trenton, but Washington had slipped away and outflanked Cornwallis by attacking and destroying the small force left behind at Princeton. Washington withdrew again when Cornwallis's main force arrived. General Washington now had his second victory. His reputation was rising and the colonists felt they could drive the British out, especially if they could get help from the French who were approached by John Adams and were beginning to show interest and give supporting arms.

The Secretary of State for the American colonies was Lord George Germain, who as Sackville and cavalry commander disgraced himself at Minden. In the intervening years he had managed to work off the shame and disgrace of Minden and was back in a position of influence. The future of America was in his hands and his chain of command, communications and strategy in the colony were failing.

The British plan was to isolate the New England states with Burgoyne to head down the Hudson River to Albany and meet up with Howe's column coming up from New York via West Point. Howe and Burgoyne's strategies were not co-ordinated, with dire results. Burgoyne marched from Canada to Lake Champlain in June, aiming to reach Albany. No major towns were on Burgoyne's route, only forts and wilderness. Burgoyne arrived at Fort Ticonderoga in July and was determined to chase out General St Clair. Burgoyne had with him loyal American regiments. Guns were sited on surrounding high ground, against everyone's advice and the bombardment forced out the Americans. Burgoyne moved south, building roads for the army through the forests. In August he sent a detachment of Brunswickers and loyal Americans to raid a supply depot at Bennington but they were defeated. Burgoyne continued south and met the American Generals Gates and Arnold outside Saratoga at Bemis Heights.

At Freeman's Farm on 19 September, Burgoyne, under heavy fire, dispatched the colonists, but could not follow up and take Bemis Heights, a stronghold of 6,000 men. The army rested and sent messages about their plight and waited for news of relief from Howe, which never came. A second battle occurred on 7 October, more ferocious this time with Brigadier Fraser being killed. Burgoyne withdrew to Saratoga and was eventually surrounded. With no relief, his force severely reduced, his supply line cut at Ticonderoga and Gates further reinforced, Burgoyne surrendered on 17 October 1777. News of Saratoga stunned Parliament and the country, but new regiments were raised, with major cities raising battalions in a manner very much like the 'Pals' battalions of 1914.

While Burgoyne was heading for the Hudson River, Howe decided to invade Pennsylvania and capture the seat of government at Philadelphia. He took his army by sea in July 1777, arriving at Chesapeake in Maryland in August after a dreadful voyage. Washington decided to make his defence of Philadelphia at Brandywine, but was defeated by Howe and had to withdraw his army again and Howe entered the city. Howe then made camp at Germantown near Philadelphia, where he stayed over winter. Washington made an unsuccessful attack on Germantown in October and withdrew to Valley Forge for the winter, where he experienced severe bad weather. At Valley Forge the Americans had the services of Major General Steuben, a Prussian volunteer who trained the Continental Army and got it into shape. Howe resigned on 4 February 1778 to be replaced by General Clinton, with Cornwallis as second in command. The French – influenced by John Adams as negotiator – signed a treaty with the colonists on 6 February 1778 and the British strategy now changed. France, still reeling after the loss of Canada and India, supported the Americans and declared war on Britain in June 1778.

Britain decided that more reinforcements were to be sent out, but major land operations were to be curtailed, New York would be the base of operations, the Royal Navy was to harass the coastline and activities in the south – especially Georgia – were to recommence. The French would be engaged in the Caribbean. Clinton and his whole army moved out of Philadelphia in June 1778 making for New York with a baggage train 12 miles long. The Americans caught up with the tail of the column at Monmouth's Courthouse and General Lee made a half-hearted attack, only for Washington to come up and rally his men.

The British decided to sail on to New York with Admiral Lord Howe. The French Navy joined the Americans and tried to capture Newport, Rhode Island, but failed. Troops from New York were sent in November to St Lucia to stop the French, but the French captured St Vincent and Grenada. An expedition to the south under Archibald Campbell with 3,500 men landed in Georgia and met up with Major General Prevost from East Florida to capture Savana. A civil government was resurrected in Georgia, but the expected local loyalist support did not materialise. Spain now entered the war on the side of the Americans.

A new front was opened when Clinton sailed from New York on Boxing Day 1779 with over 8,000 men and ninety ships to invade South Carolina, his target being Charleston. A dreadful storm caused havoc and nine transports were lost. At Charleston the Americans surrendered after a one-month siege on 12 May 1780, returning South Carolina to British control. Clinton issued proclamations and granted pardons, requesting oaths of allegiance to gain local support. He left with half his army for New York on 8 June, leaving Cornwallis in charge of the south.

Cornwallis garrisoned Charleston and split his force for different tasks. He took troops to Camden and General Gates decided to attack him but failed, even though he outnumbered Cornwallis four to one. Gates was replaced by Nathanael Greene. Cornwallis decided to invade North Carolina. He left Camden in September and marched through North Carolina to Charlotte. A small force of loyalists were sent out to King's Mountain, but were defeated and there was no local support.

Cornwallis decided to return again to Winnsboro, South Carolina – about 60 miles away – for a rest and repair. He wanted to know Clinton's intentions and when Major General Leslie would be arriving with his reinforcements. Cornwallis left Winnsboro in early January and continued his march north, linking up with General Leslie and his 2,400 troops. His weary army gradually diminished as he left troops to guard his route.

In contrast Greene's army was expanding as he passed each town, followed by Cornwallis. Outnumbered by Greene, Cornwallis still managed to defeat him at Guildford Courthouse in March 1781. Cornwallis's army – now 1,435 strong – was dreadfully short of supplies and was forced to march on into Virginia; by April Cornwallis had reached the coast at Wilmington. In May he marched on to Petersburg near Chesapeake, where he found much needed reinforcement. General Benedict Arnold had changed sides and had replaced General Philips. Cornwallis's 4,500 men were further reinforced with 1,700 from Clinton.

Cornwallis received conflicting instructions from Clinton about building a base for the Royal Navy in Chesapeake and he heard grim news about advancing French and American troops. He took his small army of 6,000 men to Yorktown in August and started to fortify it. Yorktown was ideal for resupply by the Royal Navy and possible evacuation. The French fleet under Admiral de Grasse had arrived with 3,000 French regulars and twenty-nine ships. Admiral Graves RN was still in New York, which eliminated any support for Cornwallis who was now isolated against Washington, Lafayette and Rochambeau's force from Newport; he was outnumbered more than two to one. A bombardment of Yorktown commenced on 9 October 1781; Cornwallis surrendered on the 19th. The shock brought down the government in Britain and with it the will to continue. Lord George Germain and Sir Henry Clinton were replaced.

A slow withdrawal from British outposts took place, starting with Savana in July 1782. A treaty was agreed with the colonists in November 1782. British troops withdrew from Charleston in December 1782 and finally New York in November 1783. The Royal Navy beat the French at the Battle of the Saints in April 1782, ensuring British supremacy in the Caribbean. While Britain's attention was distracted, the Spanish had a rerun at Gibraltar and lost again. Under siege by land, but resupplied by Admiral Rodney, General Elliot kept the Spanish out from April 1781 until February 1783, even when the French joined in.

The Treaty of Paris (Versailles) in 1783 formally recognised American independence. A number of loyal American colonist regiments were put on the British establishment after the loss of the colony, but were disbanded after a few years. Loyalists either stayed, coming to terms with the colonists, moved to Canada, or even returned to Britain. During the long struggle the 71st to 105th Foot were raised only to be disbanded, with the exception of the 73rd and 78th Foot (Adams, p.51). Raised in 1777 and 1778 as Highland regiments, the 73rd and 78th Foot were renumbered 71st and 72nd Foot in 1786 and remained on the establishment to the present time.

Territorial Titles

In July 1782, a Royal Warrant decreed that numbered regiments could take a county title, which might possibly be used as a major recruiting area. For example, the 16th Foot became the 16th (Buckinghamshire) Foot and the 47th Foot became the 47th (Lancashire) Foot. Those regiments who were reluctant to make the change were given an arbitrary title. Some regiments already had a recognised name in addition to the regimental number. The 1st (The Royal Scots Regiment) kept its title as did many other regiments with recognised names such as the Queen's Own Royal Regiment of Foot. Some regiments opted for the same county name, so there had to be something to differentiate them:

9th (East Norfolk) Foot	54th (West Norfolk) Foot
6th (1st Warwickshire) Foot	24th (2nd Warwickshire) Foot
12th (East Suffolk) Foot	63rd (West Suffolk) Foot

13th (1st Somersetshire) Foot	40th (2nd Somersetshire) Foot
19th (1st Yorkshire North Riding) Foot	65th (2nd Yorkshire North Riding) Foot
33rd (1st Yorkshire West Riding) Foot	51st (2nd Yorkshire West Riding) Foot
38th (1st Staffordshire) Foot	64th (2nd Staffordshire) Foot
45th (1st Nottinghamshire) Foot	59th (2nd Nottinghamshire) Foot

India: Maratha and Gurkha Wars

The Maratha States extended across central India with five main rulers and assorted princes and warlords. Two of the rulers, the most senior Peshwa of Poona, who ruled Hyderabad, and the Gaikwar of Baroda, were friendly to the British. The area was constantly in chaos. The First Maratha War (1779–82) was solely an East India Company conflict. The First Maratha War (1803–05) for the British Army (Second Maratha War for the EIC) started when Holkar the Rajah of Indore defeated the Peshwa. The Peshwa had to seek British support and Major General Wellesley restored the Peshwa in his capital at Poona. The three Maratha rulers, the Rajah Holkar at Indore, the Rajah Scindia of Gwalior and Rajah of Berar at Nagpore, formed a Maratha Confederacy against the British.

The Governor General ordered General Lord Lake to invade from the north, with Wellesley from the south-west. The first Maratha fort to be under siege was Ahmedugger in August 1803 and was held by French-led Scindia forces with Arab mercenaries. This walled city was a formidable task for Wellesley, with the very narrow entrance under heavy fire. After the first unsuccessful attempt to storm the heavily guarded gate failed with heavy casualties, Colin Campbell – a lieutenant in the 78th Highlanders – decided upon a different approach to the problem. He scaled the difficult ground and the wall and proceeded to climb through the window at the side of the entrance into the fort. With supporting soldiers he fought his way through to open the gate from the inside (Holmes, p.73).

At the Battle of Assaye (23 September), Wellesley completely outflanked the Scindia's force under European officers. Wellesley located a hidden ford across the river Kaitna and took the enemy from the rear. The enemy were in confusion having to turn their front. Wellesley's army of 4,500 with the 78th Foot and 74th Foot reinforcing his flanks were vastly outnumbered, facing 40,000. The battle was successful, but it was a costly victory with over 1,500 killed, wounded or missing. Wellesley's army was now supported by Colonel Stevenson's wing and they succeeded against the combined forces of Scindia and the Rajah of Berar at Argaum in November and at the siege of Gawilghur in December.

While Wellesley was advancing north, General Lord Lake captured the fortress of Ally Ghur and then Delhi in September. Finally Lake's victory at Laswari and the storming of Holkar's city of Deig brought hostilities to a close with peace terms agreed. Gujarat, Delhi and Meerut all came under British rule.

The Second Maratha War or Pindari War (Third Maratha War for the EIC) took place from 1817–19. The Pindari were troublesome tribal Pathan (ethnic Afghan) warlord mercenaries who behaved as bandits and had established themselves with the Marathas, who still bore a grudge against the British. Colonel Burr of the East India Company defeated the discontented Peshwa, chief of the Maratha Confederacy at Kirkee and the Maratha forces were again defeated at Nagpore. The Marquess of Hastings's army finally defeated Holkar at Maheidpoor. The Maratha territory of central India came under British rule, with its borders up to what is now the Pakistan border. After Scindia there was a series of juvenile leaders, whose rule was consistently contested, which did not stabilise the area. When further problems arose in 1843, the Governor General sent Sir Hugh Gough's army to subdue the Marathas once more, with battles at Maharajpore and Punniar in the Gwalior Campaign.

The Second Maratha War was the first war during which Gurkha battalions served with the British. The city-state of Gorkha was a feudal hill village in western Nepal. Under King Prithwi Narayan Shah, King of the independent Kingdom of Gorkha, the Gorkhas invaded the Kathmandu valley in 1767 and the local regents pleaded for assistance. The East India Company sent 2,400 troops to subdue Prithwi, but the Indian troops suffered heavily in the malaria-infested lowlands of the Terai district and made no impression. When Kathmandu fell, Prithwi became king of Nepal in 1768.

King Prithwi and the Gurkhas had copied western military methods, especially the British in India and were a mighty foe, the army having been built up over twenty-six years. Expansion continued and when Prithwi died in 1775, the pace of expansion did not slacken. The lack of defined boundaries encouraged the Gurkhas to invade the East India Company's territory. Their newly annexed territories and incursions, especially into Oudh in 1813, were causing friction between the East India Company and Nepal. The Gurkhas controlled the area from the border with Kashmir in the west to Bhutan in the east. Lord Minto, Governor General of Bengal, protested against the expansion and demanded a withdrawal of the Gurkhas, but all negotiations failed. When the area was reinvaded and eighteen police officers were killed, including the local British officer in Bhutawal, Lord Moira (later Lord Hastings) the new Governor General of Bengal, declared war on Nepal. He sent a task force of 22,000 and the Anglo-Nepalese War (1814–16) ensued.

The Gurkhas of Nepal were found to be ferocious soldiers, disciplined and steady under fire, and the British soon had respect for them. The Nepalese had a better supply system as they knew the mountainous country. The British could not use artillery or cavalry effectively in such conditions, and their tactics, as had been shown when fighting Native Americans, were unsuited to the terrain. The British invasion force of regular British troops and sepoys attacked Nepal from the east and west confronting 16,000 Nepalese soldiers. The two-column attack had mixed fortunes. The British suffered defeats in the attack from the east. Under Generals Wood and Marley the British were forced to retreat. The west attack, under Generals Gillespie and Ochterlony, suffered high casualties. Gillespie captured Dehra Dun, but got held up at the stronghold of Kalunga fort and was killed leading the attack. Brigadier General Ochterlony had more success with his western column and outmanoeuvred the Gurkha General Amah Singh Thapa at Malaun in April, who retreated. Peace was soon negotiated.

The second phase of the war started when the Nepalese failed to honour their 1815 agreement. Ochterlony, now Major General, together with 35,000 British, sepoy and Sikkim troops, approached Makwanpur. There was a major battle at Jaithak in March 1816 and the Gurkha General Thapa was defeated. Again, peace was arranged before the advance on Kathmandu. Ochterlony was so impressed by the valour of the Gurkhas that he allowed their General Amah Singh Thapa to march away with his troops and weapons. At the subsequent Treaty of Sagauli in 1816, Kathmandu had to have a British resident officer and Nepal was accepted as independent but had lost Sikkim, Kumaon, Terai and Garwal. The Gurkhas from the hill tribes were allowed to join the army in India and as many as 3,000 followed the flag and formed Gurkha brigades. During the Indian Mutiny the Gurkhas demonstrated their intense loyalty to the British, a service that would continue up to the present time, with great sacrifice in the two world wars and the award of a total of twenty-six Victoria Crosses.

Coalitions Against France (First and Second)

The second battalion of the 42nd Foot raised in 1779 was made into the 73rd Highland Foot in 1787 and the following regiments were also raised – the 74th Highland Foot, 75th Highland Foot, 76th Foot (Hindoostan) and 77th Foot. These new regiments were to be supported by the East India Company but only the 76th saw service in India. The 79th Foot raised in 1778 was finally disbanded in 1789. Following the French Revolution of 1789, the new republic declared war on Britain, Austria, the Netherlands and Spain and there was a real threat of invasion. The French Revolutionary Wars (1793–1802) were fought like the Seven Years' War, on many fronts, and with the addition of Napoleon's efforts, conflict in Europe would last until 1815. Nearly sixty new regiments were raised – the 78th Foot up to the 135th Foot (Adams, p.52), mainly for the duration of the war, except that most would be disbanded from 1795 to 1797. The Royal Navy was very short of men and nine army regiments were used aboard ships, the 2nd, 11th, 25th, 29th, 30th, 69th, 86th, 2/90th Foot, 97th and 118th Foot.

The First Coalition of European States against France lasted from 1793 to 1797. France invaded Belgium and Austria responded, being first on the scene. Britain was unprepared for war; such was the lack of troops that only a brigade of guards without artillery were sent to face the French. Shortages of muskets, uniforms and other equipment, together with untrained, scratch battalions added to the difficulties (Homes, p.29). Eventually, the Duke of York with an army of 10,000 British, Hanoverians and Hessians would join forces with Austria's Prince of Coburg and deploy against the French.

At Lincelles in August 1793, Major General Lake with 1,200 men of the Guards Brigade successfully stormed the French redoubts. The position was defended by 5,000 French and was retaken by the Guards after the Dutch lost it. The French then laid siege to the port of Nieuport and 1,300 of the King's Shropshire Light Infantry and Hessian troops defended it for ten days against 12,000 French until relieved. After wintering, a new campaign started. Cavalry action at Villers-en-Cauchies in April 1794, Beaumont and then Willems earned Battle Honours. The infantry had their chance at Tournai, where the brigades of 14th, 37th and 53rd Foot secured Tournai's flank and turned the balance. The second winter was more severe with the French pressing the British in difficult conditions. The army retreated through Holland and Germany in the snow and reached Bremen in early 1795 in a state of chaos, with 6,000 evacuated.

Quite a number of infantry regiments received a Battle Honour depicted as a Naval Crown with the date inscribed '1st June 1794' (the Glorious First of June battle) 'St Vincent 1797' (the Battle of Cape St Vincent) and 2 April 1801 (the Battle of Copenhagen) where even detachments of the Royal Artillery took part. In the West Indies, five British brigades under General Grey captured Martinique, Trinidad, and St Lucia. In India, Pondicherry was captured again from the French by the 1st Madras Europeans, an East India Company regiment. Holland was occupied by the French in 1795, which gave an opportunity for the capture of the Cape of Good Hope. In the Dutch East Indies, the new Dutch alliance with France gave the French access to important ports in the Moluccas. A naval expedition with the 1st Madras Europeans soon captured Amboyna and Banda in 1796 and Ternate in 1801. The regiments not disbanded were the 78th Foot to the 90th Foot and the 98th Foot and 100th Foot were renumbered 91st Foot in 1796 and 92nd Foot in 1798. The 93rd Foot was re-formed in 1800 and all of these sixteen regiments would remain on the establishment.

Napoleon was given command of the campaign in Egypt and occupied Malta and landed at Alexandria in 1798 with 12,000 men. Napoleon defeated the Egyptians at the Battle of the Pyramids leaving his fleet at Aboukir Bay. Nelson destroyed his fleet at the Battle of the Nile. Napoleon took his army into Syria and was stopped at Acre, which was reinforced by the British. Sir Sydney Smith with an Anglo-Turkish force withstood a two-month siege and thwarted Napoleon's invasion. Napoleon soon returned to France to become First Consul. Under the terms of the Second Coalition of European powers, opposed to the spread of revolutionary ideas and the expansion of the French Empire, Britain sent out an army of 12,000 under Sir Ralph Abercromby in 1801 to chase the French out of Egypt. The British landed at Aboukir Bay and Abercromby was mortally wounded. The Battle of Alexandria followed and the British advanced up the Nile and captured Cairo. It was at Alexandria that the 28th Foot (North Gloucestershires) in two lines had to ward off a heavy French attack from both sides. With one rank turned about they fought back to back, stood their ground and defeated the French. Their heroics were marked by their being allowed to wear a smaller back cap badge in addition to the normal front cap badge. When the Gloucestershire regiments amalgamated, the tradition continued.

All of Egypt was now under British control. All of the regiments involved were awarded the Sphinx superscribed 'Egypt' to be used as required on Battle Honours or badges. The Treaty of Amiens brought an end to the Second Coalition and the Revolutionary Wars, but only briefly, as Napoleon was on the march. The Treaty of Amiens of 1802 meant that all conquests were handed back (including the Cape of Good Hope to the Dutch) except for Trinidad and Ceylon. The Dutch East Indies acquisitions were also returned. The French left Egypt and the famous Rosetta Stone went to the British Museum as spoils of war.

Administrative Changes: The Duke of York's Reforms

Prime Minister William Pitt saw the need to overhaul the army and appointed a Secretary of State for War with Cabinet rank. Henry Dundas, appointed as the new Secretary of State for War in 1794, Prince Frederick, Duke of York (second son of George III and the 'Grand Old Duke') as Commander-in-Chief, and Pitt the Younger as Prime Minister, saw through a number of changes to the stewardship of the British Army.

Long overdue reorganisations were made after the disasters of the Flanders Campaign of 1793–94 and just in time for the war with France, which would last for over twenty years. The Duke, who had not shone in matters of strategy in Flanders, found his feet in overhauling the army, introducing the first reforms since Marlborough. The Commander-in-Chief would now look after most army services and also control promotion (see Appendix 1). This was the most significant reform to date. The Board of Ordnance, who used to advise the Cabinet, would however continue. Commission by purchase would continue, but was controlled with limits on promotion. The Duke tackled man-management and introduced a more humane approach, which allowed Sir John Moore to introduce new methods and tactics at Shorncliffe. The Duke believed that:

> … true discipline proceeds from trust and that the King's commission was an honour and not a social privilege – the timely interference of the officer … his personal intercourse and acquaintance with his men (which are surely to be repaid by the soldiers' confidence and attachment) and above all his personal example. (Ascoli, p.36)

The Rules and Regulations for the Movement of His Majesty's Infantry – a booklet issued in 1792 and largely ignored by the army, whose battalions drilled differently and issued orders as determined by their colonel – was henceforth enforced by the Duke, so that all orders and movements became uniform.

NINETEENTH CENTURY

Military College Formation

The Royal Artillery and Royal Engineers had had their Royal Military Academy at Woolwich since 1741 to train officer cadets. General John Le Marchant, a cavalry officer, saw the need to train young officers and founded the Royal Military College in 1800. The senior department trained existing officers for staff duties and it would later become the Staff College, Camberley. A junior department was formed in 1802 to train gentlemen cadets to become junior officers for the infantry and cavalry. This got off to a slow start providing only four officers out of every hundred commissioned at the time of the Peninsular War. This college moved to Sandhurst in 1812 and would be joined by the senior department in 1821. General Le Marchant, who became its Lieutenant Governor, was killed at Salamanca in 1812. The two colleges merged to become the Royal Military Academy Sandhurst in 1947.

Coalitions Against France (Third, Fourth and Fifth)

The peace after the Treaty of Amiens was short-lived and Britain declared war on France in May 1803. The Napoleonic Wars (1803–15) would last until the defeat of Bonaparte at Waterloo. The 94th Foot and 96th Foot were re-formed in 1802, but only lasted to 1817 when they were again disbanded, having no connections with modern regiments. The 95th was raised as a new rifle regiment. Such was the effectiveness of the French skirmishers that there were not enough light troops to match them, and the following regiments were converted to light infantry between 1803 and 1815: 43rd Foot, 51st Foot, 52nd Foot, 68th Foot, 71st Foot, 85th Foot and 90th. The 96th Foot to the 104th Foot regiments were raised (Adams, p.53).

The Cape of Good Hope was recaptured by Sir David Baird. The Third Coalition of European powers against Napoleon was set up in 1805. Naples sought support from Britain, and Sir John Stuart with 5,000 troops defeated the French General Reynier's corps of 6,000 at Maida in July 1806. During the Fourth Coalition of 1806, Arthur Wellesley (later Wellington) was given a small command under Lord Cathcart in an expedition to Copenhagen, whose neutrality was in doubt; the British did not want the Danish fleet of twenty-seven ships to fall into the hands of Napoleon, who had no fleet after Trafalgar. 18,000 troops sailed under Admiral Gambier and General Lord Cathcart. Wellesley had the 43rd Foot, 95th Rifles, 52nd Foot and 92nd Highlanders. There was little fighting and after a bombardment of Copenhagen the Danes surrendered in September 1807.

In South America, both Uruguay and Rio de la Plata (later Argentina) were controlled by Spain, and the South American market looked appealing as a conquest, especially since Spain had sided with France. In 1806, Colonel Beresford (later Wellington's General) captured Buenos Aires, much to the delight of the merchants in Britain. His success however was short-lived and the small force was soon captured. The 71st Regiment or Foot lost both Colours and they are encased on the wall in the Nieestra Senora de Rosario Chapel inside the church in Defensa Street as witnessed by author.A larger expedition under General Auchmuty was sent out and finding that Buenos Aires could not be recaptured, he took Montevideo instead. General Whitelocke took over as Commander-in-Chief South America and was tasked to recapture Buenos Aires. He approached the city in thirteen columns and met fierce resistance from the local criollas troops.The redcoats had no answer to the pouring of burning oil from the rooftops.Whitelocke made a complete mess of the attempt and had to capitulate, being forced to withdraw not only from Buenos Aires, but Montevideo as well. His troops took a dim view of his generalship and Craufurd (later Wellington's General) wanted to have him shot.

On return to England Whitelocke was court-martialled and cashiered.The Fifth Coalition of Britain and Austria against France in 1809 committed themselves to invade the Low Countries to take pressure off the Austrians. In July 1809, the government sent an expedition of 40,000 troops to Walcheren Island under the Earl of Chatham.The purpose of opening this third front against Napoleon (Copenhagen, was the first front and Spain was the second) was to capture the naval base at Antwerp and block the Scheldt.While the troops were aboard the fleet they heard that the Austrians had been beaten at Wagram, but the assault on Walcheren as a staging post before Antwerp continued. Flushing was captured but the army was devastated by 'Walcheren Fever'.The army suffered nearly 11,000 sick by September and the intended attack on Antwerp was cancelled. 4,200 died of fever, with the sick and dying landing at south coast ports.The disaster brought down the government. Expeditions were again sent to the Dutch East Indies, and Amboyna, Banda and Ternate were recaptured in 1810.

The War of 1812

The war with Revolutionary France in 1793 brought about a British blockade of France which interfered with legitimate American trade. Furthermore, the Royal Navy were stopping and delaying American ships to look for deserters from the Royal Navy. America was particularly upset about its prosperous trade of tobacco, cotton and grain being delayed or lost through missing wind and tide due to these hold-ups.The situation deteriorated when Napoleon introduced his Continental System of more blockades with continental ports closed to British trade. After the Battle of Trafalgar, Napoleon had no navy to enforce his blockade and Britain continued to stop neutral ships and even impressed men who were not British deserters. Britain, now very much alone in Europe, expected America to give support, or at least suspend trade with France. A nervous Canada was keenly watching events in America, and the militia even in 1808 were advised 'to keep themselves in constant readiness in case Jonathan should attempt an invasion' (Caffrey p.105).

Britain was at loggerheads with the United States and each country issued a number of Embargo Acts or Decrees and Orders in Council to justify and define their maritime policy. A number of maritime incidents occurred when American nationals were killed, which inflamed the situation. One that especially caused concern was when a shot from HMS *Leopard* over the bows of USS *Chesapeake* went hopelessly wrong and killed three sailors. Envoys of both countries were making every attempt to defuse tempers and have the Acts repealed against a series of national outbursts. The Acts were repealed only to be raised again and again and the final irony was that Britain repealed its offensive Order in Council within days of Congress declaring war. If a telegraph had been around in 1812, the war would have been averted. The jingle for this coming war was 'Free Trade and Sailors Rights'. The US declared war on Britain citing the Order in Council, impressment, blockades and violation of territorial waters.

America could hardly match the Royal Navy, but they could attack Canada. Lieutenant General Prevost was Governor General of Canada in all but name, with General Brock as Commander-in-Chief. Apart from Newfoundland, Nova Scotia and New Brunswick, Canada was split into Upper Canada of York (now Toronto) and Ontario, down to Fort Detroit, which was mainly English, and Lower Canada of Quebec and Montreal, mainly French. Britain still had a presence in America running trading posts such as Forts Niagara and Detroit, an arrangement that suited everyone. The Americans captured Fort Detroit only for it to be retaken by General Brock with friendly Indian support under Tecumseh. Tecumseh, chief of the Shawnee, attempted to unite the Indians from coast to coast and north to south against white settlers. The Indians of course had their own agenda.

There was a pause in hostilities when the British fleet brought news about the repeal of the contentious Order in Council. This news, together with peace initiatives, was brought to President Madison, who distrusted the British and told his generals to carry on fighting. General Brock now considered Niagara and did battle with the Americans at Queenstown nearby; he was killed while leading the assault. Major General Sheaffe arrived with reinforcements and the Americans surrendered.

Naval engagements saw successes for USS *Constitution* against HMS *Guerriere* and USS *United States* against HMS *Macedonian*. The Americans now started to build ships in earnest on the Great Lakes at Sackets Harbor, to contest the St Lawrence River. The Americans captured Frenchtown and Colonel Proctor of Fort Detroit was promoted to Brigadier General for repulsing them and capturing their general. The British made a successful attack on ships frozen in the ice at Ogdensburg. The American Admiral Chauncey attacked York after the thaw, and Sheaffe withdrew his troops. York surrendered after the grand magazine was blown up, killing the American general. The Americans burned the Parliament buildings and Government House. Sir James Yeo RN arrived to take charge of the British ships in the Great Lakes. Prevost now decided to attack Sackets Harbor, but failed in the attempt, withdrawing his troops. Colonel Harvey's night attack on the Americans camped at Stoney Creek was successful, capturing two generals, but with confused fighting and heavy casualties.

Commodore Yeo set about raiding available targets in Lake Ontario to entice the Americans out, but Chauncey stayed at Sackets Harbor. Sheaffe was replaced by Major General de Rottenburg who in turn was replaced by Lieutenant General Drummond. Napoleon's defeat at Leipzig allowed Britain to send more ships and troops to America. Peace moves were again afoot. The Royal Navy continued its blockade of the eastern seaboard except for the New England states (New Hampshire, Massachusetts, Rhode Island, Connecticut and Vermont), as some were on the verge of seceding from the Union, especially the more northern new state of Vermont. The Royal Navy were successful at Boston Bay, where the USS *Chesapeake* was boarded and surrendered to Captain Broke of HMS *Shannon*. The town of Plattsburg on Lake Champlain was captured unopposed and Fort Niagara was recaptured.

An attempted American assault on Montreal failed at Crysler's Farm where the Americans were defeated by Lieutenant Colonel Morrison with support from Royal Navy gunboats. Proctor's earlier success was short lived as he had a reverse at Moravian Town on the Thames River with high casualties and also the death of Tecumseh. A British attack at Oswego, which included the recently titled 'Royal' Marines and sailors, not only chased away the Americans, but also captured a huge stock of much needed food and stores. At Chippawa, Major General Riall had to withdraw but made another attempt at Lundy's Lane, which was more successful. The Americans gave up and threw their baggage into the Niagara Falls, with both sides completely exhausted (Caffrey, p.220). Vice Admiral Cochrane and Major General Ross arrived with veterans from the Peninsula to open a new front.

The British landed at Benedict with the view to attacking Washington. President Madison visited to see the ships for himself and realised that Washington was the target; it was soon evacuated. The US Army made a stand at Bladensburg but Congreve's rockets put the fear of death into the Americans and they were soon routed in full view of the President. The British called the event the 'Bladensburg Races' – General Ross's victory allowed him to walk into the capital. Although the White House was evacuated, the staff had laid out a formal meal for the expected victorious American soldiers, only for the British Army to walk in and drink the President's best Madeira. The Americans had previously burned York in Canada, so the British set fire to the presidential mansion and other buildings. The British were about to burn the Patents Office and its valuable contents, but the superintendent, Dr William Thornton, put up such a spirited defence against the outrage that it was spared.

The US Army retreated to Baltimore. Near Canada, Prevost sent Major General Robinson to capture Plattsburg, which he did, but during the accompanying naval action the Royal Navy had to strike its Colours in an engagement in Lake Champlain. Prevost had to withdraw the British from Plattsburg and incurred dissent among his veteran troops and even censure from back home. The British attack on Baltimore failed when Ross was killed and the navy could not give the promised support because of sunken hulks blocking its route. The defiance of the local militia, flying a huge flag during a bombardment of Fort McHenry, Baltimore, inspired Francis Scott Key to write the poem 'The Defense of Fort McHenry'. This was later put to the tune of a British drinking song, and under the name 'The Star-Spangled Banner' it became the National Anthem of the United States in 1931.

New Orleans was to be Great Britain's next assault. Cochrane favoured an overland approach to avoid a long run-in against coastal batteries. The Royal Navy had to ferry the troops from Ship Island in the Mississippi Sound 80 miles away, to the head of the Bayou Bienvenu, a tedious process, which took a week. Villere's Plantation was captured en route, where an escaped officer, Major Villere, fled to warn General Jackson. Jackson made a pre-emptive strike on the British, but was repulsed.

On Christmas Eve 1814 the Treaty of Ghent was signed to end the war, but it would take seven weeks for the news to arrive in America. A bombardment commenced on 1 January and the British endeavoured to widen the channel and improve their defences. The initial British assault across the river failed, because boats and start time were delayed and the landing bank was in poor condition. General Pakenham, newly arrived from England, was sent to replace Ross. The main British attack on New Orleans failed against a well-defended American position with Major Generals Gibbs and Pakenham killed. The severe casualties of 2,000 British soldiers in half an hour led to the action being called off, and the British withdrew. News of the Treaty of Ghent reached America on 11 February 1815 and was soon ratified by the President, bringing hostilities to an end. The borders between Canada and America were resolved, especially at the Great Lakes, as a result of the treaty.

The Peninsular War (Sixth Coalition)

Spain was an ally of France and allowed Napoleon's army under General Junot to enter Spain with the view to occupying Portugal. The French soon betrayed the Spanish by taking over the country and forcing the King to abdicate, appointing Joseph Bonaparte (Napoleon's brother) in his place. Both Portugal and Spain appealed to Britain for assistance, starting the Peninsular War (1808–14). Lieutenant General Sir Arthur Wellesley was given command of 9,000 troops earmarked for South America, but that venture was cancelled and he was redirected to Portugal, to be reinforced by a brigade under General Brent Spencer in Gibraltar.

After Wellesley had sailed, the government decided to enlarge the army in Portugal by sending General Sir John Moore's army, currently waiting in Sweden. Wellesley landed first at Corunna and then Oporto, where the local bishop had made a Unilateral Declaration of Independence and favoured the British. Wellesley found out that General Moore was to join him with 15,000 troops and the government had decided that Moore was senior to Wellesley. Sir Hew Dalrymple was to follow and command the British Army in Portugal with Sir Harry Burrard as his second in command.

More generals were to be sent out. With this surfeit of top brass, Wellesley wrote to a friend 'I hope I shall beat Junot before any of them arrive and then they may do as they please with me' (Glover, p.59).

Wellesley landed at Mondego Bay with the initial 15,000 troops, including Spencer's, in August. Wellesley's soldiers were nearly all infantry with half a regiment of the 20th Light Dragoons. Wellesley discovered there were 16,000 French in Portugal and expected Junot to field 12,000 with the rest in outposts and in Lisbon. The French General Delaborde intended to delay the British with his 4,000 men, and when Wellesley attacked, Delaborde moved back to a ridge south-west of Rolica. Wellesley was prepared to push him back even further without conflict, but an unprepared frontal attack by the 29th Foot precipitated a battle and had to be supported until the French retired. With Moore's reinforcements now arriving by sea, Wellesley moved towards a link-up at Vimiero.

Delaborde was also reinforced and now under Junot. Wellesley went aboard to greet Burrard who told Wellesley to stand fast until all reinforcements had landed ashore. This Wellesley was prepared to do reluctantly, but was informed during the night that the enemy was moving to attack. The 95th Rifles and 60th Foot, all with rifles in a long line, slowed the French attack and then opened up their ranks to expose the artillery. The 50th Foot stood fast against the advancing French column, who tried to deploy. The French failed and withdrew in confusion.

With the French on the run Wellesley suggested to Burrard he pursue the defeated enemy with his unused fresh troops, having no effective cavalry. Although the nearest French reinforcements were in Lisbon, Burrard refused. Dalrymple now arrived and he also refused Wellesley's request and took charge of the army. Wellesley was now outranked by two senior officers. General Kellerman approached the British and proposed a truce, allowing the French army to leave Portugal immediately and in British ships, with all their stores, munitions and booty, which included treasure chests.

The negotiations were completed and signed when Kellerman effectively duped Wellesley by requesting him to countersign the document, on the grounds that he was of equal rank to himself. Having lost the battle and effectively been chased out of Portugal, Kellerman wanted to redeem the situation a little by implicating Wellesley in the controversial agreement. Kellerman was only too aware that Wellesley had political influence. The Convention of Cintra was agreed and caused a storm in England with the senior officers recalled to explain themselves. Wellesley had already left for England. General Moore took over the army in Portugal.

At the subsequent inquiry in December it was abundantly clear that the senior officers had taken charge after the battle and the negotiations were their responsibility. The inquiry reluctantly endorsed the convention as the best means of removing the French without further battles, thanked Wellesley for his success at Vimiero and both Dalrymple and Burrard never got another command. The jury was still out over Wellesley's signature and his future was in some doubt.

General Moore took his army out of Portugal – leaving 10,000 behind in Lisbon – and headed for Salamanca with 25,000 troops, his aim being to disrupt French communications and attack Soult in Galicia. Napoleon by this time was entering Madrid. Once Napoleon had dealt with the Spanish armies, he concentrated on the British. Leaving Victor and the new King Joseph in Madrid, Napoleon marched after Moore. Moore advanced north to link up with 10,000 reinforcements under Sir David Baird in October, landing at Corunna. Soult's force was met at Sahagun where a sharp cavalry attack saw him off. When Moore found out that Napoleon had left Madrid to go after him, he realised he was outnumbered and headed for Corunna. The 200-mile march from Benavente to Corunna was particularly arduous, with mountainous terrain and narrow passes.

Moore arrived at Corunna in January 1809, with Soult on his tail. A fierce rearguard action took place and Moore was mortally wounded; the army had to be evacuated.

In April the government called upon Wellesley to command the army in the Peninsula, as he was the only general whose CV included beating the French decisively and who had already put plans forward of how to continue to hold Portugal. With 23,000 men (17,000 British, including Major General Stapleton-Cotton's cavalry and 6,000 Portuguese under Beresford) Wellesley was up against Soult with 15,000 troops in Oporto, Portugal. A further French corps under Ney in Galicia and Victor's army of 35,000 were both nearby in Spain and could reinforce Soult. There were seven French corps in Spain with a total of 280,000 troops under Mortier, Junot, Soult, St Cyr, Ney, Sebastiani and Victor (Glover, p.72). Wellesley could call on Cuesta's Spanish army, but it was unreliable. Soult in Oporto was Wellesley's first target, but Soult had destroyed all the bridges across the Douro and thought it impassable. There was a damaged ferry which could be repaired and locals directed Wellesley to hidden wine barges, which enabled the army to force a crossing.

Wellesley immediately reinforced the Bishop's seminary and secured his crossing. Soult, caught unawares, bid a hasty retreat leaving behind his artillery and stores, and Oporto was liberated. Wellesley had a problem with funds from Britain and had to wait until he could pay his troops and wagon masters. The army was already on half rations. By the time he was ready to move against Victor, the latter was near Talavera. Wellesley could call upon 50,000 troops, British, Portuguese and Spanish under Venegas and Cuesta. Victor, Sebastiani and Joseph Bonaparte had the same number of French troops. The planned attack for 23 July did not come off as Cuesta was not ready and his army was tired. Victor moved back and Cuesta was attacked by the French and shaken up. Wellesley agreed with Cuesta to stand and fight at Talavera.

In the afternoon of 28 July the initial French attack was on the Spanish, who fired a volley and immediately retreated. The French overran the baggage train, including Cuesta's carriage. During the night, three French columns broke through to the Medellin Hill, a British position, but it was retaken by the 29th Foot. At 5 a.m. a major attack on Medellin Hill occurred, preceded by a bombardment. The attacking columns were stopped by the reinforced line of infantry. A lull occurred (even an unofficial truce) where much needed water was obtained and Wellesley adjusted his position. The next French attack was successful and the line gave way only for the 48th Foot to gallantly filling the gap. The infantry rallied around the 48th Foot and threw the French back. It is no surprise that Talavera was chosen as the regimental anniversary of the 48th Foot. The British suffered 5,300 casualties, with 800 killed, but the French lost more and retired next morning. The Light Brigade and the much needed troop of Horse Artillery arrived to strengthen Wellesley's command. To prevent the French from entering Portugal and cutting off his communications with Lisbon and a possible escape route, Wellesley sent his light infantry to secure the bridges over the Tagus at Almaraz. Wellesley was raised to the peerage as Viscount Wellington of Talavera.

In 1810, Wellington decided upon the best position for the defence of Portugal. It was to be in front of the capital Lisbon, with the sea on one side and the Tagus on the other, at Torres Vedras. His chief engineer Colonel Fletcher built three lines of fortifications exploiting the rivers, damming roads to make them impassable, and with interlocking fire support. The lines of Torres Vedras would not only defend Lisbon and Portugal but any French approach would mean acute supply difficulties. As Glover put it, the French 'must either retreat, or starve' in such a restricted area.

Wellington now had 35,000 men. Marshal Massena commanded a whole army of three corps of 65,000. Massena had captured Ciudad Rodrigo from the Spanish and Almeida from the Portuguese en route. Wellington made contact at Busaco on 27 September to slow down the French with his 50,000 British and Portuguese troops. Massena made no reconnaissance and sent General Reynier's divisions up against Wellington on the ridge of the rocky summit. The French were repulsed and further attempts failed. The French withdrew and Wellington moved back to Torres Vedras 70 miles away. Wellington waited for Massena, who was stunned to see the earthworks at Torres Vedras. Massena waited a few months and received reinforcements from d'Erlon, but in March he retreated back into Spain. Massena was losing 500 men a week through illness, hunger, and attacks by irregulars. His campaign had cost him 30,000 men. Massena left and headed to Coimbra and by 4 April had all but vacated Portugal leaving behind a mass of baggage.

The following year Wellington followed Massena to Almeida. Massena unsuccessfully attacked Wellington on 3 May at Fuentes d'Oñoro and the following day but was again repulsed. The French withdrew leaving the garrison at Almeida unsupported. Wellington gave orders for the bridge to be secured, blocking the exit of the French garrison. The officer put the order in his pocket and forgot about it until the next day and the French garrison crept out unopposed. Wellington was furious and the officer responsible shot himself pending a court martial.

General Graham defeated Victor at Barrosa near Cádiz in March. Wellington sent Beresford to support Badajoz, now under siege from Soult. He arrived too late as Badajoz had surrendered. The proposed relief became a siege of the fortress in early May. Beresford heard that Soult was on his way to support Badajoz and moved out with Spanish support to confront Soult at Albuhera. The Spanish did well, holding back the initial French attack until the British divisions attacked. Rain affected the action and the French cavalry made full use of the wet conditions. Cole's brigade did exceedingly well, with the 57th at the front getting a mention in despatches. The 57th at Albuhera earned the nickname 'Die hard' when they suffered badly against the Polish Lancers when in square. 25,000 French were defeated by 36,000 British and Spanish troops. At Arroyo dos Molinos, near Badajoz, a British brigade under Howard defeated the French, capturing 1,000 prisoners. The second attempt on Badajoz in June was unsuccessful using ancient Portuguese batteries, and time ran out as Marmont and Soult were approaching and the siege was abandoned.

At the turn of the year Ciudad Rodrigo was under siege and when the siege trains were brought up in January the assault commenced. It was surrounded by two divisions with cavalry support. The fortress fell in January to the assault of the Third and Light Divisions with 2,000 prisoners taken. Major General Craufurd of the Light Division was killed. Almeida and Ciudad Rodrigo were now garrisoned by Spaniards and controlled the northern route into Spain.

Wellington now concentrated on taking Badajoz, although the threat of Soult's arrival meant he had to send Graham to prevent or stall the French General's approach. He also heard that Marshal Marmont with his army of Portugal was en route to Ciudad Rodrigo. There was clearly a need for a swift victory, and his siege train of thirty-four 24-pounders and four 18-pounders made three breaches. Having no time to further enlarge the breach Wellington sent his troops in at 10 p.m. in a four-division attack. Narrow breaches and thirty-foot walls elsewhere made Badajoz particularly difficult and the battle was slow to gain momentum. The Third Division under Picton finally broke through and Lieutenant MacPherson of the 45th Foot was first onto the tower and removed the French flag, running up his red jacket as he had no Union Jack.

Casualties were heavy, with the British losing 5,000 in the siege and 2,500 storming the breaches. Wellington now had a decision to make – either to attack Soult in the south or Marmont in the north. He chose Marmont, leaving Hill and his independent corps to disrupt Soult's communications, which he did effectively by destroying the pontoon bridge at Almaraz and cutting Soult off. Marmont was chosen as he was at Salamanca in the province of Asturias and nearer the Pyrenees, Wellington's ultimate goal. In June, Wellington entered Salamanca to a Spanish welcome and later captured the defensive forts. The main features at Salamanca were the Greater and Lesser Arapiles. The French arrived first and occupied the Greater Arapile and Wellington took the Lesser Arapile. It was at Salamanca that Wellington famously told his brother-in-law Pakenham, 'Ned, throw your division into column and drive them [the French] to the devil' (Holmes, p.166). Marmont lost the battle and 14,000 men and twenty guns, and was injured. The cavalry under Sir Stapleton Cotton did exceedingly well, but Major General Le Marchant, founder of the Staff College, was killed. Wellington entered Madrid on 12 August 1812 and was made a Marquess.

General Clausel was now in command of the French. Wellington chased him to Burgos. The siege of the castle at Burgos did not go well as Wellington had only three guns for the job and gave up in October. In a letter to the government he blamed nobody but himself. With the Spanish generals failing to support him and the renewed threat of being cut off, Wellington withdrew to Salamanca. He chose Freneda near Ciudad Rodrigo as his HQ for the winter, having joined up with Hill early in November. After Salamanca, the Spanish made Wellington Generalissimo of all Spanish troops.

In January 1813 the news of Napoleon's disaster in Russia reached Wellington. By May Wellington had left Portugal and entered Spain again to confront King Joseph and Marshal Jourdan who were trying to join up with Clausal. Wellington met Joseph at Vitoria on 21 June and the French were thoroughly beaten, losing all their baggage. Asprey praises Wellington and his generals in his biography of Napoleon:

> His divisions superbly commanded by such as Thomas Picton and Rowland Hill, struck the centre, flanks and finally the rear of the fugitive army to win a total victory, guns, caissons, wagons and carriages abandoned as troops fled in all directions.

Marshal Jourdan's baton was captured and sent to the Prince Regent. The 14th Light Dragoons captured Joseph's chamber pot and forever after used it for drinking toasts in the regimental mess. The availability of so much booty after Vitoria forestalled any pursuit of the French. Joseph was sent into exile in disgrace and Soult became Commander-in-Chief of the French Army in Spain. The road to France lay open, except for the fortresses of San Sebastian and Pamplona and Soult's dispirited army. Soult's attack at Sorauren was repulsed and he withdrew into France. San Sebastian fell after a siege at the end of August and finally Pamplona at the end of October. Battles at Nivelle River in November and Nive River in December pushed the French away from the Pyrenees. Soult attacked at St Pierre d'Irube against Hill and was defeated and fell back to Bayonne, then Orthez on the route to Toulouse and finally got to Toulouse in March. Wellington attacked Soult on 10 April 1814, Easter Sunday, and Soult was defeated and withdrew next morning. News of Napoleon's abdication brought an end to the campaign and an end to the Sixth Coalition.

Some regiments now had many battalions. By 1809 the 1st Guards had four battalions, the Coldstream and 3rd Guards two battalions each. The 1st Foot had four battalions and the 14th, 27th and 95th Foot had three battalions each. The 60th Foot with seven battalions topped the lot.

The Waterloo Campaign (Seventh Coalition)

The defeat at Leipzig in 1813 was the end of Napoleon and when the Prussians, Austrians and Russians forced him to withdraw to Paris, he abdicated in 1814 and went into exile on Elba. He later escaped, landed at Golfe-Juan on 1 March 1815 and marched to Paris. The Congress of Vienna was in session, discussing the future of Europe and the eight countries attending, Austria, Spain, France, Great Britain, Portugal, Prussia, Russia and Sweden declared Napoleon (not France) *persona non grata* and formed the Seventh Coalition, pledging to put armies in the field to stop him. It was Wellington and Blücher with his Prussians who were first on the scene in Belgium. Wellington, with the Prince of Orange, had with him British troops, Peninsular veterans, the crack King's German Legion, Dutch/Belgians, Hanoverians, Brunswickers and even Nassauers. In those few months historically referred to as the Hundred Days, Napoleon had rebuilt his army and intended to confront and divide Wellington and Blücher.

On 14 June the French reach the Sambre, and early the next morning they crossed into Belgium. During the afternoon the Prussian outposts made contact with the French. Müffling (Wellington's Prussian liaison officer) informed the British of French activity. Marshal Ney arrived and was given command of the left wing of the French Army with two corps, with the mission to take the strategically important crossroads at Quatre Bras and drive a wedge between Wellington and Blücher. Ney has the 1st Corps of d'Erlon and Reille's 2nd Corps of 45,000 men with Kellerman's cavalry and 2nd Corps cavalry of Pire. The Prussians were to assemble their army at Ligny.

In the early evening of 15 June Wellington – not knowing Napoleon's intentions or route – put his army on standby to position themselves to cover the Mons road into Brussels. Those units further out were ordered to move closer. Ney's advance cavalry patrol reached Quatre Bras and found it deserted.

Later that evening Prince Bernhard of Saxe-Weimar heard of the French occupying Charleroi driving in his piquets at Frasnes and using his initiative, occupied the crossroads at Quatre Bras, which linked Ligny to the British. Ney investigated the situation at Quatre Bras and saw Saxe-Weimer occupying houses. Ney had nearly 2,000 cavalry and one battalion immediately available, with Reille's Corps coming up. Orders were issued for Wellington's army to concentrate at Nivelles, thus allowing for a threat to Mons, in case Charleroi was a feint.

Lieutenant General Baron de Perponcher, the 2nd Dutch/Belgian divisional commander and Major General Rebecque, Chief of Staff to the Prince of Orange, ordered the 2nd Dutch/Belgian Division to arrive next morning at Quatre Bras and not Nivelles, as ordered by Wellington. They concurred that the occupation of Quatre Bras would obstruct the French advance and so allow Wellington to gather his army and keep in touch with Blücher.

In the early hours of 16 June Wellington received the Prince of Orange's news about Quatre Bras and the main French threat through Charleroi. Borrowing a map he studied the implications of Quatre Bras and exclaimed that he has been 'humbugged, by God'. Wellington went to bed but was awakened at 4.30 a.m. to receive General Dörnberg from Mons, who had arrived specifically to apologise for not reporting the situation more clearly, and that there was no threat to Mons and that the whole of the French Army was at Charleroi. Wellington changed his orders for his whole army to march to Quatre Bras.

At 10 a.m. Wellington arrived at Quatre Bras. The 2nd Dutch/Belgian Division of 8,000 troops was in position occupying Gemioncourt farm, Pireaumount farm, Bois de Bossu and the main Namur road. An hour later Ney received an order from Napoleon to occupy Quatre Bras with six divisions if he had not already done so. Finding all quiet at 1 p.m. Wellington visited Blücher and the Prussians at the windmill at Brye and confirmed that each would come to the other's aid if circumstances allowed. d'Erlon's Corps marched to support Ney at Quatre Bras.

2 p.m. saw the start of Ney's assault on Quatre Bras with an artillery bombardment followed by two divisions of Reille's corps. Bachelu and Foy pushed some of the Dutch/Belgian units back with Piré's cavalry at Bossu Wood. Gemioncourt however stood firm. Napoleon issued a further instruction to inform Ney that he (Napoleon) and Grouchy were to attack the Prussians at Ligny and that Ney was to destroy all before him at Quatre Bras and march to his aid. Jerome's division now arrived to join Ney. After an hour Wellington returned to Quatre Bras and took command. Napoleon, with Grouchy's wing of two corps, engaged the Prussians at Ligny. Napoleon sent his third order to Ney, saying 'the fate of France is in your hands'. The Dutch/Belgian 3rd Light Cavalry Brigade under van Merlen arrived at Quatre Bras. d'Erlon's Corps received an order to about turn and march to Ligny to support Napoleon.

Ney did not receive Napoleon's order until 4 p.m., at the same time as Picton's division arrived at the double with three brigades. Kempt's and Pack's brigades lined the Namur road with Best's brigade in support. They soon came under a fierce artillery bombardment. General Foy attacked Bossu Wood and Gemioncourt and chased out the Prince of Orange's Dutch, who were hopelessly outnumbered. Merlen's cavalry assault in support of the Dutch withdrawal from Gemioncourt was defeated by Pire, who charged on and reached the crossroads. The Duke of Brunswick led an attack on Gemioncourt followed by a general advance of Picton's division in echelon from the road against two large French columns. The division had to withdraw back to the road to avoid artillery and the Duke of Brunswick was killed. Wellington sought refuge in the square of the 92nd Highlanders from an attack by Piré's cavalry.

At 5 p.m. Alten's Division arrived with Halkett's brigade and Wellington sent them to form up between the Charleroi road and Bossu Wood. Kielmansegge's brigade went to Pireaumount. d'Erlon's Corps received a desperate order from Ney to return to Quatre Bras. As a final effort Ney sent Kellerman's cuirassiers against Halkett's brigade and caught the 73rd and 69th Foot out of formation, cutting them down and forcing them to seek shelter in the wood, with the 69th losing its colour. Wellington reorganised Picton's division into seven chequered square formations. Casualties and ammunition shortages forced some battalions to join together but the squares defeated three cavalry attacks.

At 6.30 p.m. Cooke's Guards arrived and secured Bossu Wood and the surrounding farms. The major positions were retaken from the French. By 9 p.m. the conflict was now under control with the British holding all positions at Quatre Bras. d'Erlon's Corps, thoroughly put out after marching backwards and forwards nearly eight hours without engagement, finally arrived too late at Quatre Bras. In total the British suffered 4,700 casualties compared to the French 4,300. Meanwhile, Napoleon was at Ligny beating the Prussians with only half his army.

Waterloo 1815

Wellington, after stopping Ney at Quatre Bras, moved back to Waterloo to defend the ridge at Mont Saint Jean. He had chosen the ground carefully with a reverse slope to protect his infantry from artillery. Before leaving Ligny Blücher had assured Wellington of his support. The Prussians marched to Wavre in good order with Marshal Grouchy following with Vandamme's 3rd and Gerard's 4th Corps. It rained all day and all night, making life miserable for both armies. Sunday 18 June arrived with Wellington's army in position on a 3-mile front; his centre was at La Haye Sainte and the château at Hougoumont, to the left was Papalotte and Smohain, and to the right was Braine L'Alleud.

Wellington had four corps: 1st Corps Prince of Orange, 2nd Corps General Hill, a reserve corps and a cavalry corps under Uxbridge. Napoleon had Marshal Ney and four infantry corps: 1st Corps d'Erlon, 2nd Corps Reille (less Girard's Division), Imperial Guard Corps Drouot, and 6th Corps Lobau (less Teste's Division). Girard and Teste were with Grouchy, supposedly to keep the Prussians at bay. Napoleon's cavalry reserve had two corps, Milhaud and Kellerman. Pajol and Exelman's Corps were with Grouchy.

Wellington had 68,000 men and 156 guns against Napoleon's 72,000 men and 246 guns, with eighty guns all lined up together in a Grand Battery. Only 30,000 of Wellington's army were British or redoubtable KGL troops. To prevent being outflanked Wellington had a further 17,000 at Tubize and Hal, approximately 10 miles away. Delayed by the wet ground Napoleon occupied himself by reviewing his troops. Wellington's tactic was to stand and defend his ridge and counter the French assault.

At 11.30 a.m. the Grand Battery started a bombardment in support of Reille's 2nd Corps' attack on Château Hougoumont. Hougoumont was left in the capable hands of Colonel Macdonnell with light troops of the Coldstream Guards, 3rd Guards and later 1st Guards with Hanoverian and Nassau Light Infantry in the perimeter garden. The attack by Prince Jerome, Napoleon's brother, was unsuccessful but some of the French managed to get inside the courtyard, but Macdonnell with Corporal Graham and others managed to close and secure the gate.

At 1.30 p.m. a ninety-minute Grand Battery bombardment began, followed by d'Erlon's 1st Corps attacking in four divisional columns on Wellington's left at Mont St Jean; d'Erlon's left flank was mauled by the KGL under Major Baring as they passed the fortified La Haye Sainte. The attack was repulsed by General Picton's 5th Division extended in line on the ridge, but General Picton was killed. At the critical moment when d'Erlon's Corps staggered against Picton and endeavoured to open out into line,

General Uxbridge sent in the heavy cavalry consisting of Somerset's Household and Ponsonby's Union Brigades and captured two eagles.

Somerset dealt with the supporting cavalry and the Union Brigade of English, Scottish and Irish regiments routed d'Erlon's division. This is when the 92nd Highlanders famously held onto the stirrups of the Royal Scots Greys, shouting 'Scotland Forever'. Smohain fell to the French but was soon evacuated as d'Erlon's Corps retired. Further attacks by d'Erlon came to nothing as Lambert's Brigade came up to support Picton's division. The first French attack on La Haye Sainte failed. Lobau's 6th Corps moved to Plancenoit to protect Napoleon's flank from the Prussians. Hougoumont was still under constant attack and the defenders were running out of ammunition until Private Brewer of the Royal Wagon Train, with his much needed tumbrel, came to the rescue. Hougoumont Château was set on fire but held out through five assaults.

At 3 p.m. Wellington moved his army 100yd back as further protection against the French artillery. The French saw this as a withdrawal and Ney ordered a massed cavalry charges of forty squadrons of 5,000 troops. Milhaud's whole 4th Cavalry Corps of eight regiments of cuirassiers and Lefebvre-Desnoette's Guard Light Cavalry of lancers and chasseurs à cheval began the attack. The British formed squares, with the gunners firing to the very last and then seeking shelter in the squares. Captain Mercer of the Royal Horse Artillery entered folklore when he refrained from entering the square of young Brunswickers, as they appeared unsteady. Mercer was alone in standing his ground and was the first to fire on the retreating cavalry. When Napoleon found out what was happening he sent in Kellerman's 3rd Corps and the Guards Heavy Cavalry. A further forty squadrons joined in and nearly 10,000 cavalry could not break the British squares after repeated attempts.

The second attack on La Haye Sainte also failed. Bulow's Prussian Corps appeared in the distance. The Prussians took Plancenoit, 1 mile from the French position, but it was retaken by the French with a regiment of the Young Guard. Plancenoit was taken once more by Bulow with Blücher now arrived. Hougoumont was reinforced and continued to hold out against a sixth attack.

At 6 p.m. La Haye Sainte finally fell as the KGL ran out of ammunition. The King's German Legion failed to retake it and lost a standard when attacked by cuirassiers. Wellington's centre was in difficulties. Gaps were closed and flank infantry and cavalry were brought to the centre. Duhesme and his Young Guard in support of Lobau regained Plancenoit from Bulow. A major Prussian assault retook Plancenoit again. Two battalions of the Old Guard took Plancenoit with an impressive controlled bayonet charge, only for the Prussians to reclaim it. Meanwhile Hougoumont held out against a seventh attack.

Napoleon sent in six battalions of his undefeated Imperial Guard against Wellington's centre at 7.30 p.m. The large column split into two waves. The first wave of grenadiers dislodged Halkett's division and two battalions were in disarray but were rallied and recovered. General Chassé brought up his Dutch Brigade of 3,000, and his horse artillery engaged the Imperial Guard with double-shotted canisters and defeated the Guards. The second wave of Chasseurs continued but was stopped, with Wellington himself telling his Guards to rise up and assault the Imperial Guards with the order, 'Maitland, now is your time.' The French fell back, but rallied and ascended the ridge again. Colonel Colborne delivered the *coup de grâce* with his advance of the 52nd who delivered volley after volley into the Imperial Guard's exposed flank, who retreated to the cry '*La Garde recule*!'

At 8.30 p.m. Wellington ordered his light cavalry after the French and then a general advance of his army. The Old Guard made a futile last stand. Wellington met Blücher at La Belle Alliance. The Prussians continue to rout the French well into the evening.

Wellington and his army stood their ground for nine long hours that day. The casualties were appalling, with 30,000 French killed or wounded, 15,000 British and 6,700 Prussians. On a regimental level the 1st Guards 3rd Battalion had eighty-four officers and men killed and 351 wounded out of 1021, 2nd Guards 2nd Battalion had fifty-five officers and men killed and 250 wounded out of 1,003, and the 27th Inniskillings had 105 officers and men killed and 373 wounded out of 698.

Post-Waterloo Changes

After Waterloo, only the three Guards Regiments, the 1st (Royal Scots) 60th and the 95th (Rifles), retained their second battalions; the others were disbanded. The 95th was taken out of the numbered regiments and renamed the Rifle Brigade. The remaining Foot regiments 96th to 104th Foot were renumbered as the 95th to 103rd Foot. The 1st Guards took the title 'Grenadier' for services at Waterloo against the French Imperial Guard. In 1816 the Waterloo Medal was issued as the first campaign medal to all ranks. In 1817 the newly numbered 94th Foot to 103rd Foot were disbanded (Adams, p.54). In 1823 the British government realised that the reduction in the strength of the army would not service the requirements of the expanding empire and sanctioned the raising of new regiments.

The number of regiments of foot increased, 94th Foot and 95th Foot in 1823, and 96th Foot to 99th Foot in 1824, with the 100th added in 1858. The 94th Foot had previously been raised and disbanded three times. It was raised again in 1793 as the Scots Brigade without a number and came onto the establishment as the 94th Foot in 1802, only to be disbanded again 1817. The 94th (Scots Brigade) had served in India at Seringapatam. The Scots or Scotch Brigade had had an unconventional existence, having been raised for service in Holland during the reign of Elizabeth I, when England had good relations with the Dutch who were trying to rid themselves of Spanish domination. The brigade was funded by the Dutch and more or less remained on the continent except during the Dutch Wars. The Dutch Scots Brigade returned to Scotland and later fought under Marlborough. During the American War of Independence, when Britain had no friends in Europe, the brigade disbanded.

In 1823 the fourth and final 94th Foot was raised mainly from the discharged soldiers of the Scots Brigade. This regiment would later form part of the Connaught Rangers.

Asia: The First Burma War, the First Afghan War and the First Chinese (Opium) War

The rivalry between upper Burma and lower Burma was resolved when King Alaungpaya came to the throne in 1753. Having united the country, his successors expanded it with incursions into Siam in 1767, Arakan in 1785 and Assam and Manipur in 1819, all on the doorstep of British north-east India. The insurgents had bases in British India and refugees were flooding into Bengal, a fact that displeased the Governor. Anglo-Burmese relations soon deteriorated and all diplomatic representations failed. The Governor General of India, Lord Amherst, was further aggravated when King Alaungpaya requested that the three richest provinces in Bengal – Assam, Arakan and Tenasserim – be ceded to Burma. A small British garrison on an island off Chittagong was slain in 1823 and a Burmese invasion of Cachar – which was under British protection in 1824 – led to the First Burma War (1824–26).

The British Army landed at Rangoon, the principal city of Lower Burma. The terrain, awful weather, and disease took their toll. Of the approximately 3,000 Europeans who died during the campaign, only 150 died from battle injuries. The King sued for peace before the British could take his capital. A peace treaty ended hostilities, with Alaungpaya left in power. The three disputed provinces were recognised by Burma to be part of British India and the exiled Burmese returned. Independence was given to Manipur and Cachar and other ports were opened for trade.

Britain controlled the sea route to India through the Royal Navy, but had no control over the inland route to India via Persia (Iran). Three states separated India from Persia: Scinde (also known as Sind), Punjab and Afghanistan. Britain therefore took an interest in Afghanistan, especially when Persia – supported by Russia – captured Herat. If Afghanistan came under Persia's influence then it would come under Russian influence and the British hold in India would be weakened.

In May 1838 the British government decided to invade Afghanistan. When Persian troops withdrew from Herat, Britain decided to support the claims of Shah Shuja to replace Dost Muhammad as Amir. Shah Shuja was both loyal to the British and also friendly toward Ranjit Singh of Punjab. Two divisions 12,000-strong from the Bombay and Bengal armies, augmented with British regulars under General Keane and with a contingent from Shah Shuja, moved along the Indus into Afghanistan and the First Afghan War (1838–42) started. 30,000 camels were required to carry stores for this 'Army of the Indus'. The army entered Kandahar unopposed and laid siege to Ghuznee.

The army entered Kabul in August 1839 and Dost Muhammad fled into exile. Some troops returned to India and visited Khelat en route in November to take issue with Mehrab Khan, the ruler of Khelat. The Khan was reluctant to accept Shuja as Amir, broke promises to give supplies and assistance to the army, and was implicated in the Baluchis harassing the army. The fortress of Khelat was attacked successfully by the British and the Khan was killed. Other resistance weakened, the Russian influence subsided, and the occupying force settled. Initially the situation was quiet – albeit with subsidies to neutral tribal chiefs – but supply trains were soon attacked and settlements besieged with disastrous results.

A change in government in Britain reviewed the cost of keeping an army in Afghanistan, plus the additional payments to the Afghan chiefs who kept the peace and the passes open, and concluded that the army should be partially withdrawn. Subsidies were cut and the tribesmen at the Khyber Pass revolted in October 1841. This escalated into general unrest and the British envoy Sir Alexander Burnes and his staff were murdered by tribesmen in November and the government purse stolen. The British were in a state of shock as their garrisons were harassed, their stores stolen and they were denied food and supplies.

Brigadier Sale left Kabul for Peshawar, India, only to be harassed en route and ended up in Jalalabad. The general unrest had allowed dissidents such as Akbar Khan, son of Dost Muhammad to arrive, take command and exert their influence and Kabul was soon under siege. The road to Kandahar was also closed off, which meant that withdrawal to the Bolan Pass was impossible. Attempts to chase away the surrounding tribesmen failed. Winter approached in 1841, food was in short supply and rationed and Sir William Macnaghten, the Viceroy's envoy and senior British adviser, negotiated for the withdrawal of the Kabul garrison to the Khyber Pass. At a meeting with Akbar Khan in early December for the safe conduct during withdrawal, Macnaghten was murdered.

Akbar Khan had vowed to destroy the British Army. An evacuation arranged for mid-December from Kabul was delayed, with shortage of food a major concern. The Kabul garrison of 4,500 soldiers, of which nearly 700 were the Essex (44th) Regiment, together with 12,000 camp followers under Major General Elphinstone, left on 6 January 1842 in freezing weather, with no tents and no guarantee of safe conduct. A dreadful seven-day ordeal took place with many skirmishes, loss of life, desertions, and women and children taken as hostages. The last stand of the 44th Foot took place at Gandamak on 12 January, Captain Souter with the regimental Colours wrapped around him as a waistcoat. The Afghans thought that he was a high-ranking official and took him hostage.

Elphinstone meanwhile was held hostage in the Afghan camp and taken in by the false promises of safe conduct, was still trying to negotiate safe passage with Akbar Khan. The only survivor, assistant surgeon Dr William Brydon from Shah Shuja's contingent, made a slow trek to Jalalabad on his dying pony. Jalalabad – under Brigadier Sale – withheld a siege for four months and at Ghuznee the British were given safe conduct to leave, but were treacherously betrayed and killed. The new Governor General of India, Lord Ellenborough, arranged for the final withdrawal of the army and was determined that the British would leave with dignity and some kind of success behind them. Major General Pollock led a punitive relieving force from Peshawar, cleared the obstruction at the Khyber Pass and raised the siege of Jalalabad in April. Major General Nott – who was garrison commander in Kandahar – then joined up with Pollock to relieve Kabul in September. Akbar Khan was killed and Pollock recaptured the lost guns and Colours, and released the civilian hostages and military prisoners. For good measure, he blew up the Kabul bazaar as retribution. Dost Muhammad returned from exile as Amir. The slaughter at Gandamak was the worse military disaster up to that time. The British withdrew from Afghanistan and left it to its own devices, as there was no longer a Russian threat.

In 1672, the East India Company secured trading rights in China at Taiwan but the Chinese forever suspicious of foreigners later restricted trading to Canton, with the Portuguese well established in Macao.

The 'factories' established by the EIC, with its Royal Charter and monopoly, in Canton continued trading Traders were very restricted to Canton only, but had to conform to unusual trading practices, enforced by the 'Guild of Chinese Merchants'. In addition, unorthodox payments to custom officials and local officials and Mandarins, together with severe taxes on shipping, which were completely at loggerheads with normal trading practices, worldwide. This was such a concern to the EIC and the British government, that the director of EIC requested the government to send a Royal envoy to the Imperial Court in Peking. Lord George Macartney was sent out in 1793 with the purpose to:

- Establish a resident minister in Peking, to advance trading
- Lift trading restrictions
- Establish many other ports for trade

Macartney, after many delays, was granted an audience with Emperor Qianlong in September 1793 where he presented the Emperor with a letter of introduction and presents from King George III, which included a portable planetarium the latest astronomy technology. Mandarins had forewarned Macartney of the protocol to Kowtow to the Emperor but Macartney just bowed. The Emperor was not impressed and Lord Macartney's mission was a failure. The second mission to establish a diplomatic envoy in China, by Lord Amherst in 1816, returned without success after similar frustrations.

The British had been traders in China for some time, with tea as the major import. The demand for tea was such that in the mid-eighteenth century, the imbalance in trade, which was paid in silver, was draining the treasury. Fortunately for the government, opium grown in India would supply the Chinese needs and ease the strain on the treasury. The Chinese became addicted to the drug, the business prospered and the income became a major part of the British economy. The Chinese government finally plucked up the courage to ban the substance, issuing an ultimatum to the traders in 1839 to hand over the whole opium cargo, the value of which was immense. Together with the impounding of the cargo, the local Chinese workers were barred from working and various restrictions were placed on the British factories.

This led to unrest and some Chinese were killed by drunken sailors, the situation escalated and the British were expelled from Canton. The British gunboat *Volage* attacked the Chinese fleet and the First Chinese (Opium) War (1839–42) began. Warships and troopships were sent out with the Cameronians and the Royal Irish Regiments, together with Bengal Volunteers. After a blockade of Canton and the capture of Dinghai, dysentery decimated the army. Sir Hugh Gough took over the command of the land forces. British teachers were abducted by Chinese and the British fleet destroyed the Chinese fleet in Macao.

During the peace negotiations, the teachers were released and the Chinese agreed to pay the British government $6,000,000 for the opium loss and war reparations, but would not agree to lease a port. 1,500 troops landed at the mouth of Canton. At the ceasefire, Britain purchased the deserted island of Hong Kong for $6,000,000 and the British were accepted as bone fide traders. The government did not like the arrangement and replaced Elliot, the government official. More troops were sent out to force the issue. Britain wanted reparations for the conflict in excess of the $6,000,000, an exchange of ambassadors and access to ports. Amoy, Ningbo, Shanghai and Nanking were sacked. At the Treaty of Nanking in August 1842, Britain got $21,000,000 for the confiscated opium and conflict costs and was allowed to trade in six cities (Travis, Hanes and Senello, p.156). Consular officials were accepted and Hong Kong was recognised as a British possession. The trade in opium was not a feature of negotiations, but the trade continued unofficially. A change in government in Britain in 1843 outlawed the opium trade, but made no attempt to stop it. The trade now accounted for 10 per cent of Britain's GDP.

India: Scinde and the First and Second Sikh Wars

Scinde in north-west India had had good relations with British India, but the two Amirs were concerned about Britain establishing permanent bases on the route to Quetta. The Amirs of Scinde – realising that the British wanted to stay in their province to access the Bolan Pass into southern Afghanistan for the transfer of troops – tore up their treaty and confronted what they thought was weakened British resolve after losses in Afghanistan. General Sir Charles Napier was sent out in 1842 to agree what was considered to be a one-sided treaty with the Amirs, favourable to Britain. Major Outram was the political agent in Scinde and was given a free hand against Napier's better judgement to negotiate the treaty. Meetings with the Amirs in Hyderabad in January dragged on and on and the Baluchis were gathering force; finally the draft treaty was signed in mid-February. Outram and his staff were threatened and insulted and next day the residency was attacked. Outram had to fight his way out against the 8,000 Baluchis.

Napier made other demands such as the cessation of Karachi and the removal of duties on troop movements. When the Baluchis massed at Hyderabad, Napier invaded and his 2,800-strong army defeated 30,000 Baluchis matchlock men trapped in a riverbed at Meeanee. The 22nd (Cheshire) Foot were the only British regiment present at the Conquest of Scinde in 1843. The Baluchis were defeated again at Hyderabad and Scinde was annexed for the Crown and took British influence up to the Afghan border. Whilst the Governor in India was pleased with the annexation, London was not and Lord Ellenborough was recalled.

The Sikh state of Lahore had established its border with British India on the Sutlej River. The Sikhs under the loyal Maharaja of the Punjab, Ranjit Singh, allowed the British Army access into northern Afghanistan via the Khyber Pass, but on his death in 1839 his successor was a child and his advisers were not so accommodating. The powerful Sikh Army, now without a controlling influence, started to flex its muscles and decided to cross the Sutlej River to pillage. By crossing the Sutlej the Sikhs had violated the 1809 border agreement, initiating the First Sikh War (1845–46). The British and Indian Army were attacked at Moodkee where the approaching clouds of dust gave General Sir Hugh Gough and his three divisions time to deploy the infantry, with the cavalry screening the Sikh Army.

After the battle the Sikhs retired to Ferozeshah where a few days later the 62nd (Wiltshire) and 80th (Staffordshire Volunteers) suffered heavy casualties in a hard-fought battle over two days. The battle had started late in the day, delayed for an additional brigade to arrive. The Wiltshire Regiment alone lost 260 men in ten minutes attacking the Sikh artillery firing grapeshot. At dawn next morning the battle recommenced after a respite and General Sir Harry Smith led the final charge, with four battalions, which finally defeated the enemy. The casualties from the two battles approached 3,000.

At Aliwal, Smith again defeated the Sikhs who were attacking his supply route and he effectively used the 16th Lancers. At Sobraon, General Sir Henry Hardinge, Governor General of Bengal, was present and considered the Sikh Army to be 'the bravest and most warlike and most disruptive enemy in Asia' (Lawrence, p.106). The Sikhs were considered to be a match for the British in discipline, training and weapons. Some said that the Sikh gunners were on a par with Napoleon's artillery – a huge compliment as gunner Napoleon knew how to use such weaponry. Gough with two divisions under Major General Sir Walter Raleigh Gilbert, and Brigadier Colin Campbell with 14,000 men faced the Sikh Army of 60,000 and fought a bloody two-day battle. Stacey's brigade of 10th (North Lincolnshire) 53rd (Shropshire) and 80th (Staffordshire Volunteers) took the brunt in the first wave against the Sikh defences. Eight regiments received Battle Honours in addition to two Indian regiments and three cavalry regiments. The British lost 2,000 and the Sikhs 10,000, who were slaughtered or drowned trying to cross the river when the bridge of boats collapsed. The Sikhs lost all their guns, but three British generals were killed. Gough entered Lahore in style with bands playing.

The Punjab came under British influence but was still allowed independent rule by the Regent. Further problems arose in the Punjab, when two British officers acting as envoys to the city of Multan were murdered and beheaded in April 1848. Insurrection spread and an initial attack on the rebels at Multan failed in August, sparking the Second Sikh War (1848–49). This action could not be postponed for cooler weather, and at the height of the Indian summer the army suffered badly. The 32nd (Cornwall) lost many soldiers with fourteen dead and 175 sick through heatstroke and dehydration. Gough crossed the Sutlej River in November 1848 with the Army of the Punjab – twenty-one regiments of infantry, eleven batteries of artillery and twelve regiments of cavalry – to restore order. Sher Singh, the Sikh leader, had 16,000 troops. The first action at Ramnager next to the River Chenab was initiated by Brigadier Cureton with his vanguard of cavalry. Gough wanted his full force to come up first but found himself catching up with Cureton's premature cavalry attacks. Cureton and Havelock – the 14th Light Dragoon colonel – were killed.

The battle started on 22 November and the Sikhs finally withdrew on 3 December. Having received reinforcements, Gough commenced to besiege Multan on 27 December. Multan finally fell and those responsible for the murders of the envoys were hanged. At the Battle of Chillianwala (13 January 1849), Gough advanced into jungle scrub and heavy artillery fire with 12,000 men against 35,000 Sikhs well dug in on a 7-mile front. It was a two-division attack, with Campbell on the left and Gilbert on the right, with Brigadier Pennycuick in reserve.

The 24th (2nd Warwickshire) advanced into the scrub and suffered badly, losing half their men but taking the Sikh gun position. The 24th lost their flank support and had to withdraw from the field in disorder following an overwhelming Sikh counter-attack and, battered by Sikh cavalry, lost their Colours. When Pennycuick's brigade withdrew, the reserve brigade closed the gap. Hogan's brigade under Colin Campbell had more success, capturing thirteen guns. The 61st (South Gloucestershire), on coming out of the jungle, charged the Sikh cavalry and then faced the Sikh infantry, capturing their battery. The 29th (Worcestershire) gained their objective losing a third of their strength. Walter Gilbert's division secured their objective but found their flank was left exposed when some of the cavalry left the battlefield. When the cavalry arrived in Chillianwala, non-combatant officers, including the padre, rallied them. Gough was so taken by the action of the chaplain that he requested the man be made a Brevet Bishop. British and Sikhs had to retire from the positions. The next day rain obliged the Sikhs to move back to Gujarat.

The casualties in the Sikh Wars and lack of leadership at Chillianwala led to the removal of Gough, to be replaced by General Charles Napier. Before Napier could arrive, Gough regrouped and waited for reinforcements from Multan. The final battle at Gujarat in 1849 was a complete victory. It was a textbook battle with the artillery dominant, an infantry assault and the retreating enemy chased by cavalry. The famous Koh-I-Noor diamond passed into British hands and the Punjab was annexed and came under British rule.

Asia: The Second Burma War, the Persian War and the Second Chinese (Opium) War

The new King of Burma rejected all previous treaties with Britain and maintained an anti-British stance. The Burmese Governors of Rangoon defiled the British flag and trade was again interrupted. The Governor General of India, Lord Dalhousie, was now back to square one. The navy seized a Burmese ship in retaliation and blocked the Irrawaddy delta. Again ultimatums flew, only to be ignored, leading to the Second Burma War (1851–53). Under Major General Godwin a much better planned invasion occurred, missing the monsoon season and allowing for time to train the soldiers to attack stockades. Rangoon was captured and also Pegu, which was annexed.

The Burmese monarch was overthrown by a coup, but in the town of Donabyu local chieftain Myat-Toon was still giving trouble and Brigadier Cheape made three attempts through the jungle to reach the stockade, garrisoned by 4,000 Burmese. He finally succeeded with an advance on the stockade led by a young progressive officer, Ensign Garnet Wolseley. Wolseley had led his unit as point on the approach and then volunteered for a storming party. This was successful on the second attempt and Wolseley was mentioned in dispatches. Lower Burma was annexed.

The Persian threat continued in Afghanistan with Persia occupying the city of Herat again in 1852. British ultimatums were successful and Persia withdrew. Persia again occupied Herat in 1856 but this time stayed put when repeated ultimatums were delivered. The Persian War (1856–57) was declared in November. A British invasion force captured the Persian port of Bushire in the Persian Gulf, and later the fortified city of Reshire. Major General Outram defeated the Persians at Kush-ab and they signed a peace treaty agreeing to withdraw from Herat.

The Treaty of Nanking was not honoured by the Chinese, who continued to harass the British factories to the extent of killing some British sailors. When the Chinese kidnapped the crew of *The Arrow*, The Second Chinese (Opium) War (1857–60) was declared. Canton was blockaded and the new British envoy Lord Elgin was sent out to China. Canton was finally captured when enough troops arrived from India. Elgin then sailed for the Bei He River in May 1858, on the approach to Peking. At the Taku Forts the British and French navy had to overcome many booms blocking their advance; the forts were taken and the fleet sailed onto Tianjin, which was occupied without resistance. The Treaty of Tianjin was ratified in June 1858, which granted the British an ambassador to Peking, more cities open to trade, missionary access, and eleven more ports opened, together with $5,000,000 war reparations. Taxes on imported goods were agreed, listing opium for the first time and therefore making it a legal trade. The terms were unsatisfactory to the Emperor of China, who continued to prevaricate over all agreements.

The British public were dismayed at the continuation of the opium trade, particularly religious groups. No sooner was the ink dry on the treaty than there was disturbance in Canton with the shelling of the residency. (Some publications designate the second half of this war to be the Third Chinese War, but the British Army Battle Honours maintain it to be the Second Chinese War.) The Chinese also reneged on the assent for a permanent ambassador in Peking, insisting it was agreed under duress. When the fleet entered Bei He again, more booms were down and this time the Taku Forts were well defended. Of the four forts, one was selected to be attacked by French and British troops. When this fort fell the other three surrendered. The booms were removed and once again the army marched to Tianjin.

The Chinese were again prepared to negotiate, rather than have foreign troops in Peking. Two British envoys under a flag of truce entered Tong Xian and were asked to go to Tianjin to negotiate with General Seng, but were arrested. They were then forced to kowtow to General Seng and were humiliated and in the coming days maltreated and starved in a similar way to other British hostages, some of whom died. Seng's 20,000 troops – mostly with bows and arrows and ancient firearms – faced 3,500 British and French soldiers at Zhangjiawan and were defeated. The Allies demanded the release of the hostages but were ignored and Peking was approached. After a pause to bring up some heavy artillery the Summer Palace on the outskirts of Peking was entered and ransacked by the French. When the British arrived they followed suit and many priceless antiques were destroyed. The envoys were released alive and the gates to Peking were finally opened on 24 October, only to reveal that the Emperor had fled. The Convention of Peking in 1860 gave the British $10,000,000 in war reparations, access to further ports, Kowloon became British, an ambassador was allowed in Peking and an apology was received from the Emperor (Travis, Hanes and Sanello, p.290).

New Zealand: The Maori Wars

In 1840, the Treaty of Waitangi was signed by all the main Maori chiefs. It had three articles. The first article ceded New Zealand to the Crown and 'all rights and powers of sovereignty over their respective territories'. In the second article, the Queen guaranteed to the chiefs, tribes and families full, exclusive and undisturbed ownership of their lands, estates, forests, fisheries and other possessions. The chiefs maintained the right to sell land to the Queen and her agents. The third article gave the Maoris Royal protection. This document became controversial, in part because of the problematic translation into Maori. Some companies made fraudulent land deals, with title deeds signed sealed and delivered, but the Maori tradition was based upon inherited right, without written documents. The first clashes occurred in the South Island when thirty Europeans were killed in 1843. Further clashes occurred at Taita and Boulcott's farm in 1846, and the First Maori War (1846–47) began.

Chief Hone Heke from North Island was the first to sign the treaty and soon regretted it when he saw the extent of European expansion. At the Maori capital Kororareka the local flagstaff was – in the eyes of the Maoris – contaminated by the raising of the Union Jack. The Maoris loyal to Heke cut it down. It was replaced again and again and still cut down. Heke was outlawed and raised support against the British. Battles occurred at Puketutu, Ohaeawai and Ruapekapeka, with 300 British killed.

Heke eventually made peace with the Governor, and the Maoris were encouraged to elect a king; King Potatau was elected in 1856. A controversial land deal was made at Waitara near New Plymouth and the chiefs continued to object to European expansion. The Governor overruled them, starting the Second Maori War, sometimes known as the Taranaki War (1860–61). Major General Pratt, in command of 3,000 troops, was defeated at the heavily defended stockade at Puketakauere and the Maoris laid siege to New Plymouth. Some Maoris withdrew to plant crops, but were then defeated at the part-built Mahoetahi stockade. Peace was again agreed, but the troops stayed. The Governor built roads and communications for a military route to Waikato and now had 20,000 soldiers, sailors, Royal Marines Light Infantry and militia. The militia's reward for joining battle was the gift of land.

The invasion of Waikato occurred in July 1863, heralding the start of the Third Maori War (1863–66). Two stockades were defeated and at Rangiriri the Maoris surrendered. The conflict moved on to the rich agricultural areas and Rangiaowhia was attacked on a Sunday with non-combatants at prayer killed, an insult that infuriated the Maoris still further. The battle at Orakau ended after three assaults and Waikato was under control. The Bay of Plenty was the next target, at Tauranga, where Cameron with 1,700 men could not manage to storm the stockade defended by 230 Maoris. The Maoris evacuated the stockade only to be defeated at Te Ranga. The war was over in April 1864 with 1,000 Maori and 700 European deaths. Disturbances continued over land promised to the militia.

The Corps of Instructors

The Corps of Instructors was founded at Hythe in Kent in 1853, to maintain and improve training standards for small arms and support weapons. It became the Small Arms School in 1919, the Small Arms School Corps in 1929 and in 1969 moved to Warminster. The sister unit, the School of Musketry was formed at the same time and is now the School of Infantry, also at Warminster in Wiltshire, near Salisbury Plain. The school's current role is 'to train selected infantrymen, instructors and commanders from all arms and services, up to the rank of Brigadier, in skill-at-arms, support weapons, communications and combined arms tactics'.

The Crimean War

In 1853, Russia had designs on Turkey (the Ottoman Empire) and access to the Mediterranean. France and Russia were granted control of the holy places by the sultan. An incident flared up in Bethlehem (under Turkish rule) where Orthodox monks under Russian protection were killed while preventing French Roman Catholic monks putting a star over the manger. The situation escalated and Russia invaded the Danubian Principalities of Moldavia and Wallachia, under the pretext of protecting Russian Orthodox Christianity from persecution. Turkey declared war on Russia. Ultimatums from the British and French governments were sent to the Russians and were ignored. When the Russian Fleet from Sevastopol sank the Turkish Fleet at Sinope, Great Britain was shocked and the Crimean War (1854–56) was declared.

Russia withdrew from the principalities, but besieged Silistria in Bulgaria. The war was noticeable for the intensely cold conditions, poor supplies and medical services. 15,700 of the 19,600 lives lost were from disease.

Five infantry divisions, Duke of Cambridge's 1st, Major General de Lacy Evans's 2nd, Lieutenant General England's 3rd, Major General Cathcart's 4th and Lieutenant General Brown's Light, were sent out under Lord Raglan together with a cavalry division under Lord Lucan consisting of the Light and Heavy Cavalry Brigades. The Anglo-French force landed at Varna (Bulgaria) in May 1854 as an advance base, awaiting diplomatic moves and instructions. With the Russians withdrawing from occupied territory, the main objective was the capture of the Russian naval base at Sevastopol.

Disease broke out in the French lines on 19 July, then in the British lines, with 10,000 dying of cholera, dysentery and fever before hostilities broke out. The original landing site chosen for the attack was the River Katcha, 7 miles north of Sevastopol. This changed to Calamita Bay, 40 miles north, to avoid an opposed landing. The invading force of 61,000 British, French and Turks landed on 14 September 1854.

The army marched off to Sevastopol with flags flying and bands playing on 19 September, but ranks soon fell out as illness took its toll and the route was littered with debris. The French marched near the coast and the British inland, with the Turks in the rear. At the hill approaching Alma, the whole of the Russian Army could be seen, all 39,000, with ninety-six guns. The French position occupied 3 miles and the British position another 3 miles with the cavalry on the flank. The difficult ground sloped down to the River Alma with steep banks in parts. The Russians's strong point opposite the British position was the Kourgane Hill, with twelve heavy guns and infantry mounted on earthworks at the Great Redoubt and lighter guns with more infantry regiments on the Lesser Redoubt to the left. There were sixteen battalions of Russian infantry and four field batteries adjacent to the redoubts.

Opposite the French position was Telegraph Hill, which included a road or track leading to the road to Sevastopol. Just after 1.30 p.m. on 20 September 1854, the Russian guns opened fire on the approaching British and French. The French attacked first, approaching the far right and occupying Telegraph Hill. They even got light troops up the precipitous track, the approach to which was thinly defended as it was deemed impassable. This successful assault terminated when the French withdrew because they could not bring guns to support. The French launched a second two-division attack to take Telegraph Hill, but could not make progress and were pinned down by the Russian fire. Raglan was now asked by the French to relieve their desperate situation with a British attack. Raglan had rejected a flanking attack and launched a frontal attack into the teeth of the Russian fire. The Light Infantry Division under Brown and 2nd Division under de Lacy Evans marched down to cross the river and assault the Great Redoubt in a line 2 miles wide and two men deep. The Royal Welch Fusiliers lost fourteen officers, of whom eight were killed. The first Victoria Crosses to be gazetted were won by their Sergeant O'Connor and Captain Bell.

The Russians set fire to a village and burning stacks of brushwood added to the confusion, reducing visibility. Formation was lost, ranks closed up as gaps appeared. The 1st Division under the Duke of Cambridge was to give support, but Cambridge hesitated, possibly owing to imprecise orders. The British leading divisions captured the Great Redoubt but with harassing fire from the Lesser Redoubt and lack of support, had to fall back in haste. Cambridge's Division of the Guards and Highland Brigades now attacked under relentless Russian fire.

The French began to get guns near and together with the British artillery, started to silence the Russian guns. The Guards and Highlanders faced Russian infantry in massive columns. The Russian columns broke and the Great Redoubt was captured for the second time. The Russians fled and Lucan wished to give chase and rout the Russians with his Light Brigade. Raglan not only refused Lucan's request, but sent Lucan strict orders for the cavalry to stand fast and not to pursue the fleeing enemy. Sir Colin Campbell, always ready to use his initiative, sent six guns of the Royal Horse Artillery after the Russians. The cavalry under Lucan and Cardigan escorting the artillery sited the guns and took advantage of the situation by attacking and taking prisoners. Raglan was fearful of the Russians making a stand and the fresh Russian cavalry destroying his own. Raglan sent a second order for the cavalry to return to their duty of escorting the guns and when this had little effect, a third order to cease pursuit forthwith. The cavalry were not impressed.

After the Battle of the Alma the Allies did not advance on to Sevastopol to take on the Russians, who were in a state of chaos, but lingered burying the dead and regrouping, as cholera was still prevalent. The British suffered 2,000 casualties and the Russians 4,500. Raglan and General Canrobert for the French, as Saint-Arnaud was dying, decided to assault Sevastopol from the other side, the south side. This was because of expected fortifications. The army made a flank march, leaving on 23 September.

At Mackenzie's Farm the next day, Lucan's cavalry and artillery led the way down difficult tracks while the infantry with Raglan were behind going through wood and scrub. The cavalry took a wrong turning and were lost; Raglan also got lost and, to make matters worse, Raglan and his staff took a route out of the forest that ran straight into a Russian column. The Russians were evacuating Sevastopol leaving behind Russian sailors, having sunk ships in the harbour. Everyone was paralysed (Woodham-Smith, p.199). Like Ney at Quatre Bras, the Russians expected stronger forces in the area and were slow to take advantage of the golden opportunity to capture the British Commander-in-Chief. Raglan was fortunate to be extracted, when the cavalry arrived with a red-faced Lucan, who was admonished by his commander. The Allies reached

Balaclava, the small port an ideal base for the army. The Royal Navy had just arrived and also brought a heavy brigade of cavalry.

Outside Sevastopol, Raglan waited with his infantry for the siege guns from the Royal Navy to commence bombardment. By this time the Russians had reinforced Sevastopol with naval personnel and guns from sunken ships. When the siege guns arrived, firing commenced on 17 October. After the battles at Balaclava, the Russians remained on Causeway Heights and Raglan continued his siege of Sevastopol.

The Russians received reinforcements and, concerned about the siege, attacked the Allies at Inkerman on 5 November. A three-pronged attack occurred at 5 a.m. in misty fog with the 2nd Division's position at Home Ridge taking the initial assault of a Russian corps. When the 2nd Division fell back, Cathcart reinforced them. The second Russian corps attacked and outflanked the British at Sandbag battery, which fell and was retaken a few times. The Russians attacked the centre, but Cambridge had reinforced it with the Guards who had to retake the battery. The British were struggling when the French reinforced the position with colonial troops of Zouaves and Algerians. When guns were brought up the Russians were chased across the river.

The British lost nearly 600 killed and 2,000 wounded. The Sandbag battery was described by the French as an abattoir. Continuation of the siege was out of the question as reinforcements were required. The weather turned foul and a three-day hurricane sank over twenty ships, one of which was carrying the British winter clothing. The winter was the worst on record and both armies suffered. When news of the success at Inkerman reached London, Raglan was promoted to Field Marshal.

The second main bombardment of Sevastopol occurred in April but the French still refused to assault. The French Commander-in-Chief resigned and was replaced by General Pelissier. The third bombardment occurred early in June with 600 guns. The outer defences of Sevastopol were captured. The French took Mamelon and the British the Quarries, but the main attack failed. Following the failure to take Sevastopol, Raglan died of ill health. His temporary replacement was Major General Simpson, his Chief of Staff, with his permanent replacement being Major General Codrington. Sevastopol finally fell on 8 September with the British attacking the Grand Sedan without success and the French taking Malakov Bastion. The Russians had had enough and withdrew, Sevastopol finally surrendering. An armistice was agreed in February 1856 and the Treaty of Paris formalised the defeat.

The Indian Mutiny

In 1833 an Act of Parliament modified the governing of India. With a new charter the East India Company ceased trading and the Governor General of Bengal governed all India and had presidencies in Bengal, Bombay and Madras. The Bengal Army had seventy-four regiments with 86,000 men, the Bombay Army twenty-nine regiments with 45,000 men and the Madras Army fifty-two regiments with 51,000 men. After the Sikh Wars, nearly all of India was under British rule.

Hindu tradition dictated that when a man died his son performed funeral rights to prevent the father being eternally damned. Rajas without a natural heir would adopt a son, who would conduct his funeral and also inherit his title and land. Lord Dalhousie, Governor General of India, introduced the 'Doctrine of Lapse' in 1848 to restrict this practice, by annexing property where no rightful male heir existed (David, *Mutiny*, p.6). The Raja of Satara's heir – adopted on his deathbed – was prevented from inheriting his land and all its revenues; instead it was confiscated by the East India Company. The same applied to Lakshmi Bai, the infamous Rani of Jhansi, whose adopted son was excluded on the death of the Raja. The Rani was so incensed that she even took her claim to Calcutta and London without success.

Other states such as Nagpur were annexed when no heir existed. Also dispossessed was Nana Sahib, the adopted son of the last Peshawar of the Maratha Confederacy in Bithur. In the state of Oudh (Lucknow its capital) the new King Wajid Ali Shah – who for a long time had been guilty of maladministration – had his land annexed by the Company, on the grounds that he was not fit to rule. The vast majority of sepoys were from Oudh.

The Hindu practice of *sati*, whereby wives threw themselves or were forced to throw themselves onto the funeral pyres of their husbands, had been made illegal in 1829. The Hindus were becoming concerned at the British meddling with their customs and culture and the annexation of Oudh was particularly infuriating. Within the ranks of the army there was discontent amongst the sepoys, with grievances over poor pay and accommodation. Opportunities to better their lot through prize money and plunder were becoming less frequent. The sepoys's promotion prospects were limited in the Indian regiments, who recruited only Europeans. Saul David describes it thus:

> The inadequacy of career prospect for Indian soldiers was particularly acute in the Bengal army, because its system of promotion was based upon length of service rather than merit. In Bombay and Madras the opposite was true.

It was no coincidence that in Bengal, fifty-four regiments mutinied in whole or in part, while only three in Bombay and none in Madras did so. The Commander-in-Chief India had widened the recruitment base, removing all objections to recruitment from particular respectable castes. Particularly galling was 'The General Service Enlistment Order of 1856'. This order ensured sepoys would have to travel overseas if requested. For some castes, travelling over the sea was taboo. Sir Henry Lawrence, Chief Commissioner for Oudh, informed Lord Canning of his misgivings about this order.

The new Enfield rifle – which had been introduced in the Crimea – found its way to India in 1856 with hot climate trials by the 60th Rifles. The old ball was replaced by the new Minié bullet. The tight-fitting bullet had three grooves, which had to be greased to facilitate the loading drill. The moulds were sent to India for manufacture and assembly of the cartridge at the various ordinance depots. The paper cartridge contained a single bullet and a powder charge and was wrapped with a conventional greased paper, which was both damp proof and easier to ram. During the loading drill, the soldier had to bite the end off the wrapping in order to pour the powder into the rifle.

In January 1857 some Bengal Native Infantry sepoys were sent to Dum Dum arsenal to practise with the new Enfield. Rumours spread that the grease contained beef and pork fat and thus was offensive to both Muslims and Hindus, and this fed the rumour that all sepoys would be converted to Christianity. These fears were acknowledged by the authorities, who allowed the sepoys to grease their own bullets 'in house' with vegetable fat or beeswax during the manufacture of the cartridges, but this did not allay the fears. General Anson Commander-in-Chief India, on a visit to Ambala in March, told the assembled sepoys that there was no intention to interfere with their religion and caste system.

On 29 March 1857 Mangal Pandey, a sepoy of the 34th Bengal Native Infantry, attempted to kill a European officer and raise a mutiny, but no sepoys supported him. The 19th BNI was disbanded on 31 March, as it was implicated in sedition and Pandey was hanged at Barrackpure on 8 April. The 34th BNI were disbanded on 6 May for passive mutiny. Unrest continued and was spreading from the military to the civilian population; houses were burnt down and European civilians maltreated.

Lord Canning, the new Governor General of India, was aware of the sepoys's concerns and amended the loading procedure of the Enfield rifle to break off the cartridge in place of biting. With a copy of the new firing drill, the commanding officer (CO) of the 3rd Bengal Light Cavalry lined up his ninety elite skirmishers at Meerut on 24 April to practise loading the new rifle. When offered the new cartridges, all but five refused them. At the subsequent court of inquiry, it was demonstrated that the bullets had been greased 'in house' by sepoys with no offensive fat and that the wrapping paper was the same as for the previous ball ammunition and therefore the refusal was collective disobedience. The skirmishers were all sentenced to ten years with loss of pension. The rebels were taken in chains to the local jail, escorted by the 60th Rifles and 6th Dragoon Guards.

On 10 May the 3rd Bengal Light Cavalry Regiment mutinied and ran amok, killing fifty British officers and civilians and releasing the prisoners. They were soon joined by other Bengal Native Infantry and the Indian Mutiny, or First War of Independence (1857–59) began. The telegraph office in Delhi got wind of trouble at Meerut and sent a message to Ambala – British Army HQ – on 11 May, that the sepoys were burning bungalows and killing people. A further message about the mutiny of the 3rd Bengal Light Cavalry Regiment was forwarded to Lahore, where Sir John Lawrence, Chief Commissioner for the Punjab, acted promptly by consulting the military and civil authorities.

The initial reaction was to order civilians to take refuge and stop the issue of rifles and percussion caps to Indian regiments. Lawrence arranged to disarm the local garrison early next morning. This was completed by the 81st Regiment of Foot and artillery, who stood to, fully armed and loaded at Mian Mir, when the three regiments of Bengal Native Infantry and the 8th Bengal Light Cavalry were ordered to ground arms.

At the other end of the Punjab in Peshawar, news of the mutiny arrived the same day. The post office and strategic points were secured. The local five regiments were paraded and disarmed without incident. The remaining regiment was at Hoti Mardan and Brigadier Nicholson went out with the 70th Regiment of Foot and a loyal cavalry regiment to disarm them. The cavalry challenged the rebels who turned and fought. 120 were killed and 120 captured, the rest fleeing to Kashmir. The captured sepoys were all to be executed, but eventually forty were selected to be blown from the guns. A Punjab moveable column under Brigadier Neville Chamberlain headed for Delhi with Nicholson taking charge when Chamberlain joined Barnard's staff (David, *Mutiny*, p.146). After the mutiny at Meerut the 60th Rifles restored order but the mutineers fled the 36 miles to Delhi.

The last of the Mogul Emperors, Bahadur Shah II, had long ceased to reign over an empire, and was titled the 'King of Delhi'. He was in retirement with a British pension in the Red Fort. The rebel 3rd Bengal Light Cavalry from Meerut soon forced their way into the fort and sought support from the King. After an initial rejection, the king gave his support and they declared him Emperor. The Delhi Brigade of the 38th, 54th and 74th BNI, were the only defence and they mutinied except for isolated detachments. British officers were killed including the colonel of the 54th BNI. Some sepoys remained loyal and supported the British attempts to secure the gates. Overwhelmed by the arrival of two regiments of mutineers from Meerut, the British officers defending the Delhi magazine had a difficult job and after a fierce defence had to blow the magazine, the biggest in upper India. Lieutenants Willoughby, Forrest and Raynor were awarded VCs and Delhi was evacuated and left to the rebels.

The rebels set about killing Christians and destroying churches and cemeteries. Groups of Europeans made their way to Ambala and Meerut. Fifty Europeans were interned in the bowels of the Red Fort, but the mutineers found them and massacred all but five of them who were Muslims. General Anson had at his immediate disposal for the 1,000 miles from Delhi to Calcutta the 53rd Foot and 84th Foot (Calcutta), 10th Foot (Dinapore), 32nd Foot (Lucknow), and the 3rd Bengal European Fusiliers at Agra. He could call on the 43rd Foot and 1st Madras European Fusiliers (Madras), the 35th Foot (Pegu Burma), and the 2nd Bombay European Fusiliers (Bombay). There was the possibility of additional support from the 64th Foot and 78th Highlanders (Persia), the 90th Foot (China expedition), the 5th Foot (Mauritius), the 93rd Foot (Cape Town), the 48th Foot, 57th Foot and 71st Highlanders (Malta), and finally the 8th Hussars (England).

Anson's immediate task was to secure the arsenals in the Punjab with the 61st, the 81st and some of the 8th Foot. From the British Army's winter headquarters in Simla he sent the 75th Foot and the 1st and 2nd Bengal European Fusiliers to Ambala and the 9th Lancers and Sirmoor Ghurka has to meet up with them at Meerut.

These reinforcements were for the relief of Delhi. With the mutiny speedily turning into a civil war, help from friendly maharajas was sought and most maintained their loyalty.

By end of May, mutinies had occurred across the whole of Oudh in north India and notably in Meerut, Delhi, Ferozepore, Aligarh, Agra, Lucknow and Bareilly. In June it spread to Nimach, Benares, Cawnpore, Jhansi, Allahabad and Gwalior, and in July to Indore, Sagar, Azimgarh and Dinapore. In addition to the cities, many garrison towns mutinied. With one or two exceptions the mutiny had not spread any further south and the maharajas and princes had remained loyal. Under siege were Delhi, Lucknow, Cawnpore and the Europeans in Agra's Red Fort. Sir Henry Lawrence (brother of Sir John) was in Lucknow with the 32nd (Cornwall) Foot, preparing for a siege, contrary to the advice of his military commander, on whom he had to pull rank. The brigadier was of the opinion that his sepoys would remain loyal. Lawrence removed the magazine and made a fortress out of the Residency, in which the British took refuge on 30 June. The sepoys did mutiny and the brigadier was killed. Lawrence was later killed by a shell.

Colonel Neill moved his troops along the trunk road to secure Benares and Allahabad in early June with Allahabad becoming the new British base. General Anson died of cholera and Lieutenant General Sir Patrick Grant from the Madras presidency was nominated as his temporary replacement until Sir Colin Campbell arrived as Commander-in-Chief India. Until Grant arrived from Madras, General Barnard commanded the Delhi Relief Force. Barnard also died of cholera and General Reed was now commander of the Delhi Relief Force. Reed soon resigned due to ill health and General Wilson took charge as the fourth commander in three months.

In Cawnpore, General Wheeler was bottled up preparing for a siege with 200 British regulars, mainly 32nd (Cornwall) 84th (York and Lancaster) with artillery, and nearly 900 civilians. Two regiments had mutinied and two were suspect. The dispossessed Prince Nana Sahib was in charge of the rebels who opened the attack on 6 June. Food and water ran out and appeals to Lucknow failed as they had their own problems. By 23 June 4,000 rebels surrounded the entrenchment and continued the attack. One third had been killed when Nana Sahib offered terms. He wanted guns, ammunition and treasure for granting safe passage.

Wheeler negotiated terms with Nana Sahib for his group to leave by boat down river to Allahabad on 27 June. Instead of the promised safe conduct, they were treacherly ambushed at Sati Chaura Ghat and many were killed or drowned, including General Wheeler himself. Only four survived the boat trip. A few senior officers and 125 women and children were imprisoned in a bibighar for some weeks. Other fugitives elsewhere were also rounded up and when the relieving army under General Havelock approached the city, on 15 July all were slaughtered. Seventy-three women and 124 children were butchered and thrown naked down a well.

When Havelock arrived he found that Nana Sahib had left for Lucknow, leaving Brigadier Neill to seek vengeance on Cawnpore. Havelock's force was decimated by engagements and illness and had to return to Cawnpore to await reinforcements.

The new Commander-in-Chief India, Sir Colin Campbell, now the sixth, took over in August 1857. One of his tasks was to bring an end to the siege of Delhi. Delhi had attracted quite a number of mutineers in part because of its Mogul history, and 40,000 rebels faced a 7,000-strong Delhi Relief Force camped outside on the ridge under General Wilson. The majority of the relief force had to force-march 30 miles a day for three weeks from the Punjab to reach the city. The rebels's morale inside Delhi was deteriorating because they had no effective leaders and the British retaliatory action with superior weapons had unnerved them. In August three rebel brigades totalling 10,000 left Delhi, the Jhansi, Bareilly and Nimach Brigades gave up, but this still left quite a forbidding number in defence.

When the siege train finally arrived, the siege of Delhi could finally be raised after so many delays. Four batteries were dug in with a total of fifty guns and mortars. Wilson had 10,000 troops of which only 3,000 were European.

The bombardment began on 12 September and Delhi was stormed on 14 September by four columns with a fifth in reserve. The first column led by Brigadier Nicholson attacked the Kashmir Bastion and Ajmir Gate; the second column led by Brigadier Jones attacked the Water Bastion and Kabul Gate; the third column led by Colonel Campbell attacked the Kashmir Gate and Jama Masjid Mosque; the fourth column led by Major Reid attacked the suburbs and Kashmir Gate; and the fifth column in reserve was led by Brigadier Longfield. The cavalry under Brigadier Hope Grant was to prevent any rebel flanking movements. Brigadier Nicholson, a most promising officer, was wounded and died a few days later.

The King of Delhi was captured and exiled to Rangoon and his two sons were shot. The British losses over the six days of fighting were 992 killed and 2,845 wounded out of a force of 10,000 (David, *Mutiny*, p.305). After Delhi, Cawnpore was the priority, but information from Lucknow – which was under siege – indicated that they could not last out. Havelock relieved Lucknow on 26 September after an eighty-seven-day siege, with heavy losses including two brigade commanders. The 78th Highlanders led the way.

The relieving force could not leave Lucknow for Cawnpore and so it remained inside, still under siege but extending the defences beyond the Residency. A further threat came from Tatya Tope, at the head of the previously friendly 15,000 Gwalior contingent, which advanced on Cawnpore. When reinforcements arrived from overseas, Sir Colin Campbell gave Lucknow his first priority as food was in short supply.

The 93rd Highlanders and 53rd (Shropshire) were the lead regiments to storm the large fortified gardens, the Sikandarbagh, and then the final barrier, the Shah Najaf mosque. The first black man to be awarded a VC was at the relief of Lucknow. Lieutenant Young and the rating Hall manned the last 24-pounder after all guns and crews were destroyed. After half a day, under constant fire, they finally broke through, much to the relief of Campbell. Both received the VC and were part of the Shannon Brigade supporting Royal Navy guns. Hall, a son of a freed slave, was from Canada and had joined the Royal Navy. A total of twenty-one Victoria Crosses, the highest for one engagement, were awarded for the Relief of Lucknow (Billière, p.337). Victoria Crosses were won by the 78th Highlanders (8), 93rd Highlanders (6), and the 53rd Shropshire (5). Lucknow was relieved on 17 November. The 32nd (Cornwall) Foot was given the title 'Light Infantry' for their gallantry at the siege of Lucknow and later would become the Duke of Cornwall's Light Infantry. The regiment lost fifteen officers and 364 men killed and eleven officers and 198 men wounded, winning four Victoria Crosses.

The second siege lasted sixty-one days. Campbell decided to evacuate Lucknow of friendly residents and wait for reinforcements. Havelock was informed of his knighthood but died of dysentery within days of being relieved. Campbell now headed for Cawnpore where he had heard that the garrison was under attack by Tatya Tope and had fled the city. The rebel Gwalior contingent under Tatya Tope was reinforced by Nana Sahib's force, under his brother Bala Rao. Campbell recaptured Cawnpore in December and the rebels were destroyed with many guns captured, but the rebel leaders had escaped to Kalpi. By 1858 Campbell had 46,000 British, 10,000 Punjabis and 58,000 Indian troops. In January the visiting Prime Minister of Nepal offered Campbell 8,000 Gurkhas in twelve regiments and these were used in the final relief of Lucknow.

In February Campbell renewed his offensive against Lucknow and the city finally fell on 15 March 1858. Lord Canning, now residing in Allahabad, issued his Oudh proclamation on 14 March, which ordered the confiscation of all land in Oudh unless the local rulers were seen to be loyal to the Crown and the annexation of the land of all rebel leaders.

General Sir Henry Rose in Central India now marched to Jhansi. The Rani of Jhansi was in a predicament. All the evidence seems to suggest that the Rani had no part in the initial mutiny in early June, when the garrison mutinied and murdered sixty Europeans after promising them safe conduct. The Rani had explained her actions and the British had forbidden her to have any effective army of her own to subdue the rebels. Any assistance she gave to the rebels was under duress, as they threatened the destruction of her palace and her life. The British wanted the Rani to restore order and continue to rule, collecting taxes and revenues until the situation improved. The Rani restored order with the help of her father but when a dispute occurred with neighbouring leaders, with Jhansi under siege, the Rani could not get any help from the British who were hard-pressed elsewhere.

The Rani sought help from a neighbouring Raja whose loyalty to the Crown was suspect and this disturbed Lord Canning. The Rani wrote to Rose's commissioner, again stating her innocence and enquiring how she would be judged, but her request produced no reaction. The Rani was damned if she supported the British and damned if she supported the mutiny. It was nine months since the massacre at Jhansi and the Rani had written three letters to the authorities and had ruled her state for the Crown without British help and now General Rose was at the gates of Jhansi. As the Rani could get no guarantee that her case would be considered sympathetically, it is not surprising that she eventually sided with the rebels.

When Rose arrived at Jhansi, he found that Tatya Tope with 15,000 of the Gwalior contingent had come to give support on the Betwa. Tope was defeated but moved back to Kalpi. The Rani defended Jhansi and when it fell on 3 April, she too went to Kalpi. Rose followed and beat both the Rani and Tatya Tope at Kunch and at Kalpi. The mutineers now entered Gwalior to try and persuade the pro-British Maharaja Scindia to join the rebellion, but he refused. The final demise of the Rani occurred at the battle at Kotah-ki-Serai, just outside Gwalior. She was killed by a trooper of the 8th Hussars on 17 June but Tatya Tope escaped. The rebel force now meandered over 3,000 miles over nine months, marching into Indore and Nagpore with the view to raising a rebellion. Campbell's tactic was to chase them into the Nepal Terai district, which was disease-ridden and where they would get no help from the Nepalese. Tatya Tope was betrayed and hanged in April 1859. Bala Rao died of disease and Nana Sahib escaped but was reported to have died. Peace in India was declared by Canning on 8 July 1859. The Victoria Cross was awarded to 182 recipients. Coincidentally, both the youngest and oldest recipients were awarded during the Mutiny: Lieutenant W. Raynor of the Bengal Veteran Establishment, Indian Army, aged 62, and drummer T. Flinn, aged 15 (Billiere, p.16). The casualties in India were 2,600 killed and 8,000 died of sunstroke or disease.

Queen Victoria announced the abolition of the East India Company with the Crown running India and a Viceroy to replace the Governor General. The Peel Committee was set up to overhaul the Indian Army and to recommend changes in the light of the mutiny. A Staff Corps was to be set up for each of the three presidencies, and all native infantry regiments were to be based on the irregular system with six European officers. Regimental positions were to be regarded as staff appointments, with appropriate pay, commanding officers were to have increased power to punish and reward, and promotions were to be based on efficiency rather than seniority. Uniforms were to be more suitable, and the shako and leather stock were abolished. The native army was to consist of different nationalities and castes, and all enlistment would be for general service.

Recruitment moved from Oudh to the Punjab and Nepal (David, p.399). The nine European infantry regiments (and three cavalry) recruited and funded by the East India Company were taken onto the British establishment in 1858, but stayed in India and continued to be funded by India. Queen Victoria in a proclamation of 1861 made the senior regiment Royal, one from each presidency. They were finally numbered and titled as follows in 1862:

101st Royal Bengal Fusiliers, from the 1st Bengal European Fusiliers
104th Bengal Fusiliers from the 2nd Bengal European Fusiliers
107th Bengal Infantry Regiment from the 3rd Bengal European Light Infantry
102nd Royal Madras Fusiliers from the 1st Madras European Fusiliers
105th Madras Light Infantry Regiment from the 2nd Madras European Light Infantry
108th Madras Infantry Regiment from the 3rd Madras European Infantry Regiment
103rd Royal Bombay Fusiliers from the 1st Bombay European Fusiliers
106th Bombay Light Infantry from the 2nd Bombay European Light Infantry
109th Bombay Infantry Regiment from the 3rd Bombay European Infantry Regiment

As mentioned earlier, the 103rd Royal Bombay Fusiliers have a long history, having been raised in the time of Charles II to garrison Bombay, which he acquired by marriage. It should be noted that the strength of the British Army during major conflicts increased to meet demands, with the raising of numbered regiments of foot only for most of them to be disbanded at the end of hostilities. The 105th Regiment of Foot for example, has had four reincarnations, having been raised during the Seven Years' War, the War of American Independence and the French Revolutionary Wars, to be disbanded each time. The 105th Madras Light Infantry is its fourth and final incarnation.

Africa: The Abyssinian and (First, Second and Third) Ashanti Wars

Britain had trading posts and forts on the Gold Coast and had good relations with the Fante tribe and agreed to give them protection. When the Ashanti tribes north of the Gold Coast were making inroads into Fante territory and slaughtering the occupants of forts and trading posts, Governer Sir Charles McCarthy with a small force of 500 went to negotiate with the Ashanti and was defeated. McCarthy was killed and his skull used as a drinking cup. The Fante were unreliable and were no match for the ferocious 10,000 Ashanti warriors. Fighting went on for a number of years, but a British/Fante force finally subdued the Ashanti, bringing an end to the First Ashanti War (1823–31).

When King Theodore II of Abyssinia had a dispute with Europeans, he held British and German residents and envoys hostage. Negotiations failed and a punitive expedition was sent out under Sir Robert Napier, fresh from China where he had been a divisional commander, heralding the start of the Abyssinian (Ethiopian) War (1867–68). The mission to release the prisoners was a very difficult logistical expedition. Napier had to supply his British and Indian troops with European, Hindu and Muslim meals. Also he had to haul a 9-pounder breech-loading gun and two mortars the best part of 400 miles across difficult mountainous terrain, building roads en route.

The King's fortress at Magdala was stormed with heavy casualties for the Abyssinians, but none of Napier 15,000 force was killed and the King committed suicide. The 3rd Dragoon Guards, King's Own, Duke of Wellington's and Sherwood Foresters all took part. The silver Royal 'Proclamation Drum' was captured, reputed to be 1,000 years old, and is now jointly held in the officers's messes of the participating regiments.

On the Gold Coast, the British government sent out a local Governor, Captain George Maclean, to administer the region. The infamous blood-curdling fetishes and slavery of the Ashanti were tolerated by Maclean, and he did bring peace between the Fante and Ashanti for a number of years. Maclean was reluctant to 'civilise' the Ashantis, much to the annoyance of London.

Further conflict between the Fante and Ashanti broke out in 1863 (the Second Ashanti War, 1863–64) after Ashantis crossed the border, and matters came to a head when a large force of Ashanti warriors invaded a new British trading post acquired from the Dutch at Elmina on the coast. Disease meant that Maclean had to withdraw his West Indian troops and there was no satisfactory outcome.

Following the invasion of Elmina in Britain's recently purchased Dutch Gold Coast by the Ashanti, General Garnet Wolseley was invited out to defend the territory, and he took with him as advisers a number of young forward-thinking officers known as 'the Ashanti Ring' (later the Wolseley Ring). Wolseley's mission was for his officers to command local forces and defeat the Ashanti. When he arrived he found that the local forces were unreliable and asked for troops from Britain. In the Third Ashanti War (1873–74) Wolseley commanded 4,000 troops, including the Black Watch, Rifle Brigade, Welsh Fusiliers, a West Indian regiment, sailors, Royal Marines and local levies. H.M. Stanley (of Livingstone fame) joined the expedition for the *New York Herald.*

The objective was to march the 150 miles to seize the capital at Kumasi. Wolseley, having experienced the difficulty of marching in rigid uniforms while an ensign in Burma, insisted that his men marched in grey uniform and in loose order. He even issued his soldiers with his previously published *Soldiers's Pocket Book for Field Service* – a 400-page work on the rudiments of soldiering, on how to take care of oneself on active duty, conduct in the field, even whistles to be used should you get lost in the jungle.

Expecting an attack from all sides, Wolseley approached the Ashanti area with his army in a large square. Contact with the Ashanti army was made 20 miles from the capital Kumasi and the British could hardly see the attackers in the undergrowth during the twelve hours of the Battle of Ordahsu. When 15 miles from Kumasi, General Wolseley decided on a dash for the capital and a flying column left at dawn leaving unessential equipment behind. The chiefs at Kumasi surrendered without any fighting, but the King and his Golden Stool (traditionally believed to house the spirit of the Ashanti nation) had disappeared.

Envoys from the King brought 1,000 ounces of gold to the British, and Wolseley forbade looting and only selected treasures were taken back to the Queen, including the King's ceremonial umbrella. The treaty required the Ashanti to pay an indemnity of 50,000 ounces of gold, renounce claims on Elmina, the payment for use of forts was to be reviewed, they must terminate alliances with other states, open trade routes and end human sacrifice. The operation by Wolseley was so smooth, efficient and successful that Wolseley was knighted and the phrase 'Everything's all Sir Garnet' came into fashion, meaning 'all is in order'.

Africa: Natal, South Africa, (First) Boer and Zulu Wars

The huge Bantu nation had migrated from the north and established itself in southern Africa. Over centuries there were many subdivisions. The Nguni faction settled around Natal with the Tonga tribe moving north to the Pongola River and the Amaxhosa or Xhosa tribe settling south on the Fish River valley. By the 1770s the Xhosa were competing for territory with the Boers and later the British. A series of Kaffir Wars broke out when disputes arose over territory and boundaries, and the British went to the aid of the Boers. The Fifth Kaffir War (1819) was to repel a Xhosa attack on Grahamstown, Natal. Governor D'Urban decided to annex the Xhosa territory in 1834. The Sixth Kaffir War (1835) was led by Governor D'Urban and Colonel Harry Smith with a detachment from the Cape Colony against the Xhosa, who had crossed the Fish River en masse, causing mayhem among the Boers and settlers.

D'Urban wanted to push the Xhosa beyond the River Kei, but the British government took a dim view of D'Urban extending the frontiers, the borders were reinstated in 1836 and D'Urban recalled. The Boers annexed Port Natal and Durban in 1838 and started to populate the area, building the town of Pietermaritzburg. The British were concerned, as Natal on the coast was a strategically important area, its port a staging post to India. Furthermore, American missionaries and traders had arrived and joined with the Boers.

When the Boers wanted to expand into the Faku lands, the Cape Governor Sir George Napier took exception. Napier sent the 27th Foot under Captain Smith to occupy Durban and Smith was soon under siege. Although Smith received support from two ships arriving, he remained trapped.

With no further help at hand, a civilian Dick King who spoke Zulu volunteered to get help and, with a 16-year-old native retainer, had a most extraordinary journey. With two horses trailing behind, he rowed to an island, crossed it and then reached the mainland and travelled 600 miles in ten days to Grahamstown, alone, as the retainer had given up. With a company of the 27th Foot and two ships arriving with the 25th Foot, the siege (which had lasted for thirty-four days) was raised and King became a hero (Morris, p.159). A statue of him was placed on Victoria Embankment, Durban. The British decided to annex Natal with the Queen's approval and it became a British colony in 1843. British and King's German Legion settlers arrived.

The 7th Kaffir War (1846–47) or the War of the Axe started when an important Xhosa prisoner was handcuffed and his tribe freed him by chopping off the hand of the prisoner cuffed to him. The British column intended to subdue the Xhosa in retribution, but failed. A new government agreed to give some sort of independence to the Xhosa with the creation of a sub-colony, British Kaffraria, in 1847. Sir Harry Smith was appointed Governor of the Cape in 1847 and effectively Commander-in-Chief. The Transorangia was annexed as the Orange River Sovereignty and the Boers were understandably furious. Pretorius was defeated by Smith at Boomplaatz. With the Xhosa now independent, further difficulties arose in the overcrowded area with the Gaika tribe. The 8th Kaffir War (1850–53) was to defeat a rising by the disgruntled Gaika. The new Xhosa colony was found to be unsustainable and was annexed into the colony of Natal in 1866. The 9th Kaffir War (1877–78) occurred when the Gcalekas tribe attacked the friendly Fingoes and routed the local troops. When they attacked again, this time joined by the Gaika, Sir Arthur Cunynghame Commander-in-Chief and his imperial troops put down the rebellion. When President of South

Africa Nelson Mandela died in 2013 he was buried in the Xhosa tradition. He was also married in this tradition.

At Slachter's Nek in 1815, some Boers were hanged under British jurisdiction following a rebellion. When slavery was abolished in the Cape in 1834, the Boer farmers – already hostile to British rule and still seething over the hanging of the five agitators – decided to move out on their Great Trek. Between 12,000 and 14,000 Boers moved out from 1836 to 1838. The great majority of Afrikaans-speaking Dutch colonists stayed at the Cape. The Sand River Convention acknowledged the Transvaal Republic in 1852 and the Bloemfontein Convention acknowledged Transorangia as the Orange Free State for the Boers.

Transvaal was proclaimed a British Crown Colony in 1877 on the understanding that the locals were in favour. Its government was in chaos and on the verge of bankruptsy. Paul Kruger conducted a poll of the locals and concluded that they were not and contested the acquisition. He took up his complaint in London with no success. The Boers took up arms against the British and the First South African (First Boer) War (1881) began. It did not start well with am ambush at Brokhurst-Spruit where 120 British soldiers were killed at Majuba Hill 1881, the Boers gave the British a masterclass in fire and movement. With the old Boers firing to keep the British heads down, the young Boers crept up the hill. Any soldier who stood up to fire on the advancing young Boers was instantly killed as no digging in took place. The result was a disaster for the British with General Colley killed and Majuba entering into Boer folklore. At Majuba 171 of the 2nd Battalion Northamptonshires and 141 of the Gordon Highlanders were killed with 280 of the Northamptonshires and 3rd Battalion Royal Rifle Corps killed at Laings Nek. Reverses at Laing's Nek Ingogo River and Majuba Hill made the British government restore the Transvaal Republic, with Kruger as President.

By the time King Cetewayo, who ruled from 1872 to 1879, came to power, the Zulu Army (Impi) was 50,000 strong with 25,000 young warriors. The traditional throwing of spears had been outlawed by the former King Shaka, who introduced the assegai or stabbing spear. In place of frontal assaults Shaka had introduced tactics with his structured army, and bigger, stronger shields with Colours for each regiment.

The British controlled Cape Province and Natal adjacent to Zululand, while the Boers controlled Transvaal and Orange Free State. The new British High Commissioner for South African Affairs was Sir Bartle Frere, a seasoned diplomat. His mission was to work towards the confederation of the states, a sort of 'United South Africa'. Frere considered the Zulus to be a stumbling block to his dream of being the Clive of South Africa (Gardner, p.98). The residents of Natal were nervous about the might of the Zulus next door and every minor incident of Zulu aggression was magnified, especially when dissident Zulus sought refuge in Natal. There had been peace between the Zulus and Europeans for quite some time, but little insurrections had occurred. Whilst missionaries were initially welcomed by Cetewayo, he took exception to Zulu conversions.

The Zulus had had no major battles in recent years and they were unable to 'wash their spears' – the young warriors were frustrated. Frere consulted General Thesiger (later Baron Chelmsford) who replaced Cunynghame, about the military situation and a possible invasion of Zululand. Frere communicated his fears to London that the Zulus were 'out of hand' but said nothing of invasion. London instructed Frere to exercise prudence and show a spirit of forbearance in order to achieve a reasonable compromise with the Zulus. Frere wanted a war, but lacked a suitable *casus belli*. A forthcoming Boundary Commission report on the border between Transvaal and Zululand was the ideal opportunity for Frere to force a showdown. In December, Frere read out the Boundary Commission report, stating that the Zulus had sovereignty over the Blood River but then followed with an unscheduled ultimatum to the assembled Zulus, which took three hours of translation.

In all, thirteen demands were made and the Zulus had thirty days to comply. Named Zulu troublemakers were to be handed over to British justice with corresponding cattle fines; no Zulus were to be executed without trial and the Zulu army was to be disbanded; every Zulu was to be free to marry; missionaries were to be allowed to return; and a resident British envoy had to be stationed in Zululand (Morris, p.291).

Two battalions were sent out for the defence of Natal and a veto against war was sent out, but Frere had jumped the gun. On 4 January 1879, Frere published the following communiqué:

> The British forces are crossing into Zululand to exact from Cetewayo reparations for violations of British territory committed by the sons of Sihayo and others; and to enforce compliance with the promises made by Cetewayo at his coronation, for the better government of his people.

The Zulu War (1879) started with a pre-emptive strike by the British. Baron Chelmsford had 16,800 men with nine regular battalions, 2/3rd Foot, 2/4th Foot, 1/13th Foot, 1st and 2nd Battalion 24th Foot, 80th Foot, 1st and 2nd Battalion 90th Foot and the 99th Foot with the 7,000 locally raised Natal Native Contingency, 1,000 mounted colonial volunteers and even 500 renegade Zulus. Chelmsford had to deploy the equivalent of a battalion to man strategic points like Greytown, Helpmakaar and the crossing at Rorke's Drift. There were no British cavalry in the early stages and Chelmsford split his force into five columns in order to entice the Zulus to attack. Three columns entered Zululand heading for Ulundi (75 miles away) with one in reserve and one to defend Natal.

The right flanking Coastal Column (No. 1) of 4,750 men including the 2/3rd Foot and 99th Foot under Colonel Pearson crossed at the Lower Drift of the Tugela River and headed for Eshowe, following the coastal route. The Main or Central Column (No. 3) of 4,700 men including two battalions of the 24th Foot under Colonel Glyn and Chelmsford himself assembled at Helpmakaar to cross the Buffalo River at Rorke's Drift, heading northeast for Ulundi. The left-flanking Northern Column (No. 4) under Colonel Wood VC headed for Hlobane with 2,000 troops, including 1/13th Foot and

90th Foot. Colonel Rowland's Column in Reserve (No. 5) en route to Transvaal with the 80th Foot at Luneburg, kept an eye on the Swazis and Boers with 1,800 troops. The defence of Natal was given to Lieutenant Colonel Durnford's Column (No. 2) with 3,000 Natal Native Contingency. It was to be stationed at the Middle Drift of the Tugala below Kranz Kop, but Chelmsford broke up Durnford's column as it consisted of native troops.

Chelmsford invaded Zululand on 11 January 1879 and made camp at Isandlwana, where he sent Major Dartnell on a recce to find the Zulus. Dartnell reported a mass of Zulus at Nqutu plateau near the Mangeni Falls and he wished to attack. Chelmsford, believing them to be the main Zulu body, decided to reinforce Dartnell and split his central column. Chelmsford with Colonel Glyn of the 24th Foot decided to go ahead with the 2nd Battalion 24th Foot, less G Company who were out on duty. Lieutenant Colonel Pulleine remained at Isandlwana with five companies of the 1/24th Foot, G Company 2/24th Foot, 100 mounted infantry and 600 Natal Kaffirs. They were later made up to 950 Europeans and 850 natives when Lieutenant Colonel Durnford was recalled by Chelmsford, bringing the total to 1,800 men in the camp.

20,000 or perhaps 25,000 Zulus attacked and without laagering or a ready supply of ammunition, the camp was overwhelmed. The death toll was appalling – the 24th Foot lost all 602 officers and men. The Royal Artillery lost sixty-eight men, the mounted infantry volunteers lost sixty men, and Natal natives dead and missing totalled 550. Only fifty-five Europeans and 300 natives survived, with hardly any in a British uniform (Morris, p.389). Lieutenants Melvill and Coghill attempted to carry the Queen's colour to safety only for them to be killed, and the Colour disappeared into the Buffalo River. It was later retrieved and Queen Victoria requested it to be presented to her; she placed a small wreath of silver immortelles about the crown.

At the crossing of Buffalo River at Rorke's Drift 8 miles away, Lieutenant Bromhead commanded the garrison of B Company, 2nd Battalion 24th Foot, but when the senior officer at Rorke's Drift, Major Spalding, left to chase up troops at Helpmekaar, Lieutenant Chard of the Royal engineers was identified as the senior officer remaining. The garrison had eighty-four effectives with thirty-six men on sick duty. Captain Stephenson with a company of Natal Native Contingent was also present initially. When news of the disaster at Isandlwana arrived at Rorke's Drift, Chard realised that to attempt to withdraw to Helpmekaar would take up too much time, especially as the sick would have to be moved and their slow progress would be an invitation to the Zulus to overtake and overwhelm them. The decision was made to stand and defend with 350 men. Chard made the best of the defence by stacking mealie bags and biscuit boxes into a few perimeter defences, and laagering by inserting his two wagons into the walls.

When 4,000 Zulus arrived, Stephenson fled with his NNC leaving a very thin red line of one company of 24th Foot with a few attachments, making a total of 140 men. The Zulus attacked just after 5 p.m. testing the defences, then concentrated on the hospital which had a series of unconnected rooms that had to be opened up in a desperate evacuation. The hospital was eventually evacuated and late in the night caught fire and burned down. The attack continued into the night.

The Zulus gave up early in the morning on the approach of Chelmsford's column, which had returned to Isandlwana but moved on at 4.30 a.m. to support Rorke's Drift. Fifteen men were killed, with nine seriously injured and 20,000 rounds spent. The disaster at Isandlwana was offset by the valour of Rorke's Drift and eleven VCs were awarded.

The Coastal Column had a difficult march to Eshowe, a forward British base. When the news of Isandlwana reached Pearson, he realised his left flank was exposed and on reaching Eshowe found himself under siege from 6,000 Zulus. The Northern Column under Wood and Lieutenant Colonel Buller made their way to Hlobane. There they found a Zulu training base and a hidden stock of cattle. Wood was asked by Chelmsford to make diversionary attacks to relieve the pressure on Pearson. The attack on Hlobane Mountain by Buller and Russell's mounted troops up the narrow tracks at night ended in failure and they retired to Kambula with heavy casualties from both the Zulus on Hlobane and from a whole Zulu Impi who just happened to be en route from Ulundi. The subsequent Zulu Impi attack on Kambula was defeated by the infantry.

The invasion of Zululand was now postponed while Chelmsford awaited reinforcements and regrouped. His first task was to relieve Eshowe, which was done in March. Reinforcements arrived with four major generals, four infantry and two cavalry regiments, 21st Foot, 57th Foot, 60th Rifles, 91st Highlanders, 1st King's Dragoon Guards and 17th Lancers. Chelmsford's order of battle for the reinvasion:

Major General Crealock's, 1st Division, along the Coastal Column
    1st Brigade, Pearson: 2/3rd Foot, 88th Foot, 99th Foot
    2nd Brigade, Mansfield: 57th Foot, 3/60th Rifles, 91st Foot
Major General Newdigate's 2nd Division Central Column
    1st Brigade, Colonel Glyn: 2/21st Foot, 58th Foot
    2nd Brigade, Colonel Collingwood: 94th Foot, 1/24th Foot
The lost battalion 1/24th Foot at Isandlwana was re-formed by volunteers from depots
Major General Clifford VC, Inspector General and base: 2/24th Foot, 2/4th Foot
Major General Marshall, Cavalry Brigade: 1st King's Dragoon Guards and 17th Lancers
Brigadier General Wood, Flying Column: 1/13th Foot, 80th Foot, 90th Foot

The two-pronged invasion commenced on 31 May with Chelmsford's Central Column, which bypassed Isandlwana. On the following day Prince Louis Napoleon died; the Prince Imperial of France had been with the army to gain military experience. His death was a shock to Europe and added to the pressure on Chelmsford.

Wolseley was sent out to redeem the military situation should there be a need and activate the political settlement as Frere had lost his influence. Chelmsford defeated the final stand of the Zulus at Ulundi on 4 July, just before Wolseley arrived to take over.

Asia: (Second) Afghan and (Third) Burma Wars

The Russian influence was growing again in Afghanistan and the Amir Sher Ali had allowed a Russian mission to Kabul. The British government – alarmed at this intrusion – expected to be allowed to do the same. This was denied and the British took offence. The assembled mission in Peshawar (Pakistan) wanted to test the resolve of the Afghans and sent Major Cavagnari, the British Commissioner of Peshawar, to the border at the Khyber Pass. He was stopped on 21 September 1878 by Faiz Muhammad on the orders of the Amir who was naturally offended by the action. When the British government requested an apology and access for the mission and were refused, the Second Afghan War (1878–80) started with an invasion on three fronts.

The first column under General Stewart marched via the Bolan Pass to Quetta and on to Kandahar, and the second column under Lieutenant General Sam Browne marched from Peshawar to control the Khyber Pass. The third column under Major General Roberts (the junior general) was to enter the Kurram Valley. Stewart's column entered Kandahar, the Afghans having withdrawn. General Browne's task was to seize the Fort at Ali Masjid next to the Khyber Pass, but his two flanking brigades got lost. His assault was successful with Faiz Muhammad retiring to Jalalabad, followed by Browne. The third column had better success and occupied the Kurram Valley. The Afghans were blocking the head of the valley and Roberts did a flanking attack to dislodge them with the 72nd Highlanders and 5th Gurkhas and broke up the enemy position.

The main assault was against the Peiwar Kotal some distance away and Roberts and his attacking force had to spend a cold night at 9,000ft without tents, food or water (Heathcote, p.109). The assault – led by the 2nd Battalion King's Liverpool and the 5th Punjabis – routed the Afghan garrison. Amir Sher Ali fled to Russia and left his son Yakub Khan in charge of Kabul, who sued for peace; it was signed at Gandamak in May 1879. The British were now established in Afghanistan to support Khan. The British envoy, Cavagnari (now knighted) was accepted in the British Residency in Kabul and the British remained in control of the Khyber and Bolan passes, Kurram Valley and Quetta.

It was intended that British forces would be withdrawn as soon as conditions allowed. However, a disturbance broke out over pay to some Afghan soldiers and a mob attacked the British Residency. Cavagnari appeared on the balcony to appease the mob; he was killed together with all his seventy-five Punjabi guards and British aides. In response Roberts's field force at Kurram valley made for Kabul, destroying any opposition on his advance. Amir Yakub Khan had abdicated – having been implicated in Cavagnari's murder – and Roberts was now military Governor of Kabul. Roberts put out rewards for the murderers of Cavagnari and hanged the perpetrators.

Unrest continued and a general uprising was feared. When it became apparent that Afghan forces were combining against the British, Roberts sent out his three brigades to confront them, Macpherson and Baker's infantry brigades, with the cavalry brigade under Massy. While taking a short cut, Massy found the 10,000-strong Afghan Army under Muhammad Jan. Massy with his 500 troopers of the 9th Lancers conducted a fighting withdrawal to allow Roberts's force time to intervene. It was a close call. Shocked, the British force retired into Kabul where they spent quite a few days trying to dislodge the Afghan force without success.

Roberts decided to withdraw his 6,000-strong army to Sherpur in December where he had previously stocked supplies and forage. Roberts was offered terms of safe conduct out of Afghanistan but refused. After a two-week siege the 10,000 Afghans were defeated on 23 December 1879 and retired leaving 1,000 dead, to Roberts's eighteen dead. The British were reinforced the next day.

When Stewart's column was returning from Kandahar in April 1880, it was severely mauled by 15,000 Ghazis at Ahmed Khel. Stuart arrived in Kabul after killing 800 of the enemy and losing seventeen dead and took over from General Roberts. The British government looked around for a possible Amir and chose Abdur Rahman Khan (cousin of Sher Ali) in July 1880. Although he had previous connections with the Russians, the British felt they could do business with him. Ayub Khan, ruler of Herat (and brother of Yakub Khan), made a move to usurp the power of Abdur Rahman Khan and declared himself Amir. A brigade under Brigadier General Burrows left Kandahar in July and at Maiwand they were stopped and defeated by a massive Afghan army of 8,000 regulars and 15,000 tribesmen under Ayub Khan. The three infantry battalions of the 66th Foot, the 1st Bombay Grenadiers and the 30th Bombay Infantry together with two Bombay cavalry regiments and twelve guns were completely overwhelmed and the brigade destroyed. 1,000 British were killed and 168 wounded. Six guns of the Royal Horse Artillery were saved by Captain Slade and the 66th Foot made their gallant last stand with the colour still in its case.

The survivors made their way to Kandahar and via telegraph the news was read out to a shocked House of Commons the following night on 28 July. Under siege at Kandahar, General Brooke was killed. Stewart in Kabul despatched Roberts with his relief force, which became a flying column as Roberts and his force – with only pack gun batteries in support – took twenty days to travel the 280 miles from Kabul to relieve Kandahar, arriving on 31 August to find a much demoralised garrison. Roberts now took charge and was in total command in Afghanistan. He set about the task of defeating Ayub Khan, and the battle at Baba Wali Kotal, with the 92nd Highlanders and 2nd Gurkhas storming the batteries, defeated the Afghans. British losses were forty killed with more than 600 Afghans killed. The British now withdrew, the last British troops leaving in May 1881.

In Burma, the new King Theebaw continued to show hostility towards Britain by interfering with regular trade and imposing fines on the teak exporting company. Again ultimatums were issued by India and again they were refused, starting the Third Burma War (1885–87). Sir Harry Prendergast invaded with two brigades and sailed up to the new capital Mandalay and captured the King. The war was short-lived but dacoits continued to cause disruption and further brigades were sent out with a total of 30,000 troops required to put down the insurgency. Hostilities ended in 1887 when Upper Burma was annexed and incorporated into British India. Burma became a self-governing colony in 1937 and independent in 1948.

First Amalgamation 1881: Cardwell and Childers's Reforms

In the late 1870s the Secretary of State for War Viscount Cardwell instituted radical and wide-ranging reforms to the British Army, including compulsory retirement, shorter terms of enlistment and the abolition of flogging and commission purchase. The old system established a fee ranging from ensign or cornet to lieutenant colonel and the price varied from line regiments to elite Household Cavalry or Guards regiments. Some commissions were free to deserving causes. The system was abused, with commissions purchased for 5-year-old children, although not all commissions were purchased; during the French Revolutionary Wars only one officer in five purchased a commission.

Lord Cardwell, aided by the forward-thinking General Wolseley, overhauled the major difficulties in the military system, which had shown itself to be flawed, especially in the Crimea. The British Army was unprepared for major conflicts and there was a shortage of manpower for overseas garrisons. This was to be resolved by having two-battalion regiments so that one battalion could operate overseas and the second could remain in Britain with associated Militia and Volunteers.

The archaic system of purchasing commissions was replaced by promotion based upon examination or ability. The resistance against the abolition of the purchase system was immense. To reimburse officers and agents for their commission and 'investment' would cost Cardwell £8,000,000 and it was still defeated in Parliament. A determined Cardwell required a Royal Warrant finally to abolish the system (Morris, p.243). Following on from Cardwell's earlier military system reforms, regimental reorganisation took place in 1881 under Hugh Childers as Secretary of State for War and included the following changes.

Territorial titles replaced the consecutive numbering of foot regiments that had existed since 1751. Two-battalion regiments were formed by amalgamation (others being Militia and Volunteers) with the senior regiment becoming the senior battalion. Amalgamations were to be based wherever possible upon geography. Distinctions, mottoes, badges and Colours borne by one battalion would now be borne by both. Cap badges, previously with the regimental number, could now reflect the new regiment's identity without numbers.

The foot regiments that numbered 1st to 25th had already had two battalions since 1856 and therefore did not amalgamate. Similarly, the Rifle Brigade and the three Guards regiments escaped amalgamation since they already had at least two battalions. Although the 79th (Cameron Highlanders) only had one battalion, they also escaped a merger but formed a second battalion much later. The 23rd (Royal Welch Fusiliers) changed its title to the Royal Welsh Fusiliers (only to change it back again in 1920) as did the Welch Regiment. Naturally, senior regiments took precedence over junior regiments. Close neighbours, the 28th (North Gloucestershire) merged with the 61st (South Gloucestershire) to form the Gloucestershire Regiment with both battalions allowed to wear the back cap badge. Correspondingly, the 44th (East Essex) merged with the 56th (West Essex) to form the Essex, and the 57th (West Middlesex) merged with the 77th (East Middlesex) to form the Middlesex. There were also some novel title changes. Near neighbours, 32nd (Cornwall) and the 46th (South Devon) merged into the Duke of Cornwall Light Infantry. The 34th (Cumberland) and the 55th (Westmorland) formed the Border Regiment and the Sherwood Foresters were formed from the Nottinghamshire (45th Foot) and the Derbyshire (95th Foot).

The amalgamations produced some strange bedfellows. The 27th (Inniskilling) merged with the 108th (Madras Infantry) and became the Royal Inniskilling Fusiliers. Explanations are hard to find for some of the more unusual marriages. The 40th (2nd Somersetshire) and 82nd (Prince of Wales's Volunteers) became the South Lancashire Regiment. The 69th (South Lincolnshire) moved across country to merge with the 41st (Welsh) and became the Welsh Regiment. The 30th (Cambridgeshire) and the 59th (2nd Nottinghamshire) formed the West Lancashire Regiment in May, but had second thoughts and redesignated themselves the East Lancashire Regiment in July 1881. Similarly the Staffordshires reversed their seniority.

Regiments that already had two battalions generally kept the same title but the 24th Foot who distinguished themselves at Rorke's Drift – otherwise known as the 2nd Warwickshire Regiment – changed its title to the South Wales Borderers to reflect an area where they had a new recruiting depot. Similarly the 20th Foot known as the East Devonshire Regiment changed its title to the Lancashire Fusiliers after a 100-year association with that good recruiting area.

Some regiments chose city titles in place of county; the 8th (King's) became the Liverpool Regiment (King's) in May 1881 and then changed to the King's Regiment (Liverpool) in July. The 63rd (West Suffolk) and 94th Foot merged to become the Manchester Regiment. The nine infantry regiments from the dissolved East India Company were now dispersed into British regiments and the remainder formed new Irish regiments, the Royal Munster Fusiliers (101st Royal Bengal Fusiliers and 104th Bengal Fusiliers) and the Royal Dublin Fusiliers (102nd Royal Madras Fusiliers and 103rd Royal Bombay Fusiliers). The Prince of Wales's Leinster was formed from the 109th Bombay Infantry and the Prince of Wales's Royal Canadians (100th Foot).

Foot	Regiment (1st Bn)	Foot	Regiment (2nd Bn)	Regiment Title May 1881	Regiment Title July 1881
1	Royal			Lothiam (Royal Scots)	Royal Scots (Lothiam)
2	Queen's Royal			Royal West Surrey (Queen's)	Queen's (Royal West Surrey)
3	East Kent- Buffs			Kentish (Buffs)	Buffs (East Kent)
4	King's Own			Royal Lancaster (King's Own)	King's Own Royal (Lancaster)
5	Northumberland Fusiliers			Northumberland Fusiliers	Northumberland Fusiliers
6	Royal 1st Warwickshire			Royal Warwickshire	Royal Warwickshire
7	Royal Fusiliers			City of London (Royal Fusiliers)	Royal Fusiliers (City of London)
8	King's			Liverpool (King's)	King's (Liverpool)

9	East Norfolk			Norfolk	Norfolk
10	North Lincolnshire			Lincolnshire	Lincolnshire
11	North Devonshire			Devonshire	Devonshire
12	East Suffolk			Suffolk	Suffolk
13	1st Somersetshire			Somersetshire (Prince Albert's LI)	Prince Albert's LI (Somersetshire)
14	Buckinghamshire			West Yorkshire (POWO)	POWO (West Yorkshire)
15	Yorkshire East Riding			East Yorkshire	East Yorkshire
16	Bedfordshire			Bedfordshire	Bedfordshire (Hertfordshire 1919)
17	Leicestershire			Leicestershire	Leicestershire
18	Royal Irish			Royal Irish	Royal Irish
19	1st Yorkshire North Riding			North Yorkshire POWO	POWO (Yorkshire)
20	East Devonshire			Lancashire Fusiliers	Lancashire Fusiliers
21	Royal North British Fusiliers			Royal Scots Fusiliers	Royal Scots Fusiliers
22	Cheshire			Cheshire	Cheshire
23	Royal Welsh Fusiliers			Royal Welsh Fusiliers	Royal Welsh Fusiliers
24	2nd Warwickshire			South Wales Borderers	South Wales Borderers
25	King's Own Borderers			York (King's Own Borderers)	King's Own Borderers
26	Cameronian	90	Perthshire LI	Scotch Rifles (Cameronians)	Cameronians (Scotish Rifles)
27	Inniskilling	108	Madras LI	Royal Inniskilling Fusiliers	Royal Inniskilling Fusiliers
28	North Gloucestershire	61	South Gloucestershire	Gloucestershire	Gloucestershire
29	Worcestershire	36	Herefordshire	Worcestershire	Worcestershire
30	Cambridgeshire	59	2nd Nottinghamshire	West Lancashire	East Lancashire
31	Huntingtonshire	70	Surrey	East Surrey	East Surrey
32	Cornwall LI	46	South Devonshire	Duke of Cornwall's LI	Duke of Cornwall's LI
33	Duke of Wellington's	76	Regiment	Halifax (D of W's)	Duke of Wellington's WR
34	Cumberland	55	Westmoreland	Cumberland	Border
35	Royal Sussex	107	Bengal Infantry	Royal Sussex	Royal Sussex
37	North Hampshire	67	South Hampshire	Hampshire	Hampshire
38	1st Staffordshire	80	Staffordshire Volunteers	North Staffordshire	South Staffordshire
39	Dorsetshire	54	West Norfolk	Dorsetshire	Dorsetshire
40	2nd Somersetshire	82	POW Volunteers	South Lancashire	South Lancashire
41	Welsh	69	South Lincolnshire	Welsh	Welsh
42	Royal Highland (Black Watch)	73	Perthshire	Royal Highland (Black Watch)	Black Watch (Royal Highland)

43	Monmouthshire	52	Oxfordshire LI	Oxfordshire LI	Oxfordshire LI
44	East Essex	56	West Essex	Essex	Essex
45	Nottinghamshire SF	95	Derbyshire	Derbyshire (Sherwood foresters)	Sherwood Foresters (Derbyshire)
47	Lancashire	81	Loyal Lincoln V	North Lancashire	Loyal North Lancashire
48	Northamptonshire	58	Rutlandshire	Northamptonshire	Northamptonshire
49	P's CoW Hertfordshire	66	Berkshire	Berkshire (P's CoW)	P's CoW's (Berkshire)
50	Queen's Own	97	Earl of Ulster's	Royal West Kent (Queen's Own)	Queen's Own (Royal West Kent)
51	2nd Yorkshire WR (King's Own LI)	105	Madras LI	South Yorkshire (King's Own LI)	King's Own Yorkshire LI
53	Shropshire	85	Bucks V's (King's LI)	Shropshire King's LI	King's Shropshire LI
57	West Middlesex	77	East Middlesex	Middlesex (DoCO)	DoCO (Middlesex)
60	King's Royal Rifle Corps			KRRC	KRRC
62	Wiltshire	99	Lanarkshire	Wiltshire (Duke of Edinburgh's)	Duke of Edinburgh's (Wiltshire)
63	West Suffolk	96	Regiment	Manchester	Manchester
64	2nd Staffordshire	98	Prince of Wales's	South Staffordshire (PoW)	PoW (North Staffordshire)
65	2nd Yorkshire North Riding	84	York & Lancaster	York & Lancaster	York & Lancaster
68	Durham LI	106	Bombay LI	Durham LI	Durham LI
71	Highland LI	74	Highlanders	Highland LI	Highland LI
72	DoA's Own Highlanders	78	Highland Ross-shire Buffs	Seaforth Highlanders	Seaforth Highlanders Ross-shire Buffs
75	Stirlingshire	92	Gordon Highlanders	Gordon Highlanders	Gordon Highlanders
79	Cameron Highlanders		had two battallions	Queen's Own Cameron Highlanders	Queen's Own Cameron Highlanders
83	County of Dublin	86	Royal County Down	Royal Irish Rifles	Royal Irish Rifles
87	Royal Irish Fusiliers	89	Regiment	Royal Irish Fusiliers (P's V)	P's V (Royal Irish Fusiliers)
88	Connaught Rangers	94	Regiment	Connaught Rangers	Connaught Rangers
91	Argyllshire	93	Sutherland Highlanders	Sutherland & Argyll Highlanders	Argyll & Sutherland Highlanders
100	PoW's Royal Canadian	109	Bombay Infantry	PoW's Royal Canadian	PoW's Leinster (Royal Canadians)
101	Royal Bengal Fusiliers	104	Bengal Fusiliers	Royal Munster Fusiliers	Royal Munster Fusiliers
102	Royal Madras Fusiliers	103	Royal Bombay Fusiliers	Royal Dublin Fusiliers	Royal Dublin Fusiliers
	Rifle Brigade			Rifle Brigade	Rifle Brigade

POWO, Prince of Wales's Own. Li, Light Infantry. DoW's Duke of Wellington's. WR West Riding. PoW Prince of Wales. SF Sherwood Foresters. V volunteer. V's Volunteers. DoCO Duke of Cambridges Own. DoA Duke of Albany's. P's V Princess Victoria. P's CoW Princess Charlotte of Wales's. Note Argyll & Sutherland Highlanders also have Princess Louise's in its title.

Africa: The Egyptian War and Campaign and the (First and Second) Sudan Wars

General Gordon went to the upper Nile in 1873 at the invitation of the Khedive of Egypt to open it to commerce and abolish the slave trade. When the slave traders moved to Sudan in 1876, Gordon got the Khedive to extend his activities there. He was made Governor General, returning to England in 1879. When the Khedive's support waned, the rebel Arabi Pasha took over the Egyptian Army in 1882 and wanted to drive away the foreigners who were there to protect the Suez Canal. The British government was concerned about the security of the newly built canal – in which Britain had a stake – and asked General Sir Garnet Wolseley to lead an expeditionary force, signalling the start of the Egyptian War (1882), also called the Revolt of Arabi Pasha.

Landing at Ismailia, Wolseley led his two divisions against Arabi Pasha in the well-fortified Tel-el-Kebir. A night attack was chosen (under normal circumstances a precarious operation) but Sir Garnet split his force into a two-pronged frontal attack, with his artillery down the middle to prevent either wing bumping into each other in the dark. He went further and put the Naval Brigade with the artillery, whose officers navigated by the stars so nobody could get lost. Wolseley, conscious of Raglan's map reading embarrassment when lost in the woods, wanted no repeat performance. When back in England, Wolseley had said he would capture Tel-el-Kebir on 15 September. He captured it on 16 September. No Isandlwana, no Maiwand, everything was 'All Sir Garnet'.

The restored Egyptian Army with British officers under Hicks Pasha was annihilated by the Mahdi in Sudan and General Sir Gerald Graham had to besiege the port of Suakin on the Red Sea and fight at El Teb and Tamai in the First Sudan War (1884–85) in order to support the Khedive's authority in Egypt and Sudan. When a further rebellion broke out in Sudan led by the Mahdi, Gordon returned as Governor General to supervise the withdrawal of Europeans and Egyptians with only local troops. No relief force was sent out when Gordon was under siege in Khartoum in March 1884 and he was completely isolated by October.

The government delayed and it was not until August that Gladstone finally allowed a relief force to be raised under Sir Garnet Wolseley and sent on the Egyptian Campaign (Sudan) (1885–86). Wolseley had calculated that in delaying the relief force, the best level on the Nile would be missed for his boats and the Dervishes could cross the Nile and assault Khartoum. Wolseley told the War Minister that 'all the gold in England would not effect the rise and fall of the Nile' (Gardner, p.142). Major logistical problems could be foreseen – hundreds of boats would be needed to transport the army down the Nile and 8,000 camels to travel across the desert to Khartoum. The elite troops of the Grenadier, Coldstream and Scots Guards and the rest of the British Army had to do a crash course in camel riding at Korti. In besieged Khartoum, food had run out and they were down to eating horses, birds and rats.

The trek across the desert was full of incident, the most desperate being the assault on the Dervishes holding the only oasis at Abu Klea to prevent the army dying of thirst.

Wolseley's advance party arrived on 28 January, but too late – Khartoum had been taken two days earlier and Gordon had been killed. Khartoum was destroyed by the Dervishes and thousands were butchered. The British were mortified at the loss of Gordon.

The Mahdi's victory over Gordon had convinced many that he was indeed the 'Expected One'. One British general, a one-eyed veteran of the Crimea, became so irritated at the miraculous powers credited to the Mahdi that, when visited one day by an Arab delegation, he took out his glass eye, tossed it in the air, caught it and replaced it in its socket; could the Mahdi do that, he enquired? (Gardner, p.150) The First Sudan War was the last war during which the scarlet jacket of the infantry was used. Khaki as worn by the Indian troops would be the uniform of the future.

Colonel Kitchener was made Commander-in-Chief (Sirdar) of a re-formed Egyptian Army and the Khalifa now led the Dervishes on the death of the Mahdi. Unrest and slavery continued and Britain decided to send out an army under Kitchener to stamp out slavery and avenge the death of Gordon and Hicks Pasha, starting the Second Sudan War (1896–98), also known as the Reconquest of the Sudan. Kitchener, aware of the logistical problems of moving an army 450 miles across the desert, decided to build a railway from Wadi Halfa to Abu Hamed across the Nubian Desert and beyond – a distance of nearly 400 miles. This was necessary to move his 25,800-strong army – which included 8,000 regulars and Maxim machine guns – closer to Khartoum.

Near Omdurman in 1898 at Egeiga adjacent to the Nile, 50,000 Dervishes made a pre-emptive strike by charging Kitchener's army and were defeated. The army formed a semicircle and had no difficulty against the onslaught. Glover recorded 'within three hundred yards of the British … scarcely a Dervisher could live', such was the effectiveness of the Lee–Metford rifle. A countercharge by the 21st Lancers became famous because a young Winston Churchill took part. The Khalifa's army was destroyed and Khartoum was entered without any resistance. The British Army had 150 killed or wounded against 11,800 Dervishes.

Africa: The Fourth Ashanti War and the War of the Golden Stool

The new King Prempeh and his chiefs refused protection from Britain and furthermore reneged on the indemnity imposed after the 1874 war. Acts of cruelty against neighbouring tribes who sought protection continued. A delegation from Kumasi to London came to nothing. A task force in 1895 was sent under Colonel Sir Francis Scott who advanced to Kumasi and the Fourth Ashanti War (1895–96) began. The Ashanti – remembering their last defeat – did not resist and the force marched into Kumasi unopposed. Prempeh was exiled to the Seychelles. Ashanti was annexed and became part of the Gold Coast in 1896.

The War of the Golden Stool (1900) or Ashanti Expedition was initiated when British troops invaded to look for the Golden Stool (the symbol of the Ashanti people). Kumasi was now garrisoned and under British protection. King Prempeh continued in exile and this caused bitterness. The Governor of the Gold Coast, Sir Frederic Hodgson, when negotiating with the Ashanti chieftains, wanted to sit on the Golden Stool; the chieftains took it as a grave insult to the traditions of the Ashanti people. The Ashantis put the British garrison in Kumasi under siege and it was two months before it was relieved by Colonel Willcocks with 1,000 men. The Golden Stool would not be unearthed until 1920.

TWENTIETH CENTURY

Asia: The Boxer Rebellion (Third Chinese War)

The Society of Righteous and Harmonious Fists in China (known as Boxers to the British) had a hatred of foreigners and Christianity, and as western influence in their country increased they began to attack missionaries and Chinese Christians. The Boxers laid siege to the International Legations in Peking on 19 June 1900. The Chinese Imperial troops under the Empress Dowager refused to protect the compound or intervene, and Christians were killed, including the German Minister en route to negotiate. Detachments from ships reinforced the compound, and included soldiers from many countries: Britain (Royal Marine Light Infantry), United States (US Marine Corps), Germany, Russia, France, Austria, Italy and Japan.

An international relief force of 2,000 troops from the Peiho River, under Vice Admiral Seymour, were under attack from Chinese Imperial troops and Boxers en route. The relief force was finally stopped at Tientsin – 25 miles short of Peking. A larger international relief column numbering 20,000 was assembled and they marched on Peking, relieving the desperate legation on 14 August.

Africa: The (Second) Boer War

Gold was found in the Witwatersrand (the Rand) Transvaal in 1886 and naturally a great influx of immigrants arrived. The Uitlanders (as they were known) soon settled, but had no legitimacy in law under Boer rule. The infamous Jameson Raid in 1895 – led by a British colonial statesman Leander Starr Jameson and intended to spark a Transvaal uprising by disaffected Uitlanders – was a failure, and Jameson was captured by the Boers. The Boers wanted to hang Jameson but the State President Paul Kruger prevented it.

The raid galvanised the Boers further against British rule. The British government requested the Transvaal Republic to implement reforms for Uitlanders and basic rights for natives. The Boers refused and in order to establish their independence and with fond memories of Majuba, declared war on Britain on 12 October 1899, beginning the Second Boer War (1899–1902). The Boers had no regular army and no infantry; they had always held arms and grouped together in commando units as and when circumstances required when fighting natives or Zulus. They were therefore highly trained crack shots and accomplished horsemen, and Kruger had purchased the latest German Mauser rifle – which was a match for the British Lee–Enfield – together with some decent artillery.

The Boer Republics of Orange Free State and Transvaal could muster 20,000 burghers each and did not expect the British to send reinforcements all the way from Great Britain. The Boers expected a quick victory against the 5,000 British troops in the Cape Province and Natal. The government in Britain decided immediately to reinforce the British garrisons by sending 10,000 troops, mainly from India, with General White VC sent out from England in command of the Natal Field Force for the defence of Natal. The military view in Britain was that the now expected 50,000 Boer rifles had to be matched with British troops and consequently a whole army corps and cavalry division of 35,000 (later increased to 47,000) was mobilised to be sent out under Lieutenant General Redvers Buller VC.

The plan was to march on Bloemfontein, capital of the Orange Free State and then on to Pretoria, capital of Transvaal. Until the army corps arrived, White would be outnumbered by Boers. The Boers lay siege to Kimberley on 14 October where Cecil Rhodes was trapped and to Mafeking where Colonel Baden-Powell was in command. Baden-Powell had anticipated a siege and had stocked up with supplies, against the orders of his Commander-in-Chief. The Boers fired their first shot against the British garrison near Dundee at 5.40 a.m. on 20 October 1899. A British brigade under Major General Symons attacked General Meyer's commando at Talana Hill. The attack was successful but costly; Symons was fatally wounded, as was the CO of the 60th Rifles, and fifty-two men were killed and another 250 injured. If that was not bad enough, the 18th Hussars got themselves captured and Meyer's 3,000 Commandos rode off unmolested.

The next day was better. Ian Hamilton's brigade defeated Commandant Kock's Johannesburg Commando with Major General French's cavalry destroying the fleeing Boers at Elandslaagte near Ladysmith. General Yule – who had replaced Symons as CO Dundee garrison – had to seek refuge in Ladysmith, leaving Dundee and the old garrison (and their stores) to the Boers. At Rietfontein, White's Brigade suffered 114 casualties including the death of the CO of the Gloucestershires. General White also had to fall back to Ladysmith. When Boer Commandant General Joubert was seen to be assembling his troops and building a 'Long Tom' gun platform, White decided to assault with two brigades and a third column protecting his flank at Nicholson's Nek. The night attack went disastrously wrong, with the two brigades in flight back to Ladysmith and the two-battalion flanking column of 954 officers and men surrendering. The Battle of Ladysmith or 'mournful Monday' was a worse day than Majuba.

White's field force of 13,000 men and fifty guns decided to stay under siege in Ladysmith. Buller finally arrived in South Africa to find hardly any forces, with most bottled up in Ladysmith. Buller had to divide his newly arrived forces into three: Lord Methuen's Division to relieve Kimberley and Mafeking via Cape Town, Gateacre's Division – at this stage a brigade – to go via Queenstown and Bloemfontein, and Buller and the main force to defend Natal and relieve Ladysmith. Methuen's first battle was at Belmont on 23 November when his brigade chased the Boers off the ridges blocking his route. Casualties of 297 killed, missing or wounded were high, with the Grenadier Guards alone suffering thirty-six killed and a total of 137 casualties. Two days later at Graspan, a similar minor but costly victory took place. In both battles the Boers escaped more or less unscathed. To prevent Methuen crossing the Modder River, Kruger had assembled Prinsloo, Cronje's and De la Rey's Commandos of 3,000 mounted Boers. Methuen's force numbered 8,000. A ten-hour firefight took place on 28 November and the honour of the first to cross the river went to a half battalion of the North Lancashires. The Boers retreated, with acrimony brewing amongst their leaders.

Methuen's success was short-lived as the events of 'Black Week' unfolded, with each of the assaulting columns having reverses. Lieutenant General Gatacre sent his small force on a night march on 10 December to secure a railway junction at Stormberg. The guide he used was unreliable, with the result that his force was exposed 150yd from the Boers when daylight arrived and about 700 men were lost, 600 being captured. Kruger, President of Transvaal and Steyn, President of the Orange Free State met and collected their forces 6 miles to the rear of Modder River at Magersfontein where 8,000 Boers dug in to await Methuen. The British attack was a two-brigade assault in the early morning of 11 December, after an overnight compass march of 3,500 men. At the crack of dawn the two brigades were hopelessly exposed and the attack was a failure; the Highland Brigade was almost destroyed and 902 men were killed or wounded. Both Major General Wauchope – who had led the attack – and the CO of the Black Watch died.

The final tragedy in 'Black Week' was Buller's assault across the Tugala at Colenso on 15 December. The left-assaulting Hart's Brigade got into difficulty by missing the intended crossing at Bridle Drift and ending up in the loop of the river where the Boers were covering on three sides. 4,000 men of the Irish Brigade entered the loop. Hildyard's central brigade made good progress towards Colenso and the main bridge across the Tugala. Colonel Long with his twelve 15-pounder guns and six naval 12-pounders took it upon himself to get within easy range of the Boers and unlimbered at 1,250yd. While this allowed Hildyard to make good progress into Colenso, it exposed his guns terribly, and a surprised Botha set about this easy target. Colonel Long was now in severe difficulties and losing men fast. Buller sent off a galloper to tell Hart to withdraw to safety and also informed Hildyard that the attack was cancelled and he should withdraw. Buller's next problem was how to extricate Long from his exposed position. A number of brave attempts were made to retrieve the guns; one such attempt by Lieutenant Roberts earned him a posthumous VC. Two guns were saved and the remainder were left. Casualties were 143 killed, 755 wounded and 240 missing, mostly captured.

For the first time in history British troops had surrendered in numbers and the reverses were immediately front page news, shocking the nation to the core. The total casualties to date were 700 killed in action or died of wounds and 3,000 wounded. The three disasters in a week brought about a change in South Africa. Lord Roberts VC, hero of Kandahar, replaced Buller as Commander-in-Chief South Africa. His much sought after command came at the same time as Roberts was notified of his son's death at Colenso.

It was decided that a second corps was to be sent out. On the approach road to Ladysmith, Lieutenant General Warren had his route blocked by Botha. He sent Major General Woodgate to chase the Boers off Rangeworthy Hills. This was to be achieved with his Lancashire Brigade reaching the summit of Spion Kop, 1,450ft high. They marched overnight, with sappers joining them to dig trenches at the summit, but they only took twenty spades for 2,000 soldiers. Shallow trenches were dug, but in the half light of dawn they were dug at a false summit. Only a few Boers were at the summit and the Spion Kop ridge was easily secured. Botha at his HQ a mile away, realised the tactical significance of getting his troops nearer, which they did by capturing Conical Hill and Aloe Knoll, only 800yd and 400yd away. Botha had field guns and the British had none on the kop. A desperate firefight took place during the day with the brigade hopelessly exposed by the regular shelling. British artillery support from the division was ineffective as they had no line of sight with Botha's position.

Woodgate received fatal injuries and reinforcements were requested and arrived. The Dorsets and Middlesex trekked up the hill to give support. Later a diversionary attack was put in to the right of Spion Kop by the Scottish Rifles and King's Royal Rifles. When night came there was a delay in getting relief, water, spades and guns up the hill. The British were exhausted and the Boers had also had enough and evacuated their supporting position. Colonel Thorneycroft of the Mounted Infantry (local irregulars) who was acting brigadier and without knowledge of the Boers's withdrawal also had had enough and brought down the remainder of the two brigades, much to the chagrin of his supporting officers. The two brigades suffered 1,500 casualties with 243 dead piled 'three deep' (Pakenham, p.305).

A further reverse took place at Vaal Krantz with 333 casualties before Ladysmith could be relieved. When Roberts arrived in South Africa his first priority was to relieve Kimberley, as Cecil Rhodes who was trapped and threatening to surrender was giving the military commander a terrible time. Meanwhile in Mafeking, Baden-Powell was sending out uplifting reports, 'All well. Four hours bombardment, one dog killed'. The British papers published his reports and the public lapped it up. French with his cavalry was sent on a flank movement and relieved Kimberley on 15 February, after a four-month siege.

Roberts's next target was the invasion of the Orange Free State and the capture of Bloemfontein. General Cronje with his 4,000 burghers who had been dug in at Magersfontein to await Roberts decided to move back to Paardeberg and dig in there. Roberts sent Kitchener with two divisions to destroy Cronje. This he did with the

Highland Brigade making a frontal assault and the 9th Division supporting his flank. Cronje finally surrendered but the casualties were heavy – 300 killed, 900 wounded and fifty missing. This was a major defeat for the Boers and it happened on the anniversary of Majuba.

Buller had now worked his way towards Ladysmith and had to take the hills one by one, in particular Hart's Hill and Wynne's Hill. Unusually, because the injured had been lying for two or three days in the open without food or drink, a truce was called and the area was cleared. Ladysmith was finally relieved on 28 February and General White and his force could at last join the main army. Mafeking was relieved on 17 May by the Imperial Light Horse.

In Britain, Baden-Powell was a hero and the relief of Mafeking was a reason for national celebration. When the Boers complained about Baden-Powell playing cricket on a Sunday, he reminded them that the score was Mafeking 200 days not out against the bowling of Cronje and Botha (Pakenham, p.397). Roberts now advanced on to Bloemfontein, entering the city on 13 March. The next objective was Pretoria via Johannesburg, which was captured on 13 May and Pretoria on 5 June. British success continued with the surrender of Prinsloo, Commandant General of the Orange Free State and Botha's defeat by Buller. Even Kruger saw the end was near and left in October 1900.

Roberts left South Africa when he felt the job was done in December 1900. Kitchener continued as Commander-in-Chief, but a guerrilla war continued right into the next year. Final defeat for the Boers was the signing of a treaty in May 1902. The war had cost £2,000,000, involving 366,000 Imperial troops and 83,000 colonists (31,000 from Canada, Australia and New Zealand); 5,774 were killed and 16,168 died of their wounds or from disease (Pakenham p.572). Nearly every regiment in Britain took part in the conflict in South Africa, including Militia for the first time.

The Territorial Army: Esher and Haldane's Reforms

Following the Second Boer War, the British Army instituted widespread reforms. The committee known as The War Office (Reconstruction) Committee was convened in 1903, to investigate the shortcomings of the British Army and to make recommendations. Chaired by Lord Esher, The Esher Report recommended an Army Council, a General Staff, the abolition of CIC and the creation of the Chief of the General Staff. The Haldane Reforms (Secretary of State Lord Haldane) between 1906 and 1912 had little effect, however, on the strength of the army, as they mainly concerned the General Staff structure and administration. However, one significant change was the organisation of the Militia and Volunteers (and Yeomanry) into a newly designated Territorial Force with the Territorial and Reserve Forces Act of 1907 (later to be termed the Territorial Army or TA in October 1920) in anticipation of the upcoming war against Germany.

First World War

With the introduction of the machine gun, the machine gun sections of regiments were assembled into a Machine Gun Corps. The Corps had three branches in 1915, infantry, cavalry and motorised. Sections of the Household Cavalry and Guards Brigade were converted to machine gun regiments. When tanks were introduced they were covertly described as the Heavy Branch of the Machine Gun Corps.

During the First World War the Welsh Guards were the only new regiment formed, but battalion strengths increased. Regular battalions were usually numbered 1 to 4 and the Territorial Army Battalions numbered 5 to 8. The famous 'Pals' battalions took the battalion numbers into double figures. When the call came out from Kitchener to raise a New Army, the first off the mark was the Earl of Derby from Liverpool who raised four battalions from 28 August to 3 September 1914 with the assurance that those who joined together would serve together. The clerks of the White Star shipping line formed one platoon, those of Cunard another, while the Cotton Exchange staff, banks, insurance, et al formed the rest.

A whole brigade of four battalions of 4,000 men would be called the 1st, 2nd, 3rd and 4th City of Liverpool Battalions, but the War Office would allot them the more official title of the 17th, 18th, 19th, and 20th Battalions, King's (Liverpool); they would be known as the Liverpool Pals. The King's Liverpool raised nearly fifty battalions. The Northumberland Fusiliers had fifty-one battalions in the First World War, and the four Fusilier regiments of the Northumberland Fusiliers, Royal Warwickshire Fusiliers, Royal Fusiliers and Lancashire Fusiliers fielded 163 battalions between them. By mid-September, 500,000 had volunteered and by December 1914, fifty towns and cities had Pals battalions. By 1916 around 2 million had volunteered. Conscription was introduced in January 1916 (for those 18 to 51 years of age) bringing a total of 4 million into the army at war's end. 350 battalions had been raised by the War Office and a further 643 battalions raised locally as Pals. Nearly 1,000 battalions went into seventy divisions.

The war also saw many duplicate battalions raised. Volunteers from the Territorial Force could specify overseas or Home Service with different rates of pay and deployment and this required different categories of battalions with fractional numbers introduced, especially with the huge numbers volunteering. For normal overseas battalions, these would be considered first line for example 1/4th Battalion (first 4th Battalion) with the second line battalion for Home Service, designated 2/4th Battalion (second 4th Battalion) and even a third line designated 3/4th which would be used to reinforce the first and second battalions.

The King's Liverpool had multi-battalions up to and including the 10th Battalion, but those battalions numbered higher, for the New Armies were just numbered. The London Regiment had up to ninety-six battalions but with second line and third line up to battalion No. 28 and even had fourth-line battalions. For all regiments third-line fractional numbering finished on 8 April 1916 and the battalions became Reserve Battalions. 3/6th Battalion Lancashire Fusiliers became the 6th (Reserve) battalion Lancashire Fusiliers. There were three armies, Regular and Territorial Force, Kitchener's Volunteer Army (Pals) and Conscription.

An example of the carnage at the Battle of the Somme was the 1st Battalion Royal Inniskilling Fusiliers of about 650 men opposite Beaumont-Hamel, who were mown down by German machine gun fire with casualties of 568 within a few minutes, of whom 246 died (Keegan, p.220). This was the same regiment whose forebears as the 27th Foot (Inniskillings) died in square at Waterloo. The 1st Newfoundland Regiment – the only battalion from overseas – tried to take the same position at Beaumont-Hamel after the Inniskillings and they suffered the greatest loss on 1 July, with 710 killed, wounded or missing, including all the officers.

Asia: The Third Afghan War

Lord Curzon, Governor General of India had created the new North-West Frontier Province in 1901, in the area of the Khyber Pass with the seat of government in Peshawar. The new young and enlightened Amir of Afghanistan, Amanulla, established in 1919, was determined to achieve independence for Afghanistan and made his intentions known to the British by appointing all anti-British officials to his government, of whom many had Turkish and Russian connections. Amanulla even declared Afghanistan independent in April 1919.

The Amir was influenced by the weakened British military presence in India following the First World War, and also internal strife in India which was brought to the world's attention by Brigadier General Dyer's ordering the massacre of Indians at Amritsar on 11 April 1919. The Amir was inciting Indians to revolt against the British, and Peshawar was infiltrated with fifth columnists. The Amir's army, which was for defence, consisted of 50,000 regulars, 10,000 irregulars and he could call upon 80,000 tribesmen. When Afghan troops crossed the Khyber into India and occupied the Bagh springs to control the pumping station, the Third Afghan War (1919) began.

The Anglo-Indian troops in India were being run down after the war, or were at their summer depots, and the British only had eight battalions with a few Territorial battalions from the war still hanging around waiting for passage home. The army was augmented with machine guns, vehicles and aeroplanes. The first British action was to secure all the gates at Peshawar with cavalry and infantry and then threaten to cut off the water supply unless the troublemakers left, which they did. The first attack on Bagh springs was unsuccessful and a few days later General Fowler sent six battalions in and Bagh was taken by the 2nd Battalion Staffordshires and both 1st and 2nd Battalions 11th Gurkhas.

The British established a camp at Dacca and the Afghans gave them trouble in the surrounding hills. A brigade attack on the Afghan artillery took place after bitter fighting, with reserves being brought up. The Afghans were defeated and lost their guns, but then trouble started in the British rear at the Khyber. So-called friendly troops, the Khyber Rifles were not so friendly and had to be disarmed. Meanwhile down at Quetta, Lieutenant General Wapshare and his 4th Division cut off the Afghan's retreat to Kandahar and defeated them at Spin Kotal.

The final Afghan resistance was led by General Nadir Khan at Ghazni and Peiwar Kotal with fourteen battalions and forty-eight guns. When Khan moved out with 6,000 troops, Brigadier General Eustace decided to confront General Nadir Khan at Thal with his four battalions of Indian infantry. When battle commenced British reinforcements under Brigadier General Dyer had to be brought from Peshawar after a hard journey. The Afghans had also reinforced to 19,000. Before a major battle started the Amir called for a truce. Negotiations as usual were protracted and eventually the Treaty of Rawalpindi was signed, giving Afghanistan its independence. The British insisted on all Russian and Turkish advisors being expelled and the continuity of good Anglo-Afghan relations.

Between the World Wars: Infantry Changes and Geddes's Axe

In 1920 regiments were given the opportunity to redesignate their titles. Many did and the Royal Scots (Lothian Regiment) became the Royal Scots (Royal Regiment) while two Welsh regiments chose to revert to the archaic spelling, thus the Royal Welsh Fusiliers became the Royal Welch Fusiliers and the Welsh Regiment became the Welch Regiment. The newly formed Welsh Guards (1915) retained the modern spelling.

The Queen's (Royal West Surrey) became the Queen's Royal Regiment (West Surrey).
The King's Own (Royal Lancaster) became The King's Own Royal Regiment (Lancaster).
The Princess of Wales's Own (Yorkshire Regiment) became the Green Howards (Princess of Wales's Own Yorkshire Regiment).
The Loyal North Lancashire Regiment became the Loyal Regiment (North Lancashire).
The Irish Rifles became the Royal Ulster Rifles.

With the formation of the Irish Free State in 1922, five Irish regiments were disbanded. It was reported that George V wept when he was given the Colours of the Irish regiments for safekeeping at Windsor Castle.

The Royal Irish (18th)
The Connaught Rangers (89th/94th)
The Leinster (100th/109th)
The Royal Munster Fusiliers (101st/104th)
The Royal Dublin Fusiliers (102nd/103rd)

In April 1922, Sir Eric Geddes planned a major disbandment of cavalry and infantry regiments. The proposed reduction for infantry regiments was twenty-two battalions. Opposition was intense and the cavalry decided to amalgamate regiments instead. The infantry took the hit, with the disbandment of the 3rd and 4th battalions of selected regiments.

Royal Fusiliers: 3rd Battalion formed 1898, disbanded 4th Battalion formed 1900, disbanded.
Worcestershire: 3rd and 4th Battalions formed 1900, disbanded.
The Rifle Brigade: 3rd Battalion formed 1809 disbanded. The 4th Battalion formed 1857, disbanded.
Middlesex: 3rd and 4th Battalion formed 1900, disbanded.
The King's Royal Rifle Corps has had a long history of many battalions. 3rd and 4th Battalions were disbanded at this time. When raised in America in 1755 it had four battalions. The 5th Battalion was formed in 1787, disbanded 1818. The 6th Battalion was formed in 1799 and disbanded 1818. The 7th Battalion was formed in 1813, disbanded 1816. Finally the 8th Battalion was formed in 1813, disbanded 1816.
The Machine Gun Corps was disbanded.

In 1935 to commemorate the Silver Jubilee of George V, the following regiments were granted 'Royal' titles:

The Buffs (Royal East Kent Regiment)
The Royal Northumberland Fusiliers
The Royal Norfolk
The East Yorkshire (Duke of York's Own)

Second World War

As with any major conflict, like the First World War, all regiments raised new battalions. For example, Liverpool King's had fifteen battalions, Lancashire Fusiliers seventeen, battalions and York & Lancs twelve battalions. The new infantry regiments (not recognised as line regiments) formed in the Second World War were the Commando and Parachute Regiments. In June 1940 after Dunkirk, morale was low and it was of the utmost importance to find a way of hitting back at the enemy. Lieutenant Colonel Dudley Clarke (Royal Artillery) came up with the idea of a highly trained resourceful unit who could punch above their weight, similar to the Boer Commandos who gave the British Army so much trouble. Clarke put the idea to Sir John Dill, Chief of the Imperial Staff, who sold it to Churchill, who agreed. The original name was Special Service (SS) Regiments but this title had rather unpleasant connotations and Commando was accepted.

Eventually Sir Roger Keyes Admiral of the Fleet was put in command of Combined Operations as Director, with General Bourne of the Royal Marines as deputy. Lord Louis Mountbatten was made Chief of Combined Operations in October 1941 and by the end of the war twelve Commandos had been raised, numbered 1 to 12 for combined operations. Recruits were volunteers and the Commando Training Course was at Achnacarry near Fort William in Scotland, where a green beret was awarded to those who completed the course. 10 Inter Allied Commando was unique in that it had foreign soldiers in each troop. French, Dutch, Belgians, Poles, Norwegians and even X troop, who were German. They were not deployed as a unit as other Commandos, but were dispersed as specialists.

The Royal Marines also raised a number of Commandos numbered 40 to 48 RM Commando. The original Royal Marine Commando raised for the Dieppe raid was formed from volunteers and later numbered 40 Royal Marine Commando. With the desperate need for combined operations troops, the Royal Marine battalions were converted to Commandos. A total of twenty-one Commandos were raised and were brigaded as Special Service Brigades and eventually Commando Brigades as the war progressed.

Commando Brigades				
	1st Brigade	2nd Brigade	3rd Brigade	4th Brigade
Army Commando	3, 4 and 6	2 and 9	1 and 5	
Royal Marine Commando	45	40 and 43	42 and 44	41, 46, 47 and 48

7, 8 and 11 Commando were part of Layforce under Brigadier Laycock and were sent to the Middle East. They were eventually disbanded and formed the nucleus of the Middle East Commando. 12 Commando also disbanded early on in the war. After the war the Army Commandos were disbanded and the Royal Marines maintained the *Per Mara Per Terram* tradition by continuing with Commando units right up to the present day as part of the 3rd Commando Brigade.

In June 1940 Churchill ordered that 5,000 troops be parachute trained. The Russians and Germans had shown that a strike force of parachutists was effective, and yet the British Army had none on the establishment. The parachutists were to be trained at Ringway, Manchester. Parachutes were used by the RAF, but the act of despatching from an aircraft with equipment was new and had to be developed. Originally 2 Commando was raised to be a parachute unit and did the original development in parachute technology. Eventually parachute battalions were raised as part of the newly formed Air Corps, which included gliders, then parachute brigades and finally divisions.

The 1st Airborne Division ceased to exist after Arnhem and was re-formed only to be disbanded after the war. The 6th Airborne Division remained after the war, but now consisted of a re-formed 1st Parachute Brigade with the 2nd, 3rd and 5th Parachute Brigades.

1st Airborne Division				
	1st Brigade	2nd Brigade	3rd Brigade	4th Brigade
Parachute Battalions	1st, 2nd and 3rd	4th, 5th, and 6th		
1943		2nd Independent Parachute Brigade	7th, 8th, 9th	156th,10th 11th

6th Airborne Division Normandy			
	3rd Brigade	5th Brigade	6th Air landing brigade
Parachute Battalions	8th, 9th and 1st Canadian	7th, 12th & 13th	1/ Royal Ulster Rifles 2/Ox and Bucks 12/Devonshire

Re-formed 1st Airborne Division for Operation Market Garden			
	1st Brigade	4th Brigade	1st Air landing brigade
Parachute Battalions	1st, 2nd and 3rd	10th, 11th & 156th	1/Border 7/King's Own Scottish Borderers 2/ South Staffs

In 1948 a general reorganisation took place with a return to the peacetime establishment. The 6th Airborne Division was disbanded, leaving a re-formed 2nd Parachute Brigade consisting of a new 1st, 2nd and 3rd Parachute Battalions. These three battalions were from mergers or renumbering of existing battalions.

In July 1948 a second reorganisation occurred; the 2nd Parachute Brigade was redesignated the 16th Independent Parachute Brigade and consisted of 1st, 2nd and 3rd Para. The number 16 was especially chosen to recall the famous 1st and 6th Airborne Divisions. The Parachute Regiment was now on the permanent establishment when it separated from the Air Corps, which disbanded in 1949. The three battalions were presented with Colours in July 1950. Hilary St George Saunders noted: 'There is no record in the proud annals of the British Army of three battalions of the same regiment receiving their first Colours on the same day from the same hands.' The 16th Independent Parachute Brigade as a group disbanded in 1977, but the Parachute Regiment of three battalions continued in service.

Post-Second World War

By 1945, the British Army had sixty-four infantry line regiments (excluding late comers, Parachute and SAS Regiments) and five regiments of Foot Guards, which included the Irish Guards and Welsh Guards formed in 1900 and 1915 respectively. In 1946 three regiments were granted a Royal title: Royal Leicestershire, Royal Lincolnshire and Royal Hampshire. In 1946 the Guards and infantry were grouped into fourteen administrative corps or groupings and identified as A to O. Mostly the brigades were territorial, but some were specialised groups such as Light Infantry and Green Jackets. The Gurkhas would join in 1948 and would be nominated P.

1	A	Guards
2	B	Lowland
3	C	Home Counties
4	D	Lancastrian
5	E	York and Northumberland
6	F	Midland
7	G	East Anglia
8	H	Wessex
9	J	Light Infantry
10	K	Mercian
11	L	Welsh
12	M	North Irish
13	N	Highland
14	O	Green Jackets

Following the India Independence Act in 1947, the ten Gurkha regiments were split between India and the UK.

1st King George V's Own Gurkha Rifles (India)
2nd King Edward VII's Own Gurkha Rifles: two battalions (UK)
3rd Queen Alexandra's Own Gurkha Rifles (India)
4th Prince of Wales's Own Gurkha Rifles (India)
5th Royal Gurkha Rifles (Frontier Force) (India)
6th Gurkha Rifles: two battalions (UK)
7th Gurkha Rifles: two battalions (UK)
8th Gurkha Rifles (India)
9th Gurkha Rifles (India)
10th Gurkha Rifles: two battalions (UK)

Following on from the 1947 tripartite agreement between the UK, India and Nepal which determined the future of the Gurkhas, every Gurkha soldier was given the opportunity to serve with the British Army, the new Indian government, or resign. Gurkhas had the opportunity to move to other regiments as well as the British officers, who could no longer serve in the new Indian Gurkha regiments. In 1948 four regiments of Gurkhas with eight battalions and supporting arms of engineers, signals and transport came onto the British establishment. The 10th Gurkha Rifles would become the 10th Princess Mary's Own Gurkha Rifles in 1950.

In 1947, the battalions of armoured infantry during the war returned to normal service and by 1948 most second battalions had been disbanded except for the Guards, Parachute and Gurkha regiments. To meet the requirement of the forces, the National Service Act was introduced in 1947 with initially a twelve-month service effective in 1949; this was increased to eighteen months and, by the time of the Korean War, to two years. The Call-Up was at 18 years of age, unless deferred owing to, for example, an apprenticeship or higher education. Some regiments during the Korean War were allowed to raise a second battalion in 1952, only to be disbanded in 1956.

Identifying the administrative brigades by letter A to P did not go down well with the army and the scheme was modified in 1948. A Brigade of Guards, a Light Infantry Brigade, a Green Jacket Brigade, a Brigade of Gurkhas and eleven Regional Brigades were announced with regiments allocated to each brigade.

The Brigade of Guards
The Light Infantry Brigade
The Green Jackets Brigade
The Brigade of Gurkhas
and eleven Regional Brigades
- East Anglian
- Midland
- Highland
- Home Counties
- Lancastrian
- Lowland
- Mercian
- Welsh
- Wessex
- York and Northumberland
- North Irish

The army detached Fusilier regiments from other brigades to form a Fusilier Brigade in 1958. The York and Northumberland Brigade was renamed Yorkshire in 1958 and in 1958 the Midland Brigade was renamed Forester, only to be disbanded in 1963, dispersing the regiments. The infantry regiments within the brigades retained their identities. The Royal Marines 3rd Commando Brigade of 40, 42 and 45 Commando is traditionally administered by the Admiralty and does not come within the British Army organisation.

Second Amalgamation: Defence White Paper 1957

A post-Suez review and the biggest change in military policy made in modern times which would reduce the armed forces by half by 1962. After the withdrawal from Suez and from India, the army considered reducing its strength from 330,000 to 200,000. The aim of the 1957 Defence White Paper prepared by Duncan Sandys and published in April, 'New Priorities in British Defence Policy', was to overhaul the army by making it totally professional and announced that conscription was to end. National Service ended on 1 January 1960, 200,000 men having served. The army decided to reduce the line infantry of sixty-four regiments to forty-nine to compensate for the ending of conscription. Regiments were required to wear brigade cap badges, except for Guards and Gurkhas. The brigades were defined with the battalion losses nominated and in 1957 were to be:

THE BRIGADE OF GUARDS (no changes)
Grenadier Guards, Coldstream Guards, Scots Guards, Irish Guards and Welsh Guards.

THE LIGHT INFANTRY BRIGADE (to lose one battalion)
The King's Yorkshire Light Infantry, the King's Shropshire Light Infantry and the Durham Light Infantry.
A merger of the Somerset Light Infantry and the Duke of Cornwall's Light Infantry.

THE GREEN JACKETS BRIGADE (no changes)
The Oxford and Buckinghamshire Light Infantry, the King's Royal Rifle Corps and the Rifle Brigade.

THE BRIGADE OF GURKHAS (no change)
The 2nd King Edward VII's Own Gurkha Rifles, the 6th Gurkha Rifles, the 7th Gurkha Rifles and the 10th Princess Mary's Own Gurkha Rifles. (In 1959 the 6th and 7th Gurkha would be given Royal titles, 6th Queen Elizabeth's Own Gurkha Rifles and the 7th Duke of Edinburgh's Own Gurkha Rifles.)

THE EAST ANGLIAN BRIGADE (to lose three battalions)
A merger of the Royal Norfolk Regiment and the Suffolk Regiment.
A merger of the Royal Lincolnshire Regiment and the Northamptonshire Regiment.
A merger of the Bedfordshire and Hertfordshire Regiment and the Essex Regiment.

THE MIDLAND BRIGADE (no changes)
The Royal Warwickshire, the Royal Leicestershire and the Sherwood Foresters.

THE HIGHLAND BRIGADE (to lose one battalion)
The Black Watch, the Gordon Highlanders and the Argyll & Sutherland Highlanders.
A merger of the Seaforth Highlanders and the Queen's Own Cameron Highlanders.

THE HOME COUNTIES BRIGADE (to lose two battalions)
The Royal Sussex Regiment and the Middlesex Regiment (Duke of Cambridge's Own).
A merger of the Queen's Royal (West Surrey) Regiment and the East Surrey Regiment.
A merger of the Buffs (Royal East Kent Regiment) and the Queen's Own Royal West Kent Regiment.

THE LANCASTRIAN BRIGADE (to lose three battalions)
The Loyal (North Lancashire) Regiment.
A merger of the King's Own Royal Regiment (Lancaster) and the Border Regiment.
A merger of the King's Regiment (Liverpool) and the Manchester Regiment.
A merger of the East Lancashire Regiment and South Lancashire Regiment.

THE LOWLAND BRIGADE (to lose one battalion)
The Royal Scots, the King's Own Scottish Borderers and the Cameronians (Scottish Rifles).
A merger of the Royal Scots Fusiliers and the Highland Light Infantry Regiment.

THE MERCIAN BRIGADE (to lose one battalion)
The Cheshire Regiment and the Worcestershire Regiment.
A merger of the North Staffordshire Regiment and the South Staffordshire Regiment.

THE WELSH BRIGADE (no changes)
The Royal Welch Fusiliers, the South Wales Borderers and the Welch Regiment.

THE WESSEX BRIGADE (to lose two battalions)
The Gloucestershire Regiment and the Royal Hampshire Regiment.
A merger of the Devonshire and the Dorset Regiments.
A merger of the Royal Berkshire Regiment and the Wiltshire Regiment.

THE FUSILIER BRIGADE (no changes)
The Royal Northumberland Fusiliers, the Royal Warwickshire Fusiliers (a Fusilier Regiment 1963), the Royal Fusiliers and the Lancashire Fusiliers.

THE YORKSHIRE BRIGADE (to lose one battalion)
The Green Howards, the Duke of Wellington's Regiment and the York and Lancaster Regiment.
A merger of the East Yorkshire Regiment and the West Yorkshire Regiment.

THE NORTH IRISH BRIGADE (no changes)
The Royal Inniskilling Fusiliers, the Royal Ulster Rifles and the Royal Irish Fusiliers.

The Parachute Regiment would continue with three battalions. This massive reduction took place over a number of years and caused some understandable grief within the regiments. Regiments were now combined.

Large regiments initially kept their battalion subtitles or regimental numbers in an attempt to preserve their history and traditions.

1958

The West Yorkshire and East Yorkshire became the Prince of Wales's Own Regiment of Yorkshire. The Devonshire Regiment and the Dorset Regiment became the Devonshire and Dorset Regiment. The first of the large regiments to be formed was the East Anglian Regiment. The recommended amalgamations from the East Anglian Brigade would be formed into the 1st, 2nd and 3rd East Anglian Regiment. The first was the 3rd East Anglian with the 2nd and 1st following later. The 3rd East Anglian Regiment (16th/44th) was a merger of the Bedfordshire and Hertfordshire Regiment and the Essex Regiment.

The East Lancashire Regiment and South Lancashire Regiment became the Lancashire Regiment (Prince of Wales's Volunteers). The King's Regiment (Liverpool) and Manchester Regiment became the King's Regiment (Manchester and Liverpool). In 1969 it was amended to the King's Regiment. The second large regiment was formed with the Green Jackets. The Oxfordshire and Buckinghamshire LI formed the 1st Green Jackets (43rd/52nd), the King's Royal Rifle Corps formed the 2nd Green Jackets (KRRC), and the Rifle Brigade formed the 3rd Green Jackets.

1959

In 1959 the 1st East Anglian Regiment (Royal Norfolk and Suffolk) was formed from the merger of the Royal Norfolk Regiment and Suffolk Regiment. The Royal Scots Fusiliers and Highland Light Infantry became the Royal Highland Fusiliers, the South Staffordshire Regiment and North Staffordshire Regiment became the Staffordshire Regiment and the Royal Berkshire Regiment and Wiltshire Regiment (Duke of Edinburgh's) became the Duke of Edinburgh's Royal Regiment (Berkshire and Wiltshire).

The King's Own Royal Regiment (Lancaster) and Border Regiment became the King's Own Royal Border Regiment, the Somerset LI and Duke of Cornwall's LI became the Somerset and Cornwall LI, and the Queen's Royal Regiment (West Surrey) and East Surrey Regiment became the Queen's Royal Surrey Regiment.

1960

The 2nd East Anglian Regiment (Duchess of Gloucester's Own Royal Lincolnshire and Northamptonshire) formed from the merger of the Royal Lincolnshire Regiment and Northamptonshire Regiment.

1961

The Seaforth Highlanders and Queen's Own Cameron Highlanders became the Queen's Own Highlanders (Seaforth and Camerons). The Buffs (Royal East Kent Regiment) and Queen's Own Royal West Kent Regiment became the Queen's Own Buffs, the Royal Kent Regiment.

Third Amalgamation British Defence Policy 1966, Innovation of Large Regiments: 1964–70

By 1962, fifteen regiments had disappeared but further changes were necessary. The Defence White Paper 'A Traditional or a New Approach' by Dennis Healey indicated the need to withdraw British forces in Singapore, Malaysia and Persian Gulf. When the pound was devalued a strategic withdrawal of British forces 'East of Suez' was completed excluding Hong Kong and Brunei. The withdrawal from Aden in 1967 left Britain with few overseas possessions and the future of the army was with NATO. A new committee was set up to implement the Army Council's decision 'that the Infantry shall be organised into large regiments' preferring rather to encourage regiments 'to move voluntarily towards the large regiment'. Further mergers formed large regiments, based on regional brigades, with up to four battalions. The pioneer large regiments were further modified, given the title Royal, but relegated to single regimental status. The individual units within the large regiments were redesignated as battalions. Sadly some regiments were disbanded. The Cameronians and York and Lancaster were given the opportunity to merge with other regiments in 1968 but decided to disband rather than merge. The following significant changes to large regiments took place between 1964 and 1968. Later large regiments were to lose one battalion and untouched brigades to lose a regiment.

1964

Royal Anglian Regiment (former East Anglian)

1st Battalion – Royal Norfolk and Suffolk, former 1st East Anglian

2nd Battalion – (Duchess of Gloucester's Own Royal Lincolnshire and Northamptonshire) former 2nd East Anglian

3rd Battalion – (16th/44th Foot) former 3rd East Anglian

4th Battalion – Royal Leicestershire

1966

Royal Green Jackets

1st Battalion – Oxfordshire and Buckinghamshire LI (43rd and 52nd), former 1st Green Jackets

2nd Battalion – King's Royal Rifle Corps, former 2nd Green Jackets

3rd Battalion – Rifle Brigade, former 3rd Green Jackets

Queen's Regiment (former Home Counties Brigade)
1st Battalion – Queen's Royal Surrey
2nd Battalion – Queen's Own Buffs
3rd Battalion - Royal Sussex
4th Battalion – Middlesex

The battalions would continue to hold on to their own historical title as subtitles but even these were omitted in 1968. This would be the pattern for most regiments.

1968
Royal Irish Rangers (former North Irish Brigade)
1st Battalion – Royal Inniskilling Fusiliers
2nd Battalion – Royal Ulster Rifles (former Royal Irish Rifles)
3rd Battalion – Royal Irish Fusiliers

Light Infantry Regiment (former Light Infantry Brigade)
1st Battalion – Somerset and Cornwall Light Infantry
2nd Battalion – King's Own Yorkshire Light Infantry
3rd Battalion – King's Shropshire Light infantry
4th Battalion – Durham Light Infantry (disbanded six months later)

Royal Regiment of Fusiliers (former Fusilier Brigade)
1st Battalion – Royal Northumberland Fusiliers
2nd Battalion – Royal Warwickshire Fusiliers
3rd Battalion – Royal Fusiliers
4th Battalion – Lancashire Fusiliers (later disbanded in 1969)
The Fusilier mergers were voluntary

In 1968 the brigade system was phased out and was replaced by six new divisions for administrative purposes. The Guards Division, the Scottish Division, the Queen's Division, the King's Division, the Prince of Wales's Division and the Light Division were created. The senior regiment of each division determined that division's seniority, unlike the cavalry which were ranked in order of precedence. The brigade cap badges were now replaced by regimental cap badges.

GUARDS DIVISION: Former Brigade of Guards
Location: London
Grenadier Guards (two battalions)
Coldstream Guards (two battalions)
Scots Guards (two battalions)
Irish Guards
Welsh Guards

SCOTTISH DIVISION: Amalgamation of Lowland and Highland Brigades
Location: the Castle, Edinburgh
Royal Scots
Royal Highland Fusiliers
King's Own Scottish Borderers
Black Watch
Queen's Own Highlanders
Gordon Highlanders
Argyll & Sutherland Highlanders

QUEEN'S DIVISION: Former East Anglian, Fusilier and Home Counties Brigades
Location: Bassingbourn Barracks, Royston, Herts.
Queen's (four battalions)
Royal Regiment of Fusiliers (four battalions)
Royal Anglian (four battalions)

KING'S DIVISION: Former Lancastrian, North Irish and Yorkshire Brigades
Location: Imphal Barracks, York
King's Own Royal Border
King's
Prince of Wales's Own Regiment of Yorkshire
Green Howards
Royal Irish Rangers (three battalions)
Lancashire
Loyal North Lancashire
Duke of Wellington's

PRINCE OF WALES'S DIVISION: Former Mercian, Welsh and Wessex Brigades
Location: Whittington Barracks, Lichfield, Staffs.
Devonshire and Dorset
Cheshire
Royal Welch Fusiliers
South Wales Borderers
Welch
Gloucestershire
Worcestershire
Sherwood Foresters
Royal Hampshire
Staffordshire
Duke of Edinburgh's Royal

LIGHT DIVISION: Former Light Infantry and Green Jacket Brigades
Location: Peninsula Barracks, Hants
Light Infantry (four battalions)
Royal Green Jackets (three battalions)

1969

3rd Battalion Royal Irish Rangers (Royal Irish Fusiliers) disbanded
4th Battalion Light Infantry (Durham LI) disbanded
4th Battalion Royal Regiment of Fusiliers disbanded (Lancashire Fusiliers)
The Royal Regiment of Wales formed from former South Wales Borderers and the Welch Regiment.

1970

The Worcestershire and Sherwood Foresters Regiment was formed from the merger of the Worcestershire and Sherwood Foresters. The Queen's Lancashire Regiment was formed by the amalgamation of the recent Lancashire Regiment and the Loyal (North Lancashire) Regiment.

The same year saw the elimination of all remaining 4th Battalions, Middlesex (Queen's) and Royal Leicestershire (Royal Anglian). The Middlesex was reduced to a cadre company but completely disbanded in 1972.

In Northern Ireland the Hunt Report of 1969 recommended that the Ulster Special Constabulary be disbanded and the Ulster Defence Regiment be raised in its place for Home Service; it consisted of part-time and full-time soldiers from both Protestant and Catholic communities. Initially seven battalions were raised with more to follow.

The amalgamation of the Royal Hampshire regiments with the Gloucestershires was reversed by the incoming Conservative Government in 1970, with the remaining cadre company of the Hampshires brought up to strength in 1972. Also the disbandment of the Argyll & Sutherland Highlanders into a cadre company (Balaclava) in 1972 was rescinded after a ferocious public outcry and a successful 'Save the Argylls's campaign. The regiment returned to full battalion status in 1972. The non-line regiments, Parachute (three battalions) and Gurkhas (four regiments with a total of five battalions) were not allocated to a division.

Thus by 1972, of the original 110 Regiments of Foot established, the changes had reduced the army's line regiments down to twenty-eight regiments comprising thirty-nine battalions. Twenty-two regiments had one battalion, one regiment (Royal Irish Rangers) had two battalions and five regiments had three battalions: Royal Regiment of Fusiliers, Light Infantry Regiment, Queen's Regiment, Royal Green Jacket Regiment and the Royal Anglian Regiment. The strength of the regular army was 160,000.

Regiment	Battalions
Grenadier Guards	2
Coldstream Guards	2
Scots Guards	2
Irish Guards	1
Welsh Guards	1
Line Infantry	39
Parachute Regiment	3
Gurkha Regiments	5
Total	55

Fourth Amalgamation Options for Change: Defence White Paper, July 1991

After the First Gulf War, the British Army was again faced with 'peacetime' cutbacks. With the end of the Cold War and the collapse of the Warsaw Pact, the infantry was forced to reduce from fifty-five to thirty-six battalions and reduce by 44,000 men, to 116,000. The Ministry of Defence announced the Defence White Paper 'Options for Change' on 23 July 1991.

The Paper ordered that the Grenadier, Coldstream and Scots Guards were to have their 2nd battalions placed in 'suspended animation'. The Light Infantry, Royal Green Jackets, the Royal Regiment of Fusiliers and Royal Anglian Regiments were to reduce from three battalions to two. The Queen's Regiment (of three battalions) was to merge with the Royal Hampshire Regiment to form a new two-battalion regiment. The Royal Irish Rangers were to merge with the Ulster Defence Regiment (a formation composed of a mixture of Regulars and Volunteers and used for internal security in Northern Ireland). This proposed new regiment was to consist of one general regular battalion on the establishment and up to seven battalions for internal security. The Cheshire Regiment was to merge with the Staffordshire Regiment (later cancelled), the Gloucestershire Regiment was to merge with the Duke of Edinburgh's Royal Regiment, the Royal Scots was to merge with the King's Own Scottish Borderers (later cancelled), and the Queen's Own Highlanders was to merge with the Gordon Highlanders. The Gurkhas's four regiments (five battalions) were to merge into a two-battalion regiment. The new regiments are highlighted in bold below.

1992

The Royal Regiment of Fusiliers took particular exception to this second battalion loss because of their previous voluntary amalgamation into a single regiment. Their 3rd Battalion, however, was withdrawn on Minden Day. The 3rd Battalion Royal Anglian Regiment merged with the 2nd Battalion.

The Queen's Regiment merged with the Royal Hampshire Regiment to form a two-battalion regiment, the Princess of Wales's Royal Regiment.

1993

These 'Options for Change' were revised and in February 1993 the Cheshire and Staffordshire and Royal Scots and King's Own Scottish Borderers mergers were withdrawn.

Both the Light Infantry and the Royal Green Jacket Regiments considered their future role and commitment and decided to disband their 1st Battalions in 1993, merging them into the 2nd Battalions. The 2nd and 3rd Battalions were renumbered to the 1st and 2nd Battalions.

1994

The Gloucestershire Regiment merged with the Duke of Edinburgh's Royal Regiment in 1994 to form a single-battalion regiment, the Royal Gloucestershire, Berkshire and Wiltshire Regiment. The Queen's Own Highlanders merged with the Gordon Highlanders in 1994 to form a single battalion regiment, the Highlanders.

The Royal Irish Regiment

The Royal Irish Rangers merged with the Ulster Defence Regiment in 1992 to form the largest regiment in the British Army, the Royal Irish Regiment with nine battalions, and withdrew from the King's Division. The regiment also included two further battalions of the Royal Irish Rangers (TA). The two regular battalions of the Royal Irish Regiment for General Service were reduced to one battalion with the remaining seven battalions identified as Northern Ireland Resident Battalions, or 'Home Service' for short. These battalions, like the Ulster Defence Regiment from which they came, were composed of a mixture of full-time and part-time soldiers and would be operational only while the problems continued in Northern Ireland.

The 2nd Battalion Royal Irish Regiment (former Royal Irish Rangers) merged with the 1st Battalion in 1993. The same year saw the merger of the 3rd and 6th Home Service Battalions. The remaining six battalions merged into three battalions, in 2001 becoming a new 2nd Battalion, with the 3rd and 4th Battalions Royal Irish Regiment.

The Royal Gurkha Rifles

The Gurkha regiments were based in Hong Kong which was due to be handed over to China. The first stage towards a merger of the Gurkha regiments was that the two battalions of the 2nd King Edward VII's Own Gurkha Rifles were to merge into one battalion in 1992. The Royal Gurkha Rifles was formed on 1 July 1994, initially with three battalions. The 1st Battalion of the Royal Gurkha Rifles was formed from the merger of the 2nd King Edward VII's Own Gurkha Rifles and the 6th Queen Elizabeth's Own Gurkha Rifles. The 2nd Battalion was the former 7th Duke of Edinburgh's Own Gurkha Rifles, with the 3rd Battalion being the former 10th Princess Mary's Own Gurkha Rifles. The 2nd and 3rd Battalions of the Royal Gurkha Rifles merged in 1996 prior to the handing over of Hong Kong. Hong Kong was finally handed over to China on 30 June 1997, with the Royal Gurkha Rifles now based in the UK.

Unmerged Regiments

With all the changes over 300 years of service and including the 125 years of mergers since Cardwell, only five regiments have led a charmed life and avoided amalgamations.

Royal Scots	1st Foot
King's Own Scottish Borderers	25th Foot
Green Howards	19th Foot
Cheshire	22nd Foot
Royal Welch Fusiliers	23rd Foot

TWENTY-FIRST CENTURY

Fifth Amalgamation: Defence White Paper, July 2004, 'Delivering Security in a Changing World'

To meet the constraints of the Treasury, General Mike Jackson, Chief of the General Staff, made a number of proposals to achieve a reduction of the army to 102,000. The aim was to provide a 'Future Infantry Structure' which would meet the current needs of the army – in Northern Ireland, Iraq, Afghanistan and the Balkans in order to do this there were to be four fewer battalions to make the army more efficient and more deployable. Manpower shortages would be offest by single-battalion regiments, which had to be recruited from overseas, mainly from the Commonwealth. The September proposals were:

1) Reduce the number of infantry battalions from forty to thirty-six by 2008.
2) The nineteen single-battalion regiments to move to larger regiments with at least two or three battalions, using the Anglian and Royal Green Jackets as role models. The larger regiments to be given set roles and fixed locations.

3) Officers and men should be able to switch from unit to unit for expertise in specialised tasks.
4) To improve the efficiency of the army by abandoning the traditional 'Arms Plot', a routine movement of regiments every three to four years to take up different infantry or mechanised roles. This practice entailed a wasteful six-months learning curve in each new role, whilst uprooting regiments and their families. The recommended structure was announced in December 2004 with seven large regiments to be formed, mainly based upon their regional recruiting catchment areas:

Scottish Division to lose one battalion, possibly the amalgamation of the Royal Scots and the King's Own Scottish Borderers. A new large regiment called 'Royal Regiment of Scotland' and incorporating all the Scottish regiments: the Royal Scots, King's Own Scottish Borderers, Royal Highland Fusiliers, Black Watch, Highlanders and Argyll & Sutherland Highlanders as named battalions in order of seniority.

Queen's Division to lose one battalion, possibly a Fusilier battalion. A new large regiment of five battalions to include the Princess of Wales's Royals – two battalions, the Royal Regiment of Fusiliers – one battalion and the Royal Anglians – two battalions.

King's Division to lose one battalion, possibly the amalgamation of the King's Own Royal Border and the King's and to form two new large regiments – a Lancashire regiment of two battalions to include King's Own Royal Borderers, King's and Queen's Lancashire. A three-battalion Yorkshire regiment was to include the Prince of Wales's Own Regiment of Yorkshire, Green Howards and Duke of Wellington's.

Prince of Wales's Division would have no losses anticipated and would form two new large regiments – a new Midland or a Mercian Regiment of three battalions, to include the Cheshire, Worcestershire and Sherwood Foresters and Staffordshires.

A new Welsh Regiment of two battalions would combine the Royal Welch Fusiliers and the Royal Regiment of Wales.

Light Division was to lose one battalion, but to incorporate from the Prince of Wales's Division, both the Devonshire and Dorset Regiment and the Royal Gloucestershire, Berkshire and Wiltshire Regiment for possible merger into a Light Infantry role.

A new large Light Infantry Regiment would then be formed, preferably with a different title, of five battalions to include the new merged regiment ranked as the senior battalion, together with the Light Infantry's two battalions and the Royal Green Jackets's two battalions. These proposals would take some time to implement and naturally regiments fought their corner in the hope of a reprieve. In November 2005, Royal approval was given to the new titles, when the final decision was made after twelve months of consultation to ease the misery of amalgamations.

The future army structure from September 2007 looked like this:

Guards Division

The Guards Regiments

1st Battalion	Grenadier Guards
1st Battalion	Coldstream Guards
1st Battalion	Scots Guards
1st Battalion	Irish Guards
1st Battalion	Welsh Guards

Scottish Division

The Royal Regiment of Scotland: effective date March 2006

1st Battalion	Royal Scots Borderers (merger of Royal Scots and King's Own Scottish Borderers)
2nd Battalion	Royal Highland Fusiliers
3rd Battalion	Black Watch
4th Battalion	Highlanders
5th Battalion	Argyll & Sutherland Highlanders

Abbreviated: 1 SCOTS, 2 SCOTS, 3 SCOTS, 4 SCOTS, 5 SCOTS

Unlike other regiments the Scottish battalions will preserve their original titles.

Queen's Division

The Princess of Wales's Royal Regiment

1st Battalion	Princess of Wales's Royal Regiment
2nd Battalion	Princess of Wales's Royal Regiment

Abbreviated: 1 PWRR, 2 PWRR

The Royal Regiment of Fusiliers

1st Battalion	Royal Regiment of Fusiliers
2nd Battalion	Royal Regiment of Fusiliers

Abbreviated: 1 RRF, 2 RRF

The Royal Anglian Regiment

1st Battalion	Royal Anglian Regiment
2nd Battalion	Royal Anglian Regiment

Abbreviated: 1 R ANGLIAN, 2 R ANGLIAN

King's Division

The Duke of Lancaster's Regiment (King's Lancashire and Border): effective date March 2007

1st Battalion	Duke of Lancaster's Regiment

2nd Battalion Duke of Lancaster's Regiment
Abbreviated: 1 LANCS, 2 LANCS

In July 2006 as an interim measure the King's Own Royal Border Regiment, the King's and the Queen's Lancashire became the 1st, 2nd and 3rd Battalions of the new Duke of Lancaster Regiment. In March 2007 the three battalions dispersed into two battalions.

The Yorkshire Regiment: effective date June 2006

1st Battalion	Yorkshire Regiment (former Prince of Wales's Own Regiment of Yorkshire)
2nd Battalion	Yorkshire Regiment (former Green Howards)
3rd Battalion	Yorkshire Regiment (former Duke of Wellington's Regiment)

Abbreviated: 1 YORKS, 2 YORKS, 3 YORKS

Prince of Wales's Division

The Mercian Regiment: effective date September 2007

1st Battalion	Mercian Regiment (former Cheshire)
2nd Battalion	Mercian Regiment (former Worcester and Sherwood Foresters)
3rd Battalion	Mercian Regiment (former Staffordshire)

Abbreviated: 1 MERCIAN, 2 MERCIAN, 3 MERCIAN

The Royal Welsh Regiment: effective date March 2006

1st Battalion	The Royal Welsh (former Royal Welch Fusiliers)
2nd Battalion	The Royal Welsh (former Royal Regiment of Wales 24/41)

Abbreviated: 1 R WELSH, 2 R WELSH

Light Division

The Rifles: effective date February 2007

1st Battalion	The Rifles (former merger of Devonshire and Dorset and RGBW)
2nd Battalion	The Rifles (former 1st Battalion Royal Green Jackets)
3rd Battalion	The Rifles (former 2nd Battalion Light Infantry)
4th Battalion	The Rifles (former 2nd Battalion Royal Green Jackets)
5th Battalion	The Rifles (former 1st Battalion Light Infantry)

Abbreviated: 1 RIFLES, 2 RIFLES, 3 RIFLES, 4 RIFLES, 5 RIFLES

As an interim measure in 2005, the Devonshire and Dorset Regiment and the Royal Gloucestershire, Berkshire and Wiltshire Regiment were made into a light infantry regiment on Salamanca Day, 22 July.

Regiments without a Division

The Royal Irish Regiment

1st Battalion	Royal Irish Regiment

Abbreviated: 1 R IRISH

The Parachute Regiment

1st Battalion	Parachute Regiment
2nd Battalion	Parachute Regiment
3rd Battalion	Parachute Regiment

Abbreviated: 1 PARA, 2 PARA, 3 PARA

The Royal Gurkha Rifles

1st Battalion	Royal Gurkha Rifles
2nd Battalion	Royal Gurkha Rifles

Abbreviated: 1 RGR, 2 RGR

The Queen's Division's proposal for a single large regiment was rescinded and the proposed disbandment of the 2nd Battalion Royal Fusiliers did not take place, so the reduction of battalions was three.

On 16 November 2005, Her Majesty The Queen approved the titles of all the new regiments, including the Duke of Lancaster's Regiment (King's, Lancashire and Border). The attraction of the title is that it has historic roots over many centuries with the sovereign, with military skill and achievement, and with the recruiting areas of the three predecessor regiments. No other title more fittingly embraces the Royal regiment status of the three predecessor regiments, at the same time linking them to their homes in the north-west of England.

The Duchy of Lancaster is the one of only two Royal duchies in the United Kingdom. The other is the Duchy of Cornwall. The Duke of Lancaster has been the reigning sovereign since 1399.

The order of seniority of battalions within the new Rifle Regiment is strange and requires some explanation. The Devonshire and Dorset (and RBGW) as 1st Battalion is expected; the Devonshire, when 11th Foot, is the oldest regiment and therefore takes precedence. The Green Jackets follow next as 2nd Battalion (senior regiment 43rd Foot), preceding the Light Infantry (senior regiment 13th Foot). This is a surprise and stems not from seniority of original regiments of foot, which is the norm, but from seniority between formation of the Green Jackets and the Light Infantry. The Green Jackets are the oldest regiment, being formed in 1958, ten years before the Light Infantry, and therefore precedence of regiments is retained.

When the new Rifles Regiment was formed, the Light Infantry decided its own order of seniority by nominating the 2nd Battalion Light Infantry to become the 3rd Battalion the Rifles, with its 1st Battalion becoming the 5th Battalion the Rifles. This is particularly galling for the Light Infantry with the additional slotting in of the former Devonshire and Dorsets and Royal Gloucestershire, Berkshire and Wiltshire Regiment taking precedence as senior battalion.

The Royal Irish Regiment's three battalions for Home Service, the new 2nd Battalion and the 3rd and 4th Battalions, stood down from active service in September 2006 and were disbanded on 1 July 2007 when peace returned to Northern Ireland. Over 250 soldiers lost their lives serving with the UDR and the Home Service battalions of the Royal Irish Regiment during the thirty-eight years of active service during Operation Banner. It was the longest continuous deployment in the history of the British Army. The disbanding was equal to a brigade standing down, with 2,000 of the 3,000 soldiers full time.

Before disbandment in 2006, the Queen awarded a Conspicuous Gallantry Cross (CGC) to the Royal Irish Regiment in recognition of its long service and sacrifice. This award is normally for individual servicemen or women. The Royal Irish Regiment being singled out for a special award has a historical resonance: the same thing happened 300 years ago when King William rewarded the Earl of Granard's Regiment with the title Royal Regiment of Ireland for bravery at Namur. This regiment became the 18th (Royal Irish) Foot, and under Cardwell became the Royal Irish Regiment, but was disbanded in 1922 and has no connection with the present Royal Irish Regiment.

The current Royal Irish Regiment's pedigree begins with the three regiments making up the three battalions of the Royal Irish Rangers. The 2nd Battalion the Royal Irish Regiment (former 2nd Battalion Royal Irish Rangers) merged with the 1st Battalion in 1993. The title was resurrected in 2001 as a Home Service battalion supporting the police in Northern Ireland but was disbanded in 2007. The present 1st Battalion Royal Irish Regiment is the only regular regiment from Northern Ireland and carries with it the tradition and honours of the six pre-Cardwell regiments and the additional former seven battalions of the Ulster Defence Regiment. No doubt the officers's and sergeants's mess will have difficulty finding space for all the regimental mess silver from so many disbanded battalions and regiments.

The final chapter closed on Operation Banner with a commemoration service held in St Paul's Cathedral on 11 September 2008. The engagement lasted from 1969 to 31 July 2007, when the Home Service battalions disbanded. 300,000 troops took part, with 763 killed and over 6,000 injured.

Current Infantry Regiments for the Twenty-First Century

	Regiment	**Battalion**	**Division**
Grenadier Guards	1	1	Guards
Coldstream Guards	1	1	Guards
Scots Guards	1	1	Guards

Irish Guards	1	1	Guards
Welsh Guards	1	1	Guards
Royal Regiment of Scotland	1	5	Scottish
Princess of Wales's Royal Regiment	1	2	Queen's
Royal Regiment of Fusiliers	1	2	Queen's
Royal Anglian Regiment	1	2	Queen's
Duke of Lancaster's Regiment	1	2	King's
Yorkshire Regiment	1	3	King's
Mercian Regiment	1	3	Prince of Wales's
Royal Welsh Regiment	1	2	Prince of Wales's
The Rifles	1	5	Light
Royal Irish Regiment	1	1	None
Parachute Regiment	1	3	None
Royal Gurkha Rifles	1	2	None
Total	17	37	

Together with the cavalry (eleven regiments) and Royal Marine Commando (four battalions into 3rd Commando Brigade) a total of fifty-one regiments/battalions are available to meet the British Army's role at the start of the twenty-first century. The total manpower of the army is just over 100,000 with about 30 per cent (infantry and cavalry) at the sharp end. The addition of a line regiment (1st Battalion, The Rifles) in the 3rd Commando Brigade from April 2008 is a break from tradition. No line regiment has served into the 3rd Commando Brigade since its formation in 1943. Under normal circumstances an enlargement of the brigade would be achieved with the re-forming of 41 or 43 Royal Marine Commando.

Military Operations at the Turn of the Century

First Gulf War: Iraq 1990–91. Operation Desert Storm 53,500 deployed, forty-seven killed in action.

Bosnia Peacekeeping: 1992–95. Part of UN Protection Force up to 2,500 deployed and again in 2002.

Second Gulf War: Iraq 2003–11 (also known as Iraq War). Operation Telic Invasion of Iraq & defeat of Saddam Hussain, up to 46,000 troops deployed 179 KIA (killed in action). The last troops left Iraq on 23 May 2011, after eight years.

Afghanistan: 2001–04. Securing Helmand Province. Last troops left Afghanistan on 26 October 2014 after thirteen years fighting the Taliban Insurgency in Helmand Province, Southern Afghanistan. 453 KIA rooting out Taliban and Al Qaeda responsible for the 9/11 terrorist attack, where hijacked commercial planes were crashed into the World Trade Center in New York in 2001. Territorial Army was deployed with nineteen KIA.

Early Defence Reviews

The last Defence Review was in 1998. The Secretary of State for Defence in the Labour government published in February 2010 a government green paper, 'Adaptability and Partnership: Issues for the Strategic Defence Review'.

In the 2010 General Election no party had a majority so a Coalition was formed with the Conservative Party joining forces with the Liberal Democrats. The new Secretary of State for Defence, the Right Honourable Dr Liam Fox, continued with the Defence Review, but widened it to include security matters to be overseen by the new National Security Council and developed, alongside a new National Security Strategy, a comprehensive spending review. The government's major responsibility was the huge national debt and annual deficit. Dr Liam Fox said:

- There will be some major changes to force elements of all three Services to enable them to meet future force structures.
- The review will lead to reductions in manpower over the next five years across all three Services and the civilians in Defence.
- There have been two main priorities in the review:
  1. to ensure that our mission in Afghanistan is protected
  2. to make sure we emerge with a coherent defence capability in 2020.
- Defence cannot continue on an unaffordable footing. The *Strategic Defence and Security Review* aims to bring defence plans, commitments and resources into balance so that we have a coherent defence capability and a sustainable defence programme for the future.
- Tough decisions are required to reconfigure our armed forces to confront future threats whilst we also tackle the £38 billion deficit that has accumulated in the twelve years since the last Defence Review.

The Strategic Defence and Security Review

'Securing Britain in an Age of Uncertainty' details how Britain's armed forces will be reshaped to tackle emerging and future threats.

The Prime Minister, David Cameron, gave a statement to Parliament on 19 October 2010. This review is in six parts:

1. National Security Tasks and Planning Guidelines.
2. Defence.
3. The Deterrent.
4. Wider Security.
5. Alliances and Partnerships.
6. Structural Reform and Implementation.

Its foreword continued:

> Our country has always had global responsibilities and global ambitions. We have a proud history of standing up for the values we believe in and we should have no less ambition for our country in the decades to come. But we need to be more thoughtful, more strategic and more coordinated in the way we advance our interests and protect our national security. Nevertheless, because of the priority we are placing on our national security, defence and security budgets will contribute to deficit reduction on a lower scale than some other departments. The defence budget will rise in cash terms. It will meet the NATO 2 per cent target throughout the next four years.
>
> We must find more effective ways to tackle risks to our national security – taking an integrated approach, both across government and internationally, to identify risks early and treat the causes, rather than having to deal with the consequences. That is why we have established a *National Security Council* to draw this entire effort together. We will continue to give the highest priority to tackling the terrorist threat, protecting our operational capabilities, and reforming how we tackle radicalisation, while also reviewing all our counter-terrorism powers to ensure we retain only those that are necessary to protect the public, thereby safeguarding British civil liberties.
>
> Our armed forces – admired across the world – have been overstretched, this Review has started the process of bringing programmes and resources back into balance, making our armed forces among the most versatile in the world. In terms of the army, in this age of uncertainty our ground forces will continue to have a vital operational role. That is why we are determined to retain a significant, well-equipped army. We will continue to be one of very few countries able to deploy a self-sustaining, properly equipped brigade-sized force anywhere around the world and sustain it indefinitely. As the army is withdrawn from Germany, we will reduce its heavy armour and artillery, although we will retain the ability to regenerate those capabilities if need be. The introduction of new armoured vehicles, enhanced communications equipment and new strategic lift aircraft, will make the army more mobile and more flexible. It will be better adapted to face current and future threats, with the type of equipment it needs to prevail in today's conflicts.
>
> Members of the Territorial Army and the other Reserve Forces have performed outstandingly well in Afghanistan, yet again demonstrating their great value. We need to make sure that they are organised to deal with the threats of today, recognising that they were originally geared for a Cold War role. We will want to look carefully at the ways in which some other countries use and structure their reserve forces, and see what lessons we might usefully apply here. So we will conduct a review of our Reserve Forces. It will examine whether they are properly structured to enable us to make the most efficient use of their skills, experience and capabilities in the modern era. The immense contribution of our highly professional Special Forces is necessarily largely unreported. We are investing more in them to increase their effectiveness even further. We are committed to undertaking further strategic defence and security reviews every five years.

National Security Tasks and Planning Guidelines

Identify and monitor national security risks and opportunities.

Tackle at root the causes of instability.

Exert influence to exploit opportunities and manage risks.

Enforce domestic law and strengthen international norms to help tackle those who threaten the UK and our interests, including maintenance of underpinning technical expertise in key areas.

Protect the UK and our interests at home, at our border and internationally, to address physical and electronic threats from state and non-state sources.

Investment in new and flexible capabilities such as cyber to meet emerging risks and threats.

Help resolve conflicts and contribute to stability. Where necessary, intervene overseas, including the legal use of coercive force in support of the UK's vital interests, and to protect our overseas territories and people.

Provide resilience for the UK by being prepared for all kinds of emergencies, able to recover from shocks and to maintain essential services.

Work in alliances and partnerships (NATO, USA, EU) wherever possible to generate stronger responses.

Within the overall framework of the National Security Tasks, the contribution of the armed forces is further defined through Military Tasks.

The seven military tasks are:

1 Defending the UK and its Overseas Territories.
2 Providing strategic intelligence.
3 Providing nuclear deterrence.
4 Supporting civil emergency organisations in times of crisis.
5 Defending our interests by projecting power strategically and through expeditionary interventions.
6 Providing a defence contribution to UK influence.
7 Providing security for stabilisation.

The review continued:

We will invest in programmes that will provide flexibility and advanced capabilities, and reduce legacy capabilities which we are less likely to need in a world of precision weaponry, and where the battlespace increasingly involves unmanned and cyber operations.

The Strategic Defence and Security Review will deliver a major restructuring of the armed forces in order to generate future military capabilities.

Future Army Proposals

The Army will replace its four regional division HQ with a single divisional HQ composing five multi-role brigades, each brigade including reconnaissance forces, tanks, armoured, mechanised and light infantry forces plus supporting arms. One brigade will be kept at high readiness and available for operations and four brigades in support. 16 Air Assault Brigade, will be kept with supporting units, light, short-duration intervention capability, organized and trained for parachute and air assault operations and equipped ready to intervene in any new conflict with its own supporting units; man-portable and vehicle-fitted electronic warfare equipment; deployable surveillance to protect forward operating bases. The 3rd Commando Brigade (Royal Marines) will remain (2,000 troops) In order to meet this new structure the Army will:

- reduce by around 7,000 to about 95,000 personnel by 2015, but with no changes to combat units involved in Afghanistan, and an assumption, for now, of a requirement of about 94,000 by 2020;
- reduce by one the number of deployable brigades, as we restructure to five multi-role brigades;
- reduce our holdings of Challenger 2 tanks by around 40 per cent and our heavy artillery by around 35 per cent.

Overseas Bases

We will maintain our network of permanent joint operating bases, including: in Gibraltar; in the Sovereign Base Areas in Cyprus; British Forces South Atlantic Islands, based on the Falkland Islands and Ascension Island and maintaining a regular presence in South Georgia and South Sandwich Islands; and on Diego Garcia in British Indian Ocean Territory. We will also maintain our training areas in Canada, Kenya and Brunei. These help prepare our forces for operations. The UK currently also has a major military presence in Germany, with 20,000 service personnel and their families based there. For more than fifty years the Federal Government has supported the British military presence providing essential training and operational opportunities as well as basing. We therefore aim to withdraw all forces from Germany by 2020.

Manpower

We plan to make total reductions of around 17,000 service personnel by 2015:
The Royal Navy will decrease by around 5,000 personnel to a total of *c.* 30,000.
The Army by around 7,000 to *c.* 95,000.
The RAF by around 5,000 personnel to *c.* 33, 000.
The MoD Civil Service will decrease by 25,000 to 60,000 by 2015, as the requirement for civilian support decreases in line with the development of new force structures.

Wider Security

The Risk Assessment identified wider security risks we should give greatest priority to, based upon their relative likelihood and impact.

These include three of the four Tier One risks (terrorism, cyber security and civil emergencies in the form of natural hazards or accidents) as well as other important issues:

- Terrorism
- Instability and conflict overseas
- Cyber security
- Civil emergencies
- Energy security
- Organised crime
- Border security
- Counter proliferation and arms control.

Terrorism is a Tier One risk in the National Security Risk Assessment. The most significant terrorist threat to the UK and its interests overseas comes from the Al Qaeda senior leadership based in the border areas of Afghanistan and Pakistan, and their affiliates and supporters. The current threat to the UK from international terrorism is judged to be severe, meaning that an attack in this country is highly likely. The threat is becoming more diverse as groups affiliated to and inspired by Al Qaeda develop more autonomy in directing operations.

A third of the world's population now uses the internet, which has become a pervasive aspect of global commerce, communications and entertainment. But as global dependence on cyber space continues to grow, so have the opportunities for criminals to take advantage of shortcomings in cyber security. While it is impossible to put a precise figure on the direct and indirect financial losses caused by cyber criminals, we do know that the problem is growing progressively worse. For example, we know that:

- Criminal groups have already registered over 9,500 Olympic Games-related web addresses.
- There was a 14 per cent increase in online banking losses between 2008 and 2009.

Cyber Security

The number of new malicious software threats:

2002	21K	2006	140K
2003	19K	2007	0.6M
2004	69K	2008	1.7M
2005	113K	2009	2.9M

The risks emanating from cyber space (including the internet, wider telecommunications networks and computer systems) are one of the four Tier One risks to national security. These risks include hostile attacks upon the UK from other states, potential shortcomings in the UK's cyber infrastructure, and the actions of cyber terrorists and criminals. But cyber space also creates opportunities for the UK government and British businesses, which will derive benefits from the protection that effective cyber security measures bring to the UK economy. These threats and opportunities are likely to increase significantly over the next five to ten years, as our dependence on cyber space deepens.

The government will introduce a transformative national cyber security programme to close the gap between the requirements of a modern digital economy and the rapidly growing risks associated with cyber space. The National Cyber Security Programme will be supported by £650 million of new investment over the next four years, working to one national programme of activity with supporting strategies in other departments. Through this programme, we will: overhaul the UK's approach to tackling cybercrime by address deficiencies in the UK's ability to detect and defend itself against cyber attack, whether from terrorists, states, or other hostile actors. This will include: improving our ability to deliver cyber products and services; and enhancing our investment in national intelligence capabilities, focussing on the UK's centre for cyber security operations at GCHQ, (Government Communications Headquarters, British Intelligence and security building) working in cooperation with other government departments and agencies.

These two elements provide the foundation for all our activities in cyber space, including safeguarding sensitive government and military communications;

- create a new organisation, the UK Defence Cyber Operations Group, to mainstream cyber security throughout the MOD and ensure the coherent integration of cyber activities across the spectrum of defence operations

We will also work to develop, test and validate the use of cyber capabilities as a potentially more effective and affordable way of achieving our national security objectives.

The Revised Strategic Defence and Security Review (18 July 2011)

The SDSR cuts did not cut deep enough into the government's purse. The government continued to look for economies in an attempt for the MoD to balance its books. In a statement in the House of Commons on 18 July 2011, Right Honourable Liam Fox MP, the Secretary of State for Defence, announced the outcome of the MoD's three-month review and a six-month study into the future role and structure of Reserve Forces by an Independent Commission, led by Vice Chief of Defence Staff, General Sir Nicholas Houghton.

It concluded, further reductions in Regular Army personnel with an extra 10,000, making the total from the army of 17,000. By 2015 it was expected that 7,000 were to go with the remainder axed over the following five years.

The Defence Minister told the House of Commons:

> The vision of an integrated Army, would comprise a trained strength of 82,000 Regulars and at least 30,000 Reserves. By 2020, if the Territorial Army develops in the way we intend, we envisage a total force of around 112,000, with a Regular to Reserve ratio of around 70:30. This will be more in line with comparable countries such as the United States, Canada and Australia.
>
> The Reserve Forces had previously been mobilised for Iraq and now Afghanistan with thirty killed in the TA alone.
>
> The Territorial Army, the Royal Naval Reserve and the Royal Air Force Volunteer Reserve will receive £1.5 billion to improve pay, conditions and modern equipment
>
> The regular army is to be reduced from 101,000 to 84,000 by 2020 to comply with ARMY 2020, a final cut of 17,000 soldiers, with an increase in reservists from 20,000 to 30,000. The Territorial Army will now be titled Army Reserve.
>
> The redundancies will be done in four tranches:

First Tranche: announced September 2011, 2860 redundant (920 soldiers) effective Feb 2012. 1,800 troops based in Germany and units from Cyprus will return to UK Jan 2012 to RAF bases at Cottesmore and Kinross.

Second Tranche: announced 12 June 2012, 3,760 redundant to leave by 11 Dec 2012.

Sixth Amalgamations (Disbandments), 2012

The Strategic Defence and Security Review (5 July 2012)

Defence Secretary Philip Hammond announced to Parliament which battalions or regiments were to be removed from the order of battle (ORBAT). Twenty-three major army units are to be lost: two regiments from the Royal Armoured Corps (Cavalry) – five battalions from the infantry, two units Royal Regiment of Artillery, five units Corps of Royal Engineers, five units Royal Logistic Corps and one unit each from the Royal Corps of Signals, Royal Military Police, Royal Electrical & Mechanical Engineers and Army Air Corps.

<u>Proposals for the Infantry</u>

Five battalions to be taken out of Order of Battle (ORBAT).

Scottish Division. The Royal Regiment of Scotland to lose one battalion the 5th Battalion Argyll & Sutherland Highlanders which will reduced to a company size.

Queen's Division. The Royal Regiment of Fusiliers to lose its 2nd Battalion.

King's Division. The Yorkshire Regiment to lose its 2nd Battalion.

Prince of Wales's Division. The Mercian Regiment to lose its 3rd Battalion and the Royal Welsh Regiment to lose its 2nd Battalion.

Light Division. No change.

Regiments not allocated to a division. No change.

The Royal Irish Regiment, the Royal Gurkha Rifles & the Parachute Regiment.

The Royal Irish Regiment will move to the Prince of Wales's Division.

Administered by the Admiralty. No change.

3rd Commando Brigade (40, 42 & 45 Royal Marine Commando and supporting arms).

The 1st Battalion Light Infantry came out of 3rd Commando Brigade April 2013.

Third Tranche (announced 22 January 2013 and notified in June 5,300 soldiers.

Fourth Tranche (announced 23 January 2014 (1,425 soldiers).

Regiments removed by ORBAT (removed from order of battle) to reduce manpower to 82,000 regular troops and 30,000 reservists by 2018.

Royal Regiment of Scotland 5th Battalion Argyll & Sutherland Highlanders reduced to Balaclava Company for public duties, at Edinburgh and Holyrood, 5 July 2012.

Royal Regiment of Fusiliers 2nd Battalion disbanded & merging with the 1st battalion, 20 September 2014.

2nd Battalion (Green Howards) The Yorkshire Regiment disbanded. The Colonel of the Regiment subsequently decided to merge and renumber the battalions to form two regular battalions in Autumn 2013.

The 3rd Battalion (Duke of Wellington's) to become 1st Battalion and the 1st Battalion (Prince of Wales's Own) to become the new 2nd Battalion.

HRH The Duke of York, Colonel in Chief of the Yorkshire Regiment and His Grace, The Duke of Wellington (Deputy Colonel in Chief) took the salute at the parade at Battlesbury Barracks in Warminster, Wiltshire on 25 July 2013. The 3rd Battalion laid up their Colours at Halifax Minster, 20 July 2013.

Mercian Regiment 3rd Battalion disbanded 28 June 2014 at Lichfield.

Royal Welsh Regiment 2nd Battalion disbanded 3 April 2014 at Lucknow barracks Tidworth.

Transforming the British Army by General Sir Peter Wall (July 2013)

A report by General Sir Peter Wall, Chief of the General Staff, listed the new British ARMY 2020 structure which includes Army Reservists.

The components of the ARMY 2020 structure would be:

A Reaction Force (RF): Three Armoured Infantry Brigades within a division, which will be a higher readiness force undertaking short notice contingency tasks providing the Army's conventional deterrence for defence. It will be trained and equipped to undertake the full spectrum of intervention tasks and will provide the initial basis for any future enduring operation.

Each Armoured Infantry Brigade will consist of HQ (including Royal Signals), one armoured Cavalry Regiment, one Regiment of Armour, three Armoured Infantry battalions and supporting Logistics Brigade consisting of two regiments from the Royal Logistic Corps (Transport, Supplies, Ordnance & Pioneers), Army Air Corps (Command & Attack helicopters), Medical Services, Royal Engineers, REME, Artillery (including Air Defence) and Provost (Royal Military Police). Each division will have a Cavalry Regiment in reserve.

The 16th Air Assault Brigade is the UK's rapid reaction airborne force consisting of two Parachute Battalions (plus a reserve) Attack Helicopters (plus reserve), Close Support Artillery, Engineers, Signals Communication, Logistics Regiment, Medical and Air Assault Battalion REME.

An Adaptable Force (AF): Comprising a division of Regular and Reserve forces that will consist of seven Infantry Brigades and a Logistics Brigade. This will be used for a wide range of tasks, including providing headquarters and units for enduring operations, acting as the primary source of capability for Defence Engagement at home and overseas, as well as meeting standing tasks in the UK and abroad (e.g. Cyprus, Falkland Islands, Brunei and public duties).

Force Troops: Will support RF and AF and are specialised troops which will provide a wide range of capabilities from the centralised pool of Regulars and Reserve forces such as Artillery, Engineers, Logistics, Military Intelligence et al.

Infantry Regiments of the British Regular Army for ARMY 2020

Infantry

Division	Units	Bns	Bn	Regiment
Guards	1	1	1st	Grenadier
	2	2	1st	Coldstream
	3	3	1st	Scots
	4	4	1st	Irish
	5	5	1st	Welsh
Scottish	Royal Regiment of Scotland			
	6	6	1st	Royal Scots Borderers
	6	7	2nd	Royal Highland Fusiliers
	6	8	3rd	Black Watch
	6	9	4th	Highlanders

Queen's	7	10	1st	Princess of Wales Royal Regiment
	7	11	2nd	Princess of Wales Royal Regiment
	8	12	1st	Royal Regiment of Fusiliers
	9	13	1st	Royal Anglian
	9	14	2nd	Royal Anglian
King's	10	15	1st	Duke of Lancaster's
	10	16	2nd	Duke of Lancaster's
	11	17	1st	Yorkshire Regiment
	11	18	2nd	Yorkshire Regiment
Prince of Wales's	12	19	1st	Mercian Regiment
	12	20	2nd	Mercian Regiment
	13	21	1st	Royal Welsh Regiment
	14	22	1st	Royal Irish Regiment
Light	15	23	1st	Rifles
	15	24	2nd	Rifles
	15	25	3rd	Rifles
	15	26	4th	Rifles
	15	27	5th	Rifles
None	16	28	1st	Royal Gurkha Rifles
	16	29	2nd	Royal Gurkha Rifles
	17	30	1st	Parachute Regiment
	17	31	2nd	Parachute Regiment
	17	32	3rd	Parachute Regiment
	3rd Commando Brigade			
Admiralty		40		Royal Marine Commando
		42		Royal Marine Commando
		45		Royal Marine Commando

Army Reserve Infantry

Royal Regiment of Scotland	Princess of Wales Royal Regiment	Royal Regiment of Fusiliers	Royal Anglian Regiment	Duke of Lancaster's Regiment	Yorkshire Regiment
6 SCOTS (52nd Lowland)	3 PWRR	5 RRF	3 R ANGLIAN	4 LANCS	4 YORKS
7 SCOTS (51st Highland)					
Mercian Regiment	Royal Welsh Regiment	Royal Irish Regiment	Rifles	London Regiment	Parachute Regiment
4 MERCIAN	3 Royal WELSH	2 Royal IRISH	6 RIFLES 7 RIFLES	See below	4 PARA

London Regiment	HQ Company	A Company London Scottish	B Company Princess of Wales's Royal Regiment	C Company Royal Regiment of Fusiliers	D Company London Irish Rifles
Honourable Artillery Company (HAC) Formed in 1537 (ancient title) and the oldest military regiment in the British Army (possibly the world) of company strength continues with ceremonial role in Guildhall.					

Islamist State for Iraq and Levant

When the SDSR was first announced in 2010 and at each review, the government, MoD and GCHQ had firm views on who the potential enemy was: North Korea, China and possibly the new-look Russia (especially when the latter invaded Ukraine and annexed Crimea), and of course Osama Bin Laden (killed by US Special Forces in Abbottabad, Pakistan, on 2 May 2011) and his Al Qaeda, responsible for 9/11. A number of terrorist attacks by ISIL (Islamic State in Iraq and Levant) especially in 2015 led to a massive rethink, not only in the UK, but also by major powers (East with Russia and West with UK, NATO and USA). A new enemy was within our midst with access to social media to communicate their message.

ISIL or ISIS (Islamic State of Iraq and Syria) came into prominence in 2014 with their desecration of Islamic and Christian holy places. A self-declared caliphate, which took over parts of Iraq and later Syria, looked to the medieval interpretation of Sunni Islam and rejected all religious shrines of any sort. They massacred thousands who did not conform to their interpretation of Islam. They systematically destroyed holy places reducing them to rubble including ancient Christian sites. They used sledgehammers, bulldozers and explosives to destroy 100 ancient sites/shrines in 2015 including the ancient city of Palmyra, Nineveh and Hatra – recording their efforts for the world's press. Iraq's oldest Christian site, the ancient Christian Monastery of St Elijah, which had stood for 1,400 years south of Mosul, was destroyed, together with Mosul's museum. Such events shocked the world.

In August 2014 Jihadi John (an infamous masked jihadist) made his first YouTube broadcast, beheading hostages, and continued to record his macabre acts for the world's press. The world was quite appalled, and British and US intelligence agencies continued to search for him.

Events in 2015

7 January
ISIL gunmen kill twelve employees from *Charlie Hebdo* satirical magazine in Paris.

26 June
Thirty-two sunbathing tourists killed by a single terrorist on a beach in Tunisia.

13 November
Jihadi John killed in Syria by a Rapier Drone, firing a Hellfire guided missile.

13 November
Nearly 130 killed, with 350 injured, in a massacre at Eagles of Death Metal concert at Le Bataclan theatre, restaurants and outside the Stade de France during the France v. Germany friendly football match in Paris by ISIL jihadists.

17 November
Russian plane (Metrojet) full of holidaymakers from Sharm el-Sheikh, Egypt, shot down by ISIL over the Sinai desert, killing 225.

24 November
Russian military plane shot down by Turkey (NATO member) over Turkish air space.

16 November
The Prime Minister announced 1,900 more security and intelligence staff. The biggest increase in security since 9/11 in New York and 7/7 in London. A 15 per cent increase in MI5, MI6 and GCHQ, Aviation security funds would be doubled. The following day the PM suggested UK should attack the head of the snake – ISIL.

17 November
At the pre-arranged England v. France football match, Wembley was decked out in red white and blue with the emotional and symbolic singing of the 'La Marseillaise'. For the first time there were visible armed guards in the stadium.

20 November
The United Nations Security Council unanimously agreed Resolution 2249 calling on member states to take 'all necessary measures' against ISIL in Iraq and Syria and the 'global and unprecedented threat to international peace and security' (however, never mentioned bombing).

23 November
Announced by the Prime Minister David Cameron focusing on the next decade with £178 billion of military funding. Army restructuring with two strike brigades of 5,000 to tackle the threat of ISIL who he feels is trying to get nuclear weapons and other terrorists. The brigades to deploy quickly to boost the rapid reaction forces. He will ask Parliament to extend air strikes against ISIL from targets in Iraq to air strikes over Syria, where they were in greater numbers, with a vote before Christmas (USA, France and Russia were bombing ISIL targets in Syria). Barack Obama, US President, vowed to destroy ISIL, 'a bunch of killers with good social media'.

Also, the government to increase counter terrorism funding by a third to £15 billion by upgrading border systems, as well as the establishment of a National Digital Exploitation Service which will specialise in hacking seized phones, computers et al and Special Forces funding will rise to £2 billion.

Previously, such was the concern that the Syrian President, Bashar al-Assad used chemical weapons against his own people, that in August 2013 it was proposed to bomb Syria but Parliament rejected the proposal.

2 December

Vote in Parliament. Bombing of ISIL terrorists in Iraq was already taking place, but The PM wanted to extend the bombing to Syria in the light of recent atrocities and general mood and Parliament would be supportive. Parliament voted 397 for and 223 against giving a 174 majority. The PM referred to ISIL as 'medieval monsters who were plotting to kill us and radicalise our children'. The PM ruled out combat troops and stated in Parliament that there were 70,000 'moderate' Syrian forces to be relied upon to join the fight against the Islamic State.

Syrian Civil War

The political and military situation in Syria was extremely complex. In March 2011, pro-democracy protests were put down with the uprising becoming violent and by July 2011 thousands had taken to the streets. Opposition forces took up arms to defend themselves and then to attack government forces. Descending into civil war, rebel units organised themselves and approached Damascus and Aleppo in 2012 and by June 2013 the UN reported 9,000 killed. In August 2013 hundreds were killed by rockets containing SARIN. Assad blamed the rebels, but the UK amd USA considered President Assad to be a mass murderer for using chemical weapons against his own people who were in opposition to his regime. It had been said that a red line would be drawn if war crimes had occurred but no action was taken. The Syrian democratic forces which are a loose collection of Sunni Arabs, Kurds and even Syriac Christians wanted the downfall of President Assad's Alawite Shiite. For centuries there has been conflict and disagreements between the Sunnis and Shi'ites. If the situation wasn't bad enough ISIL jihadists joined the fracas. The five-year civil war has killed more than 270,000 people with 4½ million displaced fleeing to Turkey, Lebanon, and Jordan becoming a humanitarian crises. President Putin of Russia, quite independent of the West, supported Assad (as does Iran) by bombing opposition and ISIL targets in Syria (as did the French) from September 2015. The Kurds wish to carve out their own zone of influence.

Refugees fled to Turkey and the Greece and then further on into Europe forcing the EU to suspend its Schengen agreement (twenty-six EU countries with free border movement excluding the UK) on border controls. Such was the influx of refugees that the European nations were building wire fences to control their borders.

27 February 2016
Cessation of hostilities in Syria arranged by USA, Russia and UN.

5 March
Turkey government close down a newspaper critical of its methods.

14 March
With the truce into its third week, Russia announced it is pulling its aircraft out of Syria declaring job done military and requests President Assad to continue with diplomatic channels. On 28 April many are killed in Aleppo as the truce is under strain and in a catastrophic state according to UN.

Cyber Attack and Security (GCHQ)

Some attacks that made headlines:

- October 2015 TalkTalk bank account details stolen.
- November 2015 a major pharmaceuticals company hacked.
- February 2016 a 16-year-old British schoolboy unmasked as the prime suspect in a cyber attack on the US government by hacking into 30,000 employees' names and addresses of the FBI and Department of Homeland Security, with a lot of the data dumped online.
- February 2016 a group of cyber thieves, who had previously studied the bank's major transactions, broke into Bangladesh's central bank, obtaining data needed for payment transfers from Federal Reserve Bank of New York and then transferred large sums to fraudulent accounts overseas. The criminals were able to steal a total value of about $81 million from the Federal Reserve's Bangladesh account through a series of five transactions, but a typing mistake in the last transaction prevented a further $850 million loss, because a bank official being suspicious of repeated withdrawals queried the spelling of 'Foundation' as Fandation.One of the largest known bank robberies in history.

The high-street stores are spending a fortune on hardware to combat shoplifting but neglect to give equal consideration to cyber attacks. This is changing as boardrooms are discussing cyber problems.

Cyber Security Challenge Masterclasses were being set up annually by the defence industry as a series of national competitions, learning programmes and networking initiatives designed to identify, inspire and enable more people to become cyber security professionals. They are the most realistic civilian cyber-terrorist attack simulations to date staged to find the UK's future defenders (November 2015).

Forty-two of the UK's most talented amateur code-breakers had to lead the defence against a simulated cyber-terrorist plot to unleash a biological attack on the grounds of Westminster Abbey at a high-profile event. The major sponsors of these challenges are the Bank of England, BT, GCHQ, NCA BT et al, and essentially the aim is to find the best recruits.

Chancellor of the Exchequer George Osborne made a cyber security speech on 17 November 2015, at GCHQ in Cheltenham, as part of the Spending Review and Autumn Statement:

> British intelligence services will significantly step up their efforts to attack terrorists in cyberspace in the face of Islamic State militants who want to use the internet to kill people. The UK was prepared to use its digital powers to attack hackers, terrorist groups, criminal gangs and rogue states, but 'We reserve the right to respond to a cyber attack in any way that we choose'. The spectrum of capabilities could include infecting and disconnecting enemy computers or even disrupting power supplies to cause loss of life in the most extreme circumstances. Whoever hits the UK should know 'we are able to hit back'.
>
> It is right that we choose to invest in our cyber defences even at a time when we must cut other budgets. For our country, defending our citizens from hostile powers, criminals or terrorists, the internet represents a critical axis of potential vulnerability.
>
> From our banks to our cars, our military to our schools, whatever is online is also a target.
>
> The stakes could hardly be higher – if our electricity supply, or our air traffic control, or our hospitals were successfully attacked online, the impact could be measured not just in terms of economic damage but of lives lost.
>
> Isil's 'murderous brutality has a strong digital element' in which the group seeks to kill through attacks on cyber infrastructure.
>
> Isil are already using the internet for: hideous purposes, radicalization and operational planning too.
>
> However, they have not been able to use it to kill people yet by attacking our infrastructure through cyber attacks. They do not yet have that capability. But we know they want it, and are doing their best to build it.
>
> So when we talk about tackling Isil, that means tackling their cyber threat as well as the threat of their guns, bombs and knives.

The chancellor argued it would be easier and more cost effective to mount a cyber attack than to defend against one. Directly addressing cyber criminals he said:

> We will defend ourselves. But we will also take the fight to you, too. To those who believe cyber attacks can be done with impunity, I say that impunity no longer exists.
>
> Government has a duty to protect the country from hostile attack and to protect its citizens and companies from crime.

Only government can defend against the most sophisticated threats, using its sovereign capability. And that's exactly what we will do and it is this sovereign capability that brings me here, to GCHQ.

In 2010, at a time when we as a new government were taking the most difficult decisions on spending in other areas, we took a deliberate decision to increase spending on cyber.

We set up the National Cyber Security Programme and funded it with £860 million.

And for the past five years we have been creating and enhancing the structures and capabilities that Britain needs to defend itself in cyberspace.

We have invested in building our sovereign capability here at GCHQ.

We have ensured that our military systems are properly secured from cyber attack.

We have built the National Cyber Crime Unit so cyber criminals are brought to justice.

We established the Computer Emergency Response Team for the UK, and the Cyber Information Sharing Partnership so companies could share what they knew.

We developed clear guidance for businesses, including the Cyber Essentials scheme, which already has over a thousand companies accredited.

We launched a series of cyber risk reviews for companies in the Critical National Infrastructure, to identify vulnerabilities that could then be addressed.

We built cyber security into every stage of the education process.

We established Cyber First and cyber apprentices to make sure that we got the talent we needed coming into the field.

We undertake exercises so we know what to do when there is a serious cyber incident.

One such exercise took place last week – Operation Resilient Shield, a joint UK/US exercise across the financial sector (The Bank of England readies itself to put the UK's financial institutions through their paces in a new war game).

So I want to thank all those who, over the last five years, have brought us to where we are today.

We have built a world-class range of tools and capabilities that Britain needs to stay safe from cyber attack.

We are widely regarded as top or near top in the world.

Today I can announce that in 2016 we will establish a single National Cyber Centre, which will report to the Director of GCHQ and that the government is to double investment in online security to £1.9 billion.

The Centre will be a unified source of advice and support for the economy, replacing the current array of bodies with a single point of contact.

The Centre will make it easier for industry to get the support it needs from government. And make it easier for government and industry to share information on the cyber threat to protect the UK.

Reporting to GCHQ will mean the Centre can draw on the necessarily secret world-class expertise within this organisation.

> There will also be new efforts to encourage 14- to 17-year-olds to develop their cyber skills and opportunities for start-up companies to innovate in cyber technology at two new 'hubs'.

The Treasury stated that ministers will also lobby internet service providers to work with the government to stop more malware attacks and to block bad IP addresses. Osborne's speech at GCHQ was in part a response to the Paris terror attacks in 2015 that killed 130 people and injuring 368. The terrorists who committed these crimes were members of ISIS, who are notorious for using cyberspace as a means of communication, radicalisation, logistics and operations.

Osborne said that the military needed to be able to fight all the battles of the twenty-first century in cyberspace as well as those on land, sea, in the air and in space. This concept would be formalised in Osborne's new cyber strategy, which will be carried out by both GCHQ and the Ministry of Defence.

Cyber Troops 77th Brigade

Defence Minister Philip Hammond announced cyber troops in September 2013 ahead of the Conservative Party Conference, in response to cyber threats:

- Cyber attacks and crime (hacking) more common recently.
- New cyber unit to defend national security (laptop army).
- First nation to publicly raise a cyber strike capability.
- Will recruit Army Reservists.
- Will protect critical computer networks and protect vital data.
- Cyber defences not sufficient must have the means to counter-attack.
- Could launch strike in cyber space.
- Could disable enemy communications, nuclear and chemical weapons, aircraft and ships.
- Creation of Joint Cyber Reserve to support the Joint Cyber Unit in Cheltenham.
- Work at the cutting edge of national cyber defence.
- £500 million to be spent over the next few years.
- Cyber weapons will now join conventional weapons in future conflicts.
- Open to computer whizz kids that possibly fail current fitness tests.
- No military experience required, but computer (cyber experts) skills.
- Just as cavalry became mechanised, so cyber troops are the new revolution in warfare.
- We have fought by sea (Royal Navy), by land (army), by air (Royal Air Force), by land and sea (Royal Marines), and now in cyberspace.
- The Defence Minister added: 'A man with a rifle is not state-of-the-art modern warfare. A modern infantryman has more firepower than an entire platoon in Wellington's army at Waterloo.'

Raising the New Brigade of Cyber Troops, The 77th Brigade (Chindits)

The 77th Brigade was formally raised on 1 April 2015 with 2,000 troops of both Regulars and Army Reserve (more than 40 per cent) with computer skills rather than traditional military skills. This new army unit of laptop warriors will use social media to help Britain fight a modern cyber war in this information age. The new unit is called Chindits, with the British Army resurrecting the name from Major General Orde Wingate's unconventional unit which fought, sometimes behind enemy lines, in Burma during the Second World War. The new Chindits is modelled on unconventional, non-lethal, non-military methods and are named after Chinthe (brigade's cap badge), the mythical lion that guards every Burmese temple. The raising of the 77th Brigade completes the major restructuring of the army as a result of the Strategic Defence and Security Reviews (2010–15), resulting in ARMY 2020. The brigade is being created to draw together a number of existing capabilities within the Royal Navy and Royal Air Force, which are essential to meet modern challenges in future conflicts, with lessons learnt from operations in Afghanistan among others. The brigade is based at Hermitage, Berkshire, with detachments at other MoD units, and operates as well as training and working with other nations and across UK government departments, especially GCHQ.

The MoD website explains in more detail the structure of the 77th Brigade:

> 77th Brigade is a combined Regular Army and Army Reserve unit. The Reserve element draws specialists on a nationwide basis. This new Brigade aims to challenge the difficulties of modern warfare using non-lethal engagement and legitimate non-military levers as a means to adapt behaviours of the opposing forces and adversaries.
>
> In September 2014 the Security Assistance Group was formed and assumed command of the Military Stabilisation and Support Group, the Media Operations Group, 15 Psychological Operations Group and the Security Capacity Building team.
>
> In July 2015, the four individual units above were reshaped and formed the new 5 Columns of 77th Brigade:
>
> - **No.1 Column** – Planning support focusing on the behavioural analysis of actors, audiences and adversaries
> - **No. 2 Column** – Provides the detail synchronisation and delivery of effect
> - **No. 3 Column** – Provides highly deployable specialists to other parts of the armed forces and other Government organisations
> - **No. 4 Column** – Provides professional specialists in Security Capacity Building in Defence
> - **No. 5 Column** – Media Operations and Civil Affairs
> - In October 2015 No.7 Column was added:

- **No. 7 Column** – The Engineer and Logistics Staff Corps - A powerful and influential specialist Army Reserve unit providing engineering, logistics and communication consultancy to both the MOD and across government agencies.

There is not a No. 6 Column for historical reasons.

Recruitment for ARMY 2020

To maintain the Regular Army at 82,000 with an Army Reserve of 30,000 is always going to be a problem especially in the aftermath of the recent four tranches to reduce manpower. One factor in recruitment is the unit's esprit de corps, which sadly is disappearing as local regiments have merged into larger regiments (mainly Territorial) and regimental numbers have disappeared totally in the infantry, and with the Queen's Royal Lancers merging with the 9th/12th Royal Lancers another regimental number has disappeared. The 1st Queen's Dragoon Guards remains the last regiment keeping a regimental number.

Esprit de Corps (and morale) affects the cohesion of a combat unit, which may be defined by how well the unit fights and how well the unit takes losses. As Wellington said, 'will they stand?' and at Waterloo's Ohain Ridge the British Infantry certainly stood their ground (for nine long hours) against Napoleon's infantry, cavalry and finally the Imperial Guard.

Traditional factors for a unit's cohesion:

- Morale
- Training
- Equipment
- Weapons
- Support echelons
- Higher command
- Lower command
- Esprit de Corps

Good higher commanders, improving a unit's cohesion, such as Marlborough, Wellington, Nelson, Wolseley, Roberts, Montgomery, Orde Wingate and more recently Schwarzkopf, just to name a few, not only inspired their men, but took an interest in their welfare – Marlborough laying out a stock of boots and Wellington getting his men to lie down during a ferocious cannonade. At lower command level, there was Lieutenant Colonel Tim Collins, Commanding Officer of the Royal Irish Regiment, in the First Gulf War, who gave an operational speech that not only galvanised his men to go that extra mile (cohesion) but also went down in folklore for great military speeches, 'We go to liberate, not to conquer. We will not fly our flag in their country. We are entering Iraq to free a people and the only flag which will be flown in that ancient land is their own. Show respect for them …' (Thompson, p.194).

After 350 years of soldiering, the British Army is at its highest standard today, where it is considered the best in the world and good enough to be given 'point' (lead the attack) by General Schwarzkopf in the invasion of Iraq, demonstrating 100 per cent cohesion and the force is constantly fighting above its weight. The British soldier in combat, especially the infantryman at the sharp end, meets so many difficult situations that any changes in his wellbeing erodes this cohesion. As we continue in the twenty-first century, the cohesion of the British soldier as defined above is, in my view, under threat. In my opinion morale is under threat from the near-constant litigation and hounding of war veterans in Iraq and Afghanistan and the lifting of gender restrictions in front-line, close-combat roles. Both these government policies have potential to distract and discourage the traditional intake of the armed forces.

Last of the Field Marshals

After nearly 350 years of military changes, the last Field Marshal was appointed in 1994 when the strength of the army was near 120,000. It is sad that we have seen the last of the Light Infantry, Rangers, Dragoons and Horse Grenadier Guards, but with the army's strength currently at just over 82,000, we have surely seen the last of the Field Marshals.

Guards Division							
Battalion							*Raised*
1st	Grenadier Guards	Grenadier Guards 1877	Grenadier Regiment of Foot Guards 1815	1st Foot Guards 1685	Royal Regiment of Foot Guards 1665	Royal Regiment of Guards	1660
						King's Own Regiment of Foot Guards	1660
1st	Coldstream Guards	Coldstream Guards 1817		Coldstream Regiment of Foot Guards or 2nd Foot Guards 1670	Duke of Albemarle's Regiment of Foot Guards or Lord General's Regiment	General Monck's Regiment of Foot Guards	1661
1st	Scots Guards	Scots Guards 1877	Scots Fusilier Guards 1831	3rd Foot Guards 1712	Scots Regiment of Foot Guards 1686	Scottish Footguards	1661
1st	Irish Guards					Irish Guards	1900
1st	Welsh Guards					Welsh Guards	1915

Scottish Division								
Battalion				*1881 Cardwell's Reforms*	*Battalion*	*Foot Regiment*	*Pre-Cardwell*	*Raised*
Royal Regiment of Scotland formed March 2006. Reduced to four battalions in July 2012.								
1st	The Royal Scots Borderers	The Royal Scots Borderers 2006	Royal Scots (Royal) 1920	Royal Scots	2	1st	Royal Scots	1633
			King's Own Scottish Borderers 1887	King's Own Borderers	2	25th	King's Own Borderers	1689
2nd	Royal Highland Fusiliers	Royal Highland Fusiliers 1959		Royal Scots Fusiliers	2	21st	Royal Scots Fusiliers	1678
				Highland Light Infantry	1st	71st	Highland Light Infantry	1777
					2nd	74th	Highlanders	1787
3rd	Black Watch	Black Watch (Royal Highlanders) 1934		Black Watch	1st	42nd	Royal Highland	1739
					2nd	73rd	Perthshire	1779

4th	Highlanders	Highlanders 1994	Queen's Own Highlanders 1961	Seaforth Highlanders	1st	72nd	Duke of Albany's	1778
					2nd	78th	Ross-shire Buffs	1793
				Queen's Own Cameron Highlanders	1	79th	QOCH	1793
			Gordon Highlanders	Gordon Highlanders	1st	75th	Stirlingshire	1787
					2nd	92nd	Gordon Highlanders	1794
	Argyll & Sutherland Highlanders. Reduced to Balaclava Company for Public Duties	Argyll & Sutherland Highlanders		Argyll & Sutherland Highlanders	1st	91st	Argyllshire Highlanders	1794
					2nd	93rd	Sutherland Highlanders	1799
			Disbanded 1968	Cameronians (Scottish Rifles)	1st	26th	Cameronian	1689
					2nd	90th	Perthshire Light Infantry	1794

Queen's Division								
Battalion				*1881 Cardwell's Reforms*	*Battalion*	*Foot Regiment*	*Pre-Cardwell*	*Raised*
Princess of Wales's Royal Regiment formed in September 1992 with two battalions.								
1st	Princess of Wales's Royal Regiment	Queen's 1966 1st Battalion	Queen's Royal Surrey 1959	Queen's (Royal West Surrey)	2	2nd	Queen's Own Royal	1661
				East Surrey	1st	31st	Huntingdonshire	1702
					2nd	70th	Surrey	1756
2nd	Princess of Wales's Royal Regiment	Queen's 2nd Battalion	Queen's Own Buffs (Royal Kent) 1961	Buffs (East Kent) Royal 1935	2	3rd	East Kent (Buffs)	1665
				Queen's Own Royal West Kent	1st	50th	Queen's Own	1755
					2nd	97th	Earl of Ulster	1824
	3rd Battalion Queen's merged into POWRR 1992	Queen's 3rd Battalion	Royal Sussex	Royal Sussex	1st	35th	Royal Sussex	1701
					2nd	107th	Bengal Infantry	1862
		Queen's 4th Battalion disbanded 1970		Middlesex	1st	57th	West Middlesex	1755
					2nd	77th	East Middlesex	1787

		Royal Hampshire merged into POWRR 1992	Royal Hampshire 1946	Hampshire	1st	37th	North Hampshire	1702
					2nd	67th	South Hampshire	1756
Royal Regiment of Fusiliers formed in1968 wth four battalions but now one battalion								
1st	Royal Regiment of Fusiliers	Royal Northumberland Fusiliers 1935		Northumberland Fusiliers	2	5th	Northumberland Fusiliers	1674
Merge 2014	Royal Regiment of Fusiliers	Royal Warwickshire Fusiliers 1963		Royal Warwickshire	2	6th	Royal Warwickshire	1674
	3rd Battalion withdrawn Minden Day 1992			Royal Fusiliers	2	7th	Royal Fusiliers	1685
	4th Battalion withdrawn 1969 and merged with 1st, 2nd and 3rd Battalions			Lancashire Fusiliers	2	20th	East Devonshire	1688
Royal Anglian formed in 1964 with four battalions but now two battalions.								
1st	Royal Anglian	Royal Anglian 1964 1st Battalion	1st East Anglian 1959	Norfolk (Royal Norfolk) 1935	2	9th	East Norfolk	1685
				Suffolk	2	12th	East Suffolk	1685
2nd	Royal Anglian	Royal Anglian 2nd Battalion	2nd East Anglian 1960	Lincolnshire (Royal Lincolnshire) 1946	2	10th	North Lincolnshire	1685
				Northamptonshire	1st	48th	Northamptonshire	1741
					2nd	58th	Rutlandshire	1755
		Royal Anglian 3rd Battalion but merged into 2nd Battalion 1992	3rd East Anglian 1958	Bedfordshire (Bedfordshire and Hertfordshire 1919)	2	16th	Bedfordshire	1688
				Essex	1st	44th	East Essex	1741
					2nd	56th	West Essex	1755
		Royal Anglian 4th Battalion disbanded 1970	Royal Leicestershire 1946	Leicestershire	2	17th	Leicestershire	1688

King's Division								
Battalion				*1881 Cardwell's Reforms*	*Battalion*	*Foot Regiment*	*Pre-Cardwell*	*Raised*
Duke of Lancaster's Regiment (King's Lancashire and Border) formed in March 2007.								
1st	Duke of Lancaster's three battalions merged into two	King's Own Royal Border 1959		King's Own Royal (Lancaster)	2	4th	King's Own Royal	1680
				Border	1st	34th	Cumberland	1702
					2nd	55th	Westmorland	1755
		King's 1969	King's (Manchester & Liverpool) 1958	King's (Liverpool)	2	8th	King's	1685
				Manchester	1st	63rd	West Suffolk	1756
					2nd	96th	Queen's Own Germans	1824
2nd		Queen's Lancashire 1970	Lancashire 1958	East Lancashire	1st	30th	Cambridgeshire	1689
					2nd	59th	2nd Nottinghamshire	1755
				South Lancashire	1st	40th	2nd Somersetshire	1717
					2nd	82nd	POW Volunteers	1793
			Loyal (North Lancashire) 1921	Loyal North Lancashire	1st	47th	Lancashire	1741
					2nd	81st	Loyal Lincoln Volunteers	1793
Yorkshire Regiment formed June 2006. In July 2013 2nd Battalion disbanded. 3rd Battalion becomes 1st and 3rd Battalion becomes 2nd.								
2nd	Yorkshire 1st	Prince of Wales's Own Regiment of Yorkshire 1958	West Yorkshire (PWO) 1920	Prince of Wales's Own (West Yorkshire)	2	14th	Buckinghamshire Prince of Wales's Own	1685
			East Yorkshire (Duke of York's Own) 1935	East Yorkshire	2	15th	York, East Riding	1685
Disbanded 2013	Yorkshire 2nd	Green Howards 1921	Alexandra Princess of Wales's Own (Yorkshire) 1902	Princess of Wales's Own (Yorkshire)	2	19th	1st Yorkshire North Riding	1688
1st	Yorkshire 3rd	Duke of Wellington's Regiment (West Riding) 1921		Duke of Wellington's (West Riding)	1st	33rd	Duke of Wellington's	1702
					2nd	76th	Hindoostan	1787
			Disbanded 1968	York and Lancaster	1st	65th	2nd Yorkshire North Riding	1756
					2nd	84th	York & Lancaster	1793

Prince of Wales's Division								
Battalion				*1881 Cardwell's Reforms*	*Battalion*	*Foot Regiment*	*Pre-Cardwell*	*Raised*
Mercian Regiment formed in September 2007.								
1st	Mercian	Cheshire		Cheshire	2	22nd	Cheshire	1689
2nd	Mercian	Worcestershire and Sherwood Foresters 1970	Worcestershire	Worcestershire	1st	29th	Worcestershire	1694
					2nd	36th	Herefordshire	1701
			Sherwood Foresters (Nottinghamshire and Derbyshire) 1902	Sherwood Foresters (Derbyshire)	1st	45th	1st Nottinghamshire	1741
					2nd	95th	Derbyshire	1823
Disbanded 2014	Mercian	Staffordshire 1959		South Staffordshire	1st	38th	1st Staffordshire	1705
					2nd	80th	Staffordshire Vol	1793
				North Staffordshire	1st	64th	2nd Staffordshire	1756
					2nd	98th	Prince of Wales's	1824
Royal Welsh Regiment formed in March 2006.								
1st	Royal Welsh Regiment	Royal Welch Fusiliers 1920		Royal Welsh Fusiliers	2	23rd	Royal Welch Fusiliers	1689
Disbanded 2014	Royal Welsh Regiment	Royal Regiment of Wales 1969	South Wales Borderers	South Wales Borderers	2	24th	2nd Warwickshire	1689
			Welch 1920	Welsh	1st	41st	Welsh	1719
					2nd	69th	South Lincolnshire	1756

Royal Irish Regiment formed in 1992.								
Battalion		*1992*	*1968*	*1881 Cardwell's Reforms*	*Battalion*	*Foot Regiment*	*Pre-Cardwell*	*Raised*
1st	Royal Irish Regiment	Royal Irish Regiment 1st Battalion	Royal Irish Rangers 1st Battalion	Royal Inniskilling Fusiliers	1st	27th	Inniskillings	1689
					2nd	108th	Madras Infantry	1862
		merged with 1st Battalion 1993	Royal Irish Rangers 2nd Battalion	Royal Irish Rifles, Royal Ulster Rifles 1922	1st	83rd	County of Dublin	1793
					2nd	86th	Royal County Down	1793
			Royal Irish Rangers 3rd Battalion (disbanded 1969)	Royal Irish Fusiliers	1st	87th	Royal Irish Fusiliers	1793
					2nd	89th	Princess Victoria's	1793

Royal Irish Regiment and Ulster Defence Regiment									
Royal Irish Regiment formed in 1992 from the merger of the Royal Irish Rangers and the Ulster Defence Regiment with eleven battalions.									
1st	Royal Irish Regiment		1st	Former 1st and 2nd Battalion Royal Irish Rangers	General Service				
2nd Battalion disbanded 1993			2nd		General Service				
2nd Battalion Royal Irish Regiment (TA) in 2007		1993 4th/5th	4th	Royal Irish Rangers (TA)					
			5th	Royal Irish Rangers (TA)					
2007	2001	1993		Royal Irish Regiment Home Service	1991	1984	Ulster Defence Regiment Raised 1970, initially 7 battalions		
Disbanded	New 2nd Battalion Royal Irish Regiment	7th	7th	Royal Irish Regiment (City of Belfast)		7th/10th	7th	City of Belfast	1970
							10th	City of Belfast	1972
		9th	9th	Royal Irish Regiment (County Antrim)		1st/9th	1st	County of Antrim	1970
							9th	County Antrim	1972
Disbanded	3rd Battalion Royal Irish Regiment	3rd (County Down and County Armagh)	3rd	Royal Irish Regiment (County Down)			3rd	County Down	1970
			6th	Royal Irish Regiment (County Armagh)	2nd/11th		2nd	County Armagh	1970
							11th	Craigavon	1972
		8th	8th	R Irish (County Tyrone)			8th	County Tyrone	1972

<table>
<tr><td rowspan="3">Disbanded</td><td rowspan="3">4th Battalion Royal Irish Regiment</td><td rowspan="2">4th</td><td rowspan="2">4th</td><td rowspan="2">Royal Irish Regiment (County Fermanagh)</td><td rowspan="2">4th/6th</td><td rowspan="2"></td><td>4th</td><td>County Fermanagh</td><td>1970</td></tr>
<tr><td>6th</td><td>County Tyrone</td><td>1970</td></tr>
<tr><td>5th</td><td>5th</td><td>R Irish (County Londonderry)</td><td></td><td></td><td>5th</td><td>County Londonderry</td><td>1970</td></tr>
</table>

<table>
<tr><th colspan="12">Light Division</th></tr>
<tr><th>Battalion</th><th colspan="6"></th><th>1881 Cardwell's Reforms</th><th>Battalion</th><th>Foot Regiment</th><th>Pre-Cardwell</th><th>Raised</th></tr>
<tr><td colspan="12">The Rifles formed in February 2007.</td></tr>
<tr><td rowspan="9">1st</td><td rowspan="9">The Rifles</td><td rowspan="3">Devonshire and Dorset Light Infantry 2005</td><td colspan="3" rowspan="3">Devonshire & Dorset 1958</td><td>Devonshire</td><td>Devonshire</td><td>2</td><td>11th</td><td>North Devonshire</td><td>1685</td></tr>
<tr><td rowspan="2">Dorset 1951</td><td rowspan="2">Dorsetshire</td><td>1st</td><td>39th</td><td>Dorsetshire</td><td>1702</td></tr>
<tr><td>2nd</td><td>54th</td><td>West Norfolk</td><td>1755</td></tr>
<tr><td rowspan="6">RGBW Light Infantry 2005</td><td colspan="2" rowspan="6">Royal Gloucestershire, Berkshire & Wiltshire 1994</td><td colspan="2" rowspan="2">Gloucestershire</td><td rowspan="2">Gloucestershire</td><td>1st</td><td>28th</td><td>North Gloucestershire</td><td>1694</td></tr>
<tr><td>2nd</td><td>61st</td><td>South Gloucestershire</td><td>1756</td></tr>
<tr><td rowspan="4">Duke of Edinburgh's Royal 1959</td><td rowspan="2">Royal Berkshire 1921</td><td rowspan="2">Princess Charlotte of Wales's (Berkshire)</td><td>1st</td><td>49th</td><td>Prince of Wales's Hertfordshire</td><td>1743</td></tr>
<tr><td>2nd</td><td>66th</td><td>Berkshire</td><td>1756</td></tr>
<tr><td rowspan="2">Wiltshire (Duke of Edinburgh's)</td><td rowspan="2">Wiltshire (Duke of Edinburgh's)</td><td>1st</td><td>62nd</td><td>Wiltshire</td><td>1756</td></tr>
<tr><td>2nd</td><td>99th</td><td>Duke of Edinburgh's</td><td>1824</td></tr>
<tr><td rowspan="3">2nd</td><td rowspan="3">The Rifles</td><td rowspan="3">Renumbered 1st Battalion 1993</td><td colspan="2">Royal Green Jackets 2nd Battalion 1968</td><td colspan="2">2nd Green Jackets 1958</td><td>King's Royal Rifle Corps</td><td>4</td><td>60th</td><td>King's Royal Rifle Corps</td><td>1755</td></tr>
<tr><td rowspan="2">1st Battalion disbanded 1993</td><td rowspan="2">Royal Green Jackets 1st Battalion 1968</td><td rowspan="2">1st Green Jackets 1958</td><td rowspan="2">Oxfordshire and Buckinghamshire Light Infantry 1908</td><td rowspan="2">Oxfordshire Light Infantry</td><td>1st</td><td>43rd</td><td>Monmouthshire Light Infantry</td><td>1741</td></tr>
<tr><td>2nd</td><td>52nd</td><td>Oxfordshire Light Infantry</td><td>1755</td></tr>
</table>

<table>
<tr><td rowspan="2">3rd</td><td rowspan="2">The Rifles</td><td colspan="2" rowspan="2">Renumbered 2nd Battalion 1993</td><td colspan="3" rowspan="2">Light Infantry 3rd Battalion 1968</td><td rowspan="2">King's Shropshire Light Infantry</td><td>1st</td><td>53rd</td><td>Shropshire</td><td>1755</td></tr>
<tr><td>2nd</td><td>85th</td><td>Buck's Volunteers</td><td>1793</td></tr>
<tr><td>4th</td><td>The Rifles</td><td>Renumbered 2nd Battalion 1993</td><td colspan="2">Royal Green Jackets 3rd Battalion 1968</td><td>3rd Green Jackets 1958</td><td>Rifle Brigade 1920</td><td>Prince Consort's Own (Rifle Brigade)</td><td>4</td><td>95th until 1816</td><td>Rifle Brigade</td><td>1802</td></tr>
<tr><td rowspan="5">5th</td><td rowspan="5">The Rifles</td><td rowspan="5">Renumbered 1st Battalion 1993</td><td colspan="4" rowspan="2">Light Infantry 2nd Battalion 1968</td><td rowspan="2">King's Own Yorkshire Light Infantry</td><td>1st</td><td>51st</td><td>2nd Yorkshire WR</td><td>1755</td></tr>
<tr><td>2nd</td><td>105th</td><td>Madras LI</td><td>1862</td></tr>
<tr><td rowspan="3">1st Battalion disbanded 1993</td><td colspan="2" rowspan="3">Light Infantry 1st Battalion 1968</td><td rowspan="3">Somerset and Cornwall Light Infantry 1959</td><td>Somerset Light Infantry</td><td>2</td><td>13th</td><td>1st Somersetshire</td><td>1685</td></tr>
<tr><td rowspan="2">Duke of Cornwall's Light Infantry</td><td>1st</td><td>32nd</td><td>Cornwall LI</td><td>1702</td></tr>
<tr><td>2nd</td><td>46th</td><td>South Devonshire</td><td>1741</td></tr>
<tr><td colspan="4" rowspan="2"></td><td rowspan="2">Disbanded 1969</td><td colspan="2" rowspan="2">Light Infantry 1968 4th Battalion</td><td rowspan="2">Durham Light Infantry</td><td>1st</td><td>68th</td><td>Durham LI</td><td>1756</td></tr>
<tr><td>2nd</td><td>106th</td><td>Bombay LI</td><td>1862</td></tr>
</table>

<table>
<tr><th colspan="5">No Division</th></tr>
<tr><td colspan="5">Parachute Regiment</td></tr>
<tr><td>Battalion</td><td colspan="3"></td><td>Raised</td></tr>
<tr><td>1st</td><td>Parachute Regiment</td><td rowspan="3"></td><td rowspan="3">Transferred to Infantry of the Line 1949 as 3 battalions</td><td>1942</td></tr>
<tr><td>2nd</td><td>Parachute Regiment</td><td>1942</td></tr>
<tr><td>3rd</td><td>Parachute Regiment</td><td>1942</td></tr>
</table>

<table>
<tr><td colspan="11">Royal Gurkha Rifles in July 1994.</td></tr>
<tr><td>Battalion</td><td colspan="3"></td><td>Battalion</td><td colspan="3"></td><td colspan="2">Transferred to British Army 1948</td><td>Raised</td></tr>
<tr><td rowspan="4">1st</td><td rowspan="8">Royal Gurkha Rifles</td><td colspan="2" rowspan="4">Royal Gurkha Rifles</td><td rowspan="2">1st</td><td colspan="3" rowspan="2">2nd King Edward VII's Own Gurkha Rifles (Sirmoor Rifles)
Two battalions merge 1992</td><td>1st</td><td rowspan="2">2nd King Edward VII's Own Gurkha Rifles (Sirmoor Rifles)</td><td rowspan="2">1815</td></tr>
<tr><td>2nd</td></tr>
<tr><td rowspan="2">1st</td><td colspan="3" rowspan="2">6th Queen Elizabeth's Own Gurkha Rifles 1959
Two battalions merge 1969</td><td>1st</td><td rowspan="2">6th Gurkha Rifles</td><td rowspan="2">1817</td></tr>
<tr><td>2nd</td></tr>
<tr><td rowspan="4">2nd</td><td rowspan="2">2nd</td><td rowspan="2">Royal Gurkha Rifles 2nd Battalion</td><td rowspan="2">1st</td><td rowspan="2">Raised 2nd Battalion 1981 disbanded 1986</td><td rowspan="2">1st 1970</td><td rowspan="2">7th Duke of Edinburgh's Own Gurkha Rifles 1959</td><td>1st</td><td rowspan="2">7th Gurkha Rifles</td><td rowspan="2">1902</td></tr>
<tr><td>2nd</td></tr>
<tr><td rowspan="2">3rd</td><td rowspan="2">Royal Gurkha Rifles 3rd Battalion</td><td rowspan="2">1st</td><td colspan="3" rowspan="2">10th Princess Mary's Own Gurkha Rifles 1950
Two battalions merge 1969</td><td>1st</td><td rowspan="2">10th Gurkha Rifles</td><td rowspan="2">1887</td></tr>
<tr><td>2nd</td></tr>
</table>

<table>
<tr><td colspan="7">Disbanded Irish Regiments</td></tr>
<tr><td></td><td>1922</td><td>1881 Cardwell's Reforms</td><td>Battalion</td><td>Foot Regiment</td><td>Pre-Cardwell</td><td>Raised</td></tr>
<tr><td rowspan="9">With the establishment of the Irish Free State the five regiments were disbanded from the British Army</td><td>Disbanded</td><td>Royal Irish</td><td>2</td><td>18th</td><td>Royal Irish</td><td>1684</td></tr>
<tr><td rowspan="2">Disbanded</td><td rowspan="2">Connaught Rangers</td><td>1st</td><td>88th</td><td>Connaught Rangers</td><td>1793</td></tr>
<tr><td>2nd</td><td>94th</td><td>Foot</td><td>1823</td></tr>
<tr><td rowspan="2">Disbanded</td><td rowspan="2">Prince of Wales's Leinster (Royal Canadians)</td><td>1st</td><td>100th</td><td>POW Royal Canadian</td><td>1858</td></tr>
<tr><td>2nd</td><td>109th</td><td>Bombay Infantry</td><td>1862</td></tr>
<tr><td rowspan="2">Disbanded</td><td rowspan="2">Royal Munster Fusiliers</td><td>1st</td><td>101th</td><td>Royal Bengal Fusiliers</td><td>1862</td></tr>
<tr><td>2nd</td><td>104th</td><td>Bengal Fusiliers</td><td>1862</td></tr>
<tr><td rowspan="2">Disbanded</td><td rowspan="2">Royal Dublin Fusiliers</td><td>1st</td><td>102nd</td><td>Royal Madras Fusiliers</td><td>1862</td></tr>
<tr><td>2nd</td><td>103rd</td><td>Royal Bombay Fusiliers</td><td>1862</td></tr>
</table>

<table>
<tr><th colspan="7">Marines</th></tr>
<tr><td>1664</td><td colspan="6">Duke of York and Albany's Maritime Regiment of Foot or Lord High Admiral's Regiment</td></tr>
<tr><td>1685</td><td colspan="6">Prince George of Denmark's Regiment of Foot disbanded 1689</td></tr>
<tr><td>1690</td><td colspan="3">1st Marine Regiment for sea service only</td><td colspan="3">2nd Marine Regiment for sea service only</td></tr>
<tr><td>1698</td><td colspan="2">Brudenel's 1st and 2nd Marines</td><td>Seymour's 3rd Marines</td><td>Mordaunt's 4th Marines</td><td>Colt's 5th Marines</td><td>Rowe's 6th Marines</td></tr>
<tr><td>1699</td><td colspan="6">Disbanded</td></tr>
<tr><td>1702</td><td>Saunderson 1st Marines 30th Foot 1714</td><td>Villier's 2nd Marines 31st Foot 1714</td><td>Fox's 3rd Marines 32nd Foot 1714</td><td>Shannon's 4th Marines disbanded 1713</td><td>Holt's 5th Marines disbanded 1713</td><td>Mordaunt's 6th Marines disbanded 1713</td></tr>
<tr><td></td><td>Huntington's 7th Marines 33rd Foot 1715</td><td>Lucas's 8th Marines 34th Foot 1715</td><td>Donegal's 9th Marines 35th Foot 1715</td><td>Caulfield's 10th Marines 36th Foot 1715</td><td>Meredith's 11th Marines 37th Foot 1715</td><td>Coote's 12th Marines 39th Foot 1715</td></tr>
<tr><td>1703</td><td colspan="6">Seymour's or Queen's Marines (4th Foot) to 1710; 38th Foot Marines 1705</td></tr>
<tr><td>1714</td><td colspan="6">Four Invalid Company's of Marines</td></tr>
<tr><td>1739/41</td><td colspan="2">Six regiments raised dual numbered 1st to 6th Marines and 44th to 49th Foot</td><td colspan="2">Four regiments raised dual numbered 7th to 10th Marines and 50th to 53rd Foot</td><td colspan="2">Four regiments(Gooche's) in America 1741</td></tr>
<tr><td>1748</td><td colspan="6">Disbanded</td></tr>
<tr><td>1755</td><td colspan="3">Fifty companies rising to 153 companies for sea service in three divisions</td><td>Chatham Division</td><td>Portsmouth Division</td><td>Plymouth Division</td></tr>
<tr><td>1802</td><td colspan="6">Titled Royal Marines</td></tr>
</table>

<table>
<tr><th></th><th colspan="3">Royal Marines</th></tr>
<tr><td>1804</td><td colspan="3">Royal Marine Artillery introduced with an additional division at Woolwich</td></tr>
<tr><td>1855</td><td colspan="3">Corps split into Royal Marines Light Infantry (Red Marines) and Royal Marine Artillery (Blue Marines)</td></tr>
<tr><td rowspan="3">1914 to 1918</td><td colspan="3">Three Royal Naval Brigades</td></tr>
<tr><td>1st Drake / Nelson / Deal Battalions</td><td>2nd Anson / Hood / Howe Battalions</td><td>3rd Chatham / Portsmouth / Plymouth Battalions</td></tr>
<tr><td colspan="3">Royal Marines also served afloat as gun crews on capital ships</td></tr>
</table>

1923	RMLI and RMA became Royal Marines					
1939	Three Royal Marine Brigades			Introduction of Mobile Naval Base Defence Organisations		
	101st	102nd	103rd			
	3rd and 5th Battalions	1st and 2nd Battalions	7th, 8th, 9th and 10th Battalions	MNBDO 1		
				MNBDO 2		
	Royal Marines also served afloat as gun crews on capital ships					
1942	Formation of the first Royal Marine Commando later titled 40 and 41 Royal Marine Commando formed from 8th Battalion RM					
1943	Royal Marine battalions converted into Commandos					
	1st Battalion	2nd Battalion	3rd Battalion	5th Battalion	9th Battalion	10th Battalion
	42	43	44	45	46	47
1944	7th Battalion became 48 Commando Royal Marines					
1946	Disbandment of RM Commando numbers 40, 41, 43, 46, 47 and 48					
	RM Commando 44 renumbered 40					
	3rd Commando Brigade: 40, 42 and 45 Commando RM					
1950	41 RM Independent Commando raised for Korean War, disbanded 1952					
1960	41 Commando Royal Marines re-formed, disbanded 1981					
1961	43 Commando Royal Marines re-formed, disbanded 1968					
Present Time	3rd Commando Brigade					
	40 Commando Royal Marines		42 Commando Royal Marines		45 Commando Royal Marines	
	Supporting arms: 29 Commando Royal Artillery, 59 Commando Squadron Royal Engineers and Commando Logistic Regiment					
2008	1st Battalion The Rifles seconded to 3rd Commando Brigade (rescinded in 2013)					

Foot Regiments and Where Are They Now?				
Foot	*Raised*	*Change in Title*	*1881 Title*	*Where They Are Now*
1	1633	Le Régiment d' Hébron / Le Régiment Douglas Earl of Dumbarton / Royal / 1st Foot / Royal Scots	Royal Scots (Lothian)	1st Battalion Royal Scots Borderers, Royal Regiment of Scotland
2	1661	1st Tangier / Queen's / Queen Dowager's / Queen's Royal / Princess of Wales's Own / 2nd Queen's Own Royal	Queen's (Royal West Surrey)	1st Battalion Princess of Wales's Royal Regiment
3	1665	Holland / Prince George of Denmark's / Buffs / 3rd Foot East Kent – The Buffs	Buffs (East Kent)	2nd Battalion Princess of Wales's Royal Regiment
4	1680	2nd Tangier / Duchess of York and Albany's / Queen's / Queen's Consort / Queen's Marines / King's Own / 4th Foot / King's Own Royal	King's Own Royal (Lancaster)	Duke of Lancaster's Regiment
5	1674	Holland / Irish / 5th Foot / Northumberland / Northumberland Fusiliers	Northumberland Fusiliers	1st Battalion Royal Regiment of Fusiliers
6	1674	Vane's / 6th Foot / 1st Warwickshire / Royal Warwickshire	Royal Warwickshire	2nd Battalion Royal Regiment of Fusiliers
7	1685	Our Royal Regiment of Fusiliers / Our Ordinance / 7th Foot / Royal Fusiliers	Royal Fusiliers	Disbanded as 3rd Battalion Royal Regiment of Fusiliers
8	1685	Princess Anne of Denmark's / Queen's / King's / 8th Foot	King's (Liverpool)	Duke of Lancaster's Regiment
9	1685	Cornwell's / 9th Foot / East Norfolk	Norfolk	1st Battalion Royal Anglian Regiment
10	1685	Granville's / 10th Foot / North Lincolnshire	Lincolnshire	2nd Battalion Royal Anglian Regiment
11	1685	Duke of Beaufort's Musketeers / 11th Foot / North Devonshire	Devonshire	1st Battalion The Rifles (rescinded April 2013)
12	1685	Duke of Norfolk's / Earl of Litchfield's / 12th Foot / East Suffolk	Suffolk	1st Battalion Royal Anglian Regiment
13	1685	Earl of Huntingdon's / 13th Foot / 1st Somersetshire / 1st Somersetshire Light Infantry / 1st Somersetshire (Prince Albert's) Light Infantry	Somerset Light Infantry	Merged into 5th Battalion The Rifles
14	1685	Hale's / 14th Foot / Bedfordshire / Buckinghamshire – Prince of Wales's Own	Prince of Wales's Own (West Yorkshire)	1st Battalion Yorkshire Regiment
15	1685	Clifton's / 15th Foot / York / East Riding	East Yorkshire	1st Battalion Yorkshire Regiment

16	1688	Douglas's / 16th Foot / Buckinghamshire / Bedfordshire	Bedfordshire	Merged into 2nd Battalion Royal Anglian Regiment
17	1688	Richard's / 17th Foot / Leicestershire	Leicestershire	Disbanded as 4th Battalion Royal Anglian Regiment
18	1684	Earl of Granard's / Royal Regiment of Ireland / 18th Royal Irish	Royal Irish	Disbanded 1922
19	1688	Luttrell's / 19th Foot / 1st Yorkshire – North Riding – Princess of Wales's Own	Princess of Wales's Own (Yorkshire)	2nd Battalion Yorkshire Regiment
20	1688	Peyton's / 20th Foot / XXth / East Devonshire	Lancashire Fusiliers	Disbanded as 4th Battalion Royal Regiment of Fusiliers
21	1678	Earl of Mar's / Scots Fusiliers / Royal North British Fusiliers / 21st Royal Scots Fusiliers	Royal Scots Fusiliers	2nd Battalion Royal Highland Fusiliers (Royal Regiment of Scotland)
22	1689	Earl of Norfolk's / 22nd (Cheshire)	Cheshire	1st Battalion Mercian Regiment
23	1689	Lord Herbert's / Royal Regiment of Welch Fusiliers / Prince of Wales's Own Regiment of Welch Fusiliers / 23rd (Royal Welch Fusiliers)	Royal Welsh Fusiliers	1st Battalion Royal Welsh Regiment
24	1689	Dering's / 24th Foot / 2nd Warwickshire	South Wales Borderers	2nd Battalion Royal Welsh Regiment
25	1689	Earl of Leven's / Edinburgh / 25th (Sussex) / King's Own Borderers	King's Own Borderers	1st Battalion Royal Scots Borderers (Royal Regiment of Scotland)
26	1689	Earl of Angus's / 26th Foot (Cameronians) / Cameronian	Cameronians (Scottish Rifles)	Disbanded 1968
27	1689	Tiffin's / 27th (Inniskilling)	Royal Inniskilling Fusiliers	1st Battalion Royal Irish Regiment
28	1694	Gibson's / 28th Foot / North Gloucestershire	Gloucestershire	1st Battalion The Rifles
29	1694	Farington's / 29th Foot / Worcestershire	Worcestershire	2nd Battalion Mercian Regiment
30	1689	Lord Castleton's / Saunderson's Marines / Willis's 30th Foot / Cambridgeshire	East Lancashire	Duke of Lancaster's Regiment
31	1702	Villier's Marines / Goring's Marines / 31st Foot / Huntingdonshire	East Surrey	1st Battalion Princess of Wales's Royal Regiment
32	1702	Fox's Marines / Borr's Marines / 32nd Foot / Cornwall / Cornwall Light Infantry	Duke of Cornwall's Light Infantry	Merged into 5th Battalion The Rifles

33	1702	Earl of Huntingdon's / 33rd Foot / 1st Yorkshire / West Riding / Duke of Wellington's	Duke of Wellington's (WR)	3rd Battalion Yorkshire Regiment
34	1702	Lucas's / 34th Foot / Cumberland	Border	Duke of Lancaster's Regiment
35	1701	Earl of Donegall's / 35th Foot/ Dorsetshire / Sussex / Royal Sussex	Royal Sussex	Merged into Princess of Wales's Royal Regiment
36	1701	Viscount Charlemont's / 36th Foot / Herefordshire	Worcestershire	2nd Battalion Mercian Regiment
37	1702	Meredith's / 37th Foot / North Hampshire	Hampshire	Merged into Princess of Wales's Royal Regiment
38	1705	Lillingstone's / 38th Foot / 1st Staffordshire	South Staffordshire	3rd Battalion Mercian Regiment
39	1702	Goote's / 39th Foot / East Middlesex / Dorsetshire	Dorsetshire	1st Battalion The Rifles
40	1717	Philip's / 40th Foot / 2nd Somersetshire	South Lancashire	Duke of Lancaster's Regiment
41	1719	Independent Companies of Invalids / 41st Foot / Royal Invalids/ Welsh	Welsh	2nd Battalion Royal Welsh Regiment
42	1739	Black Watch / Highland / 43rd Renumbered 42nd Foot 1749 (Royal Highland) (The Black Watch)	Black Watch	3rd Battalion Black Watch (Royal Regiment of Scotland)
43	1741	54th Foot Renumbered 43rd Foot in 1751 / Monmouthshire / Monmouthshire Light Infantry	Oxfordshire Light Infantry	Merged into 2nd Battalion The Rifles
44	1741	55th Foot Renumbered 44th Foot in 1751 / East Essex	Essex	Merged into 2nd Battalion Royal Anglian Regiment
45	1741	Houghton's / 56th Foot Renumbered 45th Foot in 1751 / 1st Nottinghamshire / Nottinghamshire - Sherwood Foresters	Sherwood Foresters	2nd Battalion Mercian Regiment
46	1741	Price's 57th Foot Renumbered 46th Foot 1751/ South Devonshire	Duke of Cornwall's Light Infantry	Merged into 5th Battalion The Rifles
47	1741	Mourdaunt's / 58th Foot Renumbered 47th Foot 1751 / Lancashire	Loyal North Lancashire	Duke of Lancaster's Regiment
48	1741	Cholmondeley's / 59th Foot Renumbered 48th Foot 1751/ Northamptonshire	Northamptonshire	2nd Battalion Royal Anglian Regiment
49	1743	Trelawny's / Jamaica Volunteers / 63rd Foot / Renumbered 49th Foot 1751/ Hertfordshire / Princess Charlotte of Wales's	Princess Charlotte of Wales's Berkshire	1st Battalion The Rifles

50	1755	52nd Foot / Renumbered 50th Foot 1756/ West Kent / Duke of Clarance's / Queen's Own	Queen's Own Royal West Kent	2nd Battalion Princess of Wales's Royal Regiment
51	1755	53rd Foot / Renumbered 51st Foot 1756 / 2nd Yorkshire / West Riding Light Infantry / King's Own Light Infantry	King's Own Yorkshire Light Infantry	5th Battalion The Rifles
52	1755	54th Foot / Renumbered 52nd Foot 1756 / Oxfordshire / Oxfordshire Light Infantry	Oxfordshire Light Infantry	Merged into 2nd Battalion The Rifles
53	1755	55th Foot / Renumbered 53rd Foot 1756 / Shropshire	King's Shropshire Light Infantry	3rd Battalion The Rifles
54	1755	56th Foot / Renumbered 54th Foot 1756/ West Norfolk	Dorsetshire	1st Battalion The Rifles
55	1755	57th Foot / Renumbered 55th Foot 1756/ Westmoreland	Border	Duke of Lancaster's Regiment
56	1755	58th Foot / Renumbered 56th Foot 1756 / West Essex	Essex	Merged into 2nd Battalion Royal Anglian Regiment
57	1755	59th Foot / Renumbered 57th Foot 1756 / West Middlesex	Middlesex	Disbanded as 4th Battalion Queen's Regiment
58	1755	60th Foot / Renumbered 58th Foot 1756 / Rutlandshire	Northamptonshire	2nd Battalion Royal Anglian Regiment
59	1755	61st Foot / Renumbered 59th Foot 1756 / 2nd Nottinghamshire	East Lancashire	Duke of Lancaster's Regiment
60	1755	Loudon's / 62nd Foot / Royal American / Renumbered 60th Foot 1756 / Duke of York's Rifle Corps / King's Royal Rifle Corps	King's Royal Rifle Corps	2nd Battalion The Rifles
61	1756	2nd Battalion 3rd Foot / Renunbered 61st Foot / South Gloucestershire	Gloucestershire	1st Battalion The Rifles
62	1756	2nd Battalion 4th Foot / Renumbered 62nd Foot / Wiltshire	Wiltshire (Duke of Edinburgh's)	1st Battalion The Rifles
63	1756	2nd Battalion 8th Foot / Renumbered 63rd Foot / West Suffolk	Manchester	Duke of Lancaster's Regiment
64	1756	2nd Battalion 11th Foot / Renumbered 64th Foot / 2nd Staffordshire	North Staffordshire	3rd Battalion Mercian Regiment
65	1756	2nd Battalion 12th Foot / Renumbered 65th Foot / 2nd Yorkshire-North Riding	York & Lancaster	Disbanded 1968
66	1756	2nd Battalion 19th Foot / Renumbered 66th Foot / Berkshire	Princess Charlotte of Wales's Berkshire	1st Battalion The Rifles

67	1756	2nd Battalion 20th Foot/ Renumbered 67th Foot / South Hampshire	Hampshire	Merged into Princess of Wales's Royal Regiment
68	1756	2nd Battalion 23rd Foot / Renumbered 68th Foot / Durham / Durham Light Infantry	Durham Light Infantry	Disbanded as 4th Battalion Light Infantry Regiment
69	1756	2nd Battalion 24th Foot / Renumbered 69th Foot / South Lincolnshire	Welsh	2nd Battalion Royal Welsh Regiment
70	1756	2nd Battalion 31st Foot / Renumbered 70th Foot / Surrey / Glasgow Lowland	East Surrey	1st Battalion Princess of Wales's Royal Regiment
71	1777	1st Battalion 73rd (Highland) Renumbered 71st (Highland) / Glasgow Highland / Glasgow Highland LI / Highland Light Infantry	Highland Light Infantry	2nd Battalion Royal Highland Fusiliers (Royal Regiment of Scotland)
72	1778	78th (Highland) / Seaforth's Highlanders / Renumbered 72nd Highland) / 72nd / Duke of Albany's Own Highlanders	Seaforth Highlanders	4th Battalion Highlanders (Royal Regiment of Scotland)
73	1779	2nd Battalion 42nd Foot / Renumbered 73rd Highland / 73rd (Perthshire)	Black Watch	3rd Battalion Black Watch (Royal Regiment of Scotland)
74	1787	74th (Highland) / Assaye / 74th (Highlanders)	Highland Light Infantry	2nd Battalion Royal Highland Fusiliers (Royal Regiment of Scotland)
75	1787	75th (Highland) / Abercromby's Highlanders / Stirlingshire	Gordon Highlanders	4th Battalion Highlanders (Royal Regiment of Scotland)
76	1787	76th Foot / Hindoostan	Duke of Wellington's (WR)	3rd Battalion Yorkshire Regiment
77	1787	77th Foot / (East Middlesex) Duke of Camridge's Own	Middlesex	Disbanded as 4th Battalion Queen's Regiment
78	1793	78th (Highland) / Ross-Shire Buffs	Seaforth Highlanders	4th Battalion Highlanders (Royal Regiment of Scotland)
79	1793	79th Foot (Cameronian Volunteers) / Cameronian Highlanders / Queen's Own Cameron Highlanders	Queen's Own Cameron Highlanders	4th Battalion Highlanders (Royal Regiment of Scotland)
80	1793	80th Foot / Staffordshire Volunteers	South Staffordshire	3rd Battalion Mercian Regiment
81	1793	81st Foot / Loyal Lincoln Volunteers	Loyal North Lancashire	Duke of Lancaster's Regiment
82	1793	82nd Foot / Prince of Wales's Volunteers	South Lancashire	Duke of Lancaster's Regiment

83	1793	83rd Foot / Fitch's Grenadiers / County of Dublin	Royal Irish Rifles	Disbanded as 2nd Battalion Royal Irish Regiment
84	1793	84th Foot / York and Lancaster	York & Lancaster	Disbanded 1968
85	1793	85th (Bucks Volunteers) / Duke of York's Own Light Infantry King's Light Infantry	King's Shropshire Light Infantry	3rd Battalion The Rifles
86	1793	86th / Cuyler's Shropshire Volunteers / Leinster / Royal County Down	Royal Irish Rifles	Disbanded as 2nd Battalion Royal Irish Regiment
87	1793	87th Foot / Prince of Wales's Irish / Prince of Wales's Own / Irish Royal Irish Fusiliers	Royal Irish Fusiliers	Disbanded as 3rd Battalion Royal Irish Rangers
88	1793	88th Foot / Connaught Rangers	Connaught Rangers	Disbanded 1922
89	1793	89th Foot / Princess Victoria's	Royal Irish Fusiliers	Disbanded as 3rd Battalion Royal Irish Rangers
90	1794	90th Foot / Perthshire Volunteers / Perthshire Light Infantry	Cameronians (Scottish Rifles)	Disbanded 1968
91	1794	98th Argyllshire Highlanders Renumbered 91st / Princess Louise's Argyll Highlanders	Argyll & Sutherland Highlanders	5th Battalion Argyll & Sutherland Highlanders (Royal Regiment of Scotland)
92	1794	100th Foot Renumbered 92nd Foot / Gordon Highlanders	Gordon Highlanders	4th Battalion Highlanders (RROS)
93	1799	93rd Highlanders / Sutherland Highlanders	Argyll & Sutherland Highlanders	5th Battalion Argyll & Sutherland Highlanders (Royal Regiment of Scotland)
94	1823	94th Foot, previous title Scots Brigade	Connaught Rangers	Disbanded 1922
95	1823	95th Foot / Derbyshire	Sherwood Foresters	2nd Battalion Mercian Regiment
96	1824	96th Foot, previous title Queen's Own Germans	Manchester	Duke of Lancaster's Regiment
97	1824	97th Foot / Earl of Ulster's	Queen's Own Royal West Kent	2nd Battalion Princess of Wales's Royal Regiment
98	1824	98th Foot / Prince of Wales's	North Staffordshire	3rd Battalion Mercian Regiment
99	1824	99th (Lanarkshire) / Duke of Edinburgh's	Wiltshire (Duke of Edinburgh's)	1st Battalion The Rifles
100	1858	100th Foot / Prince of Wales's Royal Canadian	Prince of Wales's Leinster (Royal Canadians)	Disbanded 1922
101	1862	101st Foot / Royal Bengal Fusiliers from the East India Company	Royal Munster Fusiliers	Disbanded 1922

102	1862	102nd Foot / Royal Madras Fusiliers from the East India Company	Royal Dublin Fusiliers	Disbanded 1922
103	1662	103rd Foot / Royal Bombay Fusiliers from the East India Company	Royal Dublin Fusiliers	Disbanded 1922
104	1862	104th Foot / Bengal Fusiliers from the East India Company	Royal Munster Fusiliers	Disbanded 1922
105	1862	105th Foot / Madras Light Infantry from the East India Company	King's Own Yorkshire Light Infantry	5th Battalion The Rifles
106	1862	106th Foot / Bombay Light Infantry from the East India Company	Durham Light Infantry	Disbanded as 4th Battalion Light Infantry Regiment
107	1862	107th Foot / Bengal Infantry from the East India Company	Royal Sussex	Merged into Princess of Wales's Royal Regiment
108	1862	108th Foot / Madras Infantry from the East India Company	Royal Inniskilling Fusiliers	1st Battalion Royal Irish Regiment
109	1862	109th Foot / Bombay Infantry from the East India Company	Prince of Wales's Leinster (Royal Canadians)	Disbanded
95th	1802	Raised 1800 as experimental Corps of Riflemen / Rifle Corps / 95th / Rifle Brigade / Prince Consort's Own	Prince Consort's Own Rifle Brigade	4th Battalion The Rifles

Cavalry – Historical Summary

SEVENTEENTH CENTURY

To detail the lineage of the British cavalry, it is necessary to establish which regiments originated as Household Troops, Regiments of Horse, Horse Grenadiers and Dragoons. The transition to Life Guards, Horse Guards, Horse Grenadier Guards, Dragoon Guards, Dragoons, Light Dragoons, Hussars and finally Lancers can then be described, while keeping a sense of identification with regimental numbers, as at times the changes are bewildering. In particular, the constant raising, disbanding, reforming and renumbering of light dragoons, especially the 17th to 29th, is difficult to follow.

The King's Mounted Bodyguard: His Household Cavalry

On his restoration in 1660, Charles II brought with him his Royal mounted bodyguard, which had been in exile with him in Holland. These three troops – identified at the time as horse guards – were the 1st, 2nd and 3rd Troops of Life Guards of Horse, each numbering 150–200 men, and they became part of the new Standing Army in 1661 as the senior regiment of the Household Cavalry. In 1661 they became His Majesty's Own Troop, Duke of York's Troop and Monck's (later Duke of Albemarle's Troop).

The second cavalry regiment to guard the King became the Royal Regiment of Horse. This regiment originated under Cromwell in 1650 and at the Restoration was commanded by Colonel Unton Croke. The regiment was disbanded by Parliament, but soon re-formed for the King's safety, with new officers appointed. The regiment was commanded by the Earl of Oxford and with its blue livery it would later be known as the Oxford Blues or Blues. In 1661 it would be ranked as the First Horse or Royal Regiment of Horse and later Royal Horse Guards.

A 4th Troop of Life Guards of Horse was raised in 1661 with a 5th and 6th in 1664, only for the new additions to be soon disbanded. Further troops of Life Guards of Horse would be raised for service in Scotland and the Scottish Troop would be later known as the 4th Troop. In 1670, on the death of the Duke of Albemarle, the 3rd Troop became the Queen's Troop and took precedence as the 2nd Troop with the Duke of York's Troop becoming the 3rd Troop.

Horse Grenadiers

In line with the infantry's introduction of grenadiers, the cavalry followed suit. In 1678 three new troops of horse grenadiers were raised as mounted infantry, armed with the fusil (a short musket) and grenades. These troops of about sixty-six men were attached to the three troops of Life Guards of Horse. They were disbanded in 1680, but re-formed again in 1684. A similar troop of horse grenadiers (4th) was raised in 1686 and joined the Scottish Troop of Life Guards, but the whole regiment of guards and horse grenadiers were disbanded in 1689 to be replaced by William's Dutch Troop. The remaining 1st, 2nd and 3rd troops of horse grenadiers would merge into a separate regiment, a new 1st Troop in 1693 with the 2nd Troop added in 1702.

Regiments of Horse and Dragoons

The Earl of Peterborough raised a regiment of dragoons for service in Tangier in 1662, and after engaging in the first British cavalry charge against the Moors in 1680, they returned to England in 1684 as the King's Own Regiment of Dragoons, later the Royal Regiment of Dragoons or Royals and ranked 1st Dragoon Regiment. The Viscount Dundee raised a second dragoon regiment in Scotland from independent companies in 1681 as the Royal (Scots) Dragoons, later to be the Scots Greys when they changed to grey mounts in 1693 and ranked 2nd Dragoon Regiment.

Prior to Monmouth's Rebellion in 1685 a suspicious Parliament had kept the cavalry restricted to a few regiments, mainly to guard the King – the Troops of Life Guards of Horse, later known as Life Guards, the Royal Regiment of Horse (ranked 1st Horse) and two dragoon regiments, Tangier Horse and the Royal Regiment of Scots Dragoons.

Dragoons were mounted on light horses of 15 hands and were originally mounted infantry, in that they could get to a strategic point quickly, then dismount and use the musket. At Sedgemoor in 1685, Monmouth was defeated, and the Household Cavalry saw their first action. Monmouth, the pretender to the throne, gave James II the ideal excuse to expand his meagre forces.

Another impetus was to defend London from a threatened invasion by William of Orange. Twelve regiments of infantry and ten regiments of cavalry were raised in 1685. Eight cavalry regiments were identified as Regiments of Horse and named after their colonel (later to be ranked 2nd to 9th Horse) to distinguish them from dragoons. The regiments of horse were considered heavy cavalry, wearing cuirasses, swords and pistols and mounted on heavy horses measuring 16 hands. Two regiments were disbanded – the Earl of Thanet's 5th Horse in 1690 and Princess Anne of Denmark's 8th Horse in 1694, and renumbering took place. The 6th Horse was re-ranked 5th Horse and the 7th Horse was re-ranked 6th Horse. The 9th Horse was subjected to a double change being re-ranked 8th Horse and then 7th Horse and would later have the title 1st Carabineers.

The remaining two regiments raised in 1685 were dragoons: the Queen Consort's Own (also Duke of Somerset's) ranked 3rd Dragoon Regiment and Princess Anne of Denmark's (also Berkeley's) ranked 4th Dragoon Regiment. The Regiment of Scottish Dragoons (Scots Greys) was brought onto the English establishment in 1685 but James II had ensured their precedence was established in 1681. The four regiments of dragoons were ranked 1st to 4th Dragoons in 1688.

William III (William of Orange) succeeded the deposed James II in 1688. William brought with him his personal guard of one regiment of foot guards and two horse regiments. The Dutch Life Guards, 200 strong and Dutch Horse Guards, 500 strong, augmented his household cavalry, with the Dutch Life Guards becoming the Fourth Troop of Life Guards of Horse. The Earl of Devonshire raised a new horse regiment to show support for the King in 1688. It was ranked initially 10th Horse and subsequently re-ranked as the 8th Horse. This regiment became known as Ligonier's Horse.

William's presence brought about the Jacobite rebellion in Scotland and Ireland. The Jacobites refused to accept William and Mary as rightful rulers and supported the claim of James II. The Jacobites controlled Ireland and besieged Londonderry and Enniskillen in December 1688. The Protestants raised two dragoon regiments for the defence of Enniskillen and also a foot regiment, the 27th Foot (Inniskilling). Wynne's Regiment of Enniskillen Dragoons was raised in 1689 and later became the Royal Dragoons of Ireland and would be ranked the 5th Dragoons, and Sir Albert Conyngham's regiment of dragoons would be ranked the 6th Dragoons (Inniskilling). Colonel Henry Conyngham raised a further regiment in Ireland in 1693, ranked 8th Dragoons.

Colonel Richard Cunningham raised a regiment of dragoons in 1690 in Scotland, which saw service in Ireland at Aughrim and Flanders. It returned to the Scottish establishment and was disbanded in 1714 for a short period, but was revived by George I with mainly British officers in 1715 as the Princess of Wales's Own Royal Dragoons, and would be ranked 7th Dragoons. By 1694 the cavalry consisted of Household Cavalry made up of the four troops of Life Guards of Horse, the Royal Regiment of Horse (known as Horse Guards), a troop of Dutch Horse Guards, seven regiments of Horse ranked 2nd to 8th, and eight dragoon regiments.

Both the Life Guards and Horse Regiments were heavies trained for shock tactics, while dragoon regiments in principle were infantry mounted on lighter horses who could arrive at the battlefield to dismount, hold strategic positions and engage in fire. Dragoons were trained to fire from the saddle as was the custom on the continent, and also to clear obstacles. Their role was to keep up with the horse regiments until the foot regiments arrived. They would support storming parties during a siege or protect convoys. Dragoons were paid less, had less elaborate uniforms and rode horses that were about a third of the cost. A typical dragoon regiment had six troops of sixty men. During William's reign the dragoons acted as regular cavalry, staying in the saddle and using swords in place of carbines.

Sir Albert Conyngham – who raised dragoon regiments – was impressed by James's cavalry at the Boyne and wrote to the Secretary at War in 1691 demanding 'a good broad cutting sword'. Soon everyone wanted swords and carbines were neglected. During the War of the League of Augsburg, further dragoon regiments were raised and then disbanded after the conflict. At the defeat at Landen in 1693, six regiments engaged with swords and this was to become a common feature of cavalry tactics, although at Steenkirk in 1692 the Horse Grenadiers and 4th Dragoons fought after dismounting.

Mounting debt in 1697 and the ending of William's war against Louis XIV of France, together with pressure from Parliament, forced William to reduce his army. Many regiments were reduced to cadres and others were put on the Irish and Scottish establishment to divert them from the national purse. The Household Cavalry, five regiments of horse and three dragoons stayed on the English establishment and one troop of the Royal Regiment of Horse and two regiments of dragoons were placed on the Scottish establishment. The Irish establishment maintained two regiments of horse and three regiments of dragoons.

EIGHTEENTH CENTURY

In 1702 England went to war with France over the Spanish Succession (1702–15). All cavalry regiments were speedily brought up to strength. Horse Grenadiers were split into two troops, No. 1 Troop and No. 2 Troop. During Marlborough's campaign, the cavalry distinguished itself at Blenheim, Elixem and Ramillies; the regiments of horse and dragoons were indistinguishable as all stayed mounted. At Blenheim the cavalry performed admirably, especially the dragoons who routed the French household cavalry, while at Elixem, Cadogan's Horse (later 5th Dragoon Guards) captured four standards from the Bavarian cavalry. Total standards captured were nine, plus ten guns. The French Regiment du Roi was defeated by the Scots Greys and Royal Irish Dragoons at Ramillies.

Marlborough's cavalry never used carbines, and returned to wearing the cuirass breastplate under their coat, and were used as shock troops to rout a defeated enemy. Marlborough thought that the only use for the carbine (for the cavalry) was for sentry duty on the horse lines for which they could have 'but three charges of powder plus ball for each man for a campaign and that for only guarding their horses when at grass and not to be made use of in action'. From 1706 to 1713 the 13th Foot (Somerset Light Infantry) were mounted and known as Pearce's Dragoons.

Jacobite Rebellions

Queen Anne died without a direct heir, and in 1715 the Jacobites rebelled in England and Scotland. The Highlanders had early successes supporting the cause of the Old Pretender. Further regiments of dragoons were raised, of which the following six remained on the establishment. Traditionally named after their colonel – Wynne's, Gore's, Honeywood's, Bowle's, Munden's and Dormer's – they were ranked 9th to 14th Dragoons. These were the last regiments to be named after the colonel. At the Battle of Sheriffmuir five dragoon regiments were present. The battle was inconclusive and the Jacobites were in disarray. James the Old Pretender arrived in Scotland and the Jacobites renewed their effort.

General Hawley issued a pamphlet in 1728 on reviving the role of dismounted dragoons, stressing their ability to travel to areas difficult for infantry to access, such as the highlands, and their use against the Jacobites or against smugglers. Whilst this may have been a forlorn hope for cavalry seated with swords, his idea of lighter horses was ahead of its time. At Laufelt in 1747 where Saxe marched 50 miles in twenty-four hours to trump the British by occupying their intended battleground, General Ligonier led a gallant charge with the cavalry to prevent the infantry being overwhelmed. The day was lost to the French and General Ligonier was captured, but his cavalry had allowed the army to withdraw safely and in good order.

The Regimental System: The Reforms of George II

The three Royal Warrants issued affected the cavalry as well as the infantry. Household Cavalry regiments carried standards and dragoons carried a guidon. Standardisation of uniforms occurred with the abolition of colonel's crests. There were some exceptions: the 8th Regiment of Horse, which became the 7th Dragoon Guards, kept the headdress badge of its colonel, Sir J. Ligonier, right up to the amalgamation of the 7th Dragoon Guards with the 4th Dragoon Guards in 1922. The regiment had been wearing the crest of Earl Ligonier (a demi-lion issuing from a ducal coronet) for 170 years.

The cavalry were re-designated with their new numbers based on seniority. The cavalry have attempted to hold onto those numbers right up to the present time but only two regiments have retained them.

Dragoon Guards

The cavalry reorganisation resulting from these warrants was to remuster the horse regiments. The regiments of horse were to become dragoons and all dragoon regiments were to revert to their original role as mounted infantry. This caused quite a stir as naturally this was considered a kind of demotion by the horse regiments, and there was some resistance. By an ingenious compromise attributable to George II, the horse regiments were to be styled 'dragoon guards', a prestigious title which suggested parity with the Household Cavalry (Cooper, p.101).

The 2nd, 3rd and 4th Regiments of Horse became the 1st, 2nd and 3rd Dragoon Guards in 1746 with the remaining Regiments of Horse renumbered the 1st, 2nd, 3rd and 4th Irish Horse and then the 4th, 5th, 6th and 7th Dragoon Guards in 1788. The dragoon guards would therefore be numbered one less than their ranking as regiments of horse in 1694.

The oldest dragoon regiments – now designated 1st (Royal) Dragoons and 2nd Royal North British Dragoons (Scots Greys) – took exception to this mounted infantry regulation. They were aware of their status and reputation and considered that a dragoon fought on his horse and wanted it to stay that way. This adherence to tradition was underlined nearly 200 years later, in 1941, when they were the last cavalry regiments to dismount and become mechanised. The 6th Dragoons (Inniskillings) also stayed mounted and the remaining dragoon regiments reverted to their unpopular mounted infantry role. Even Napoleon at a much later date had difficulty with his dragoons dismounting. In 1767 the 2nd Dragoon Guards used bay-coloured mounts and would be known by their unofficial title of the Queen's Bays (the title became official in 1872).

Horse Guards and Horse Grenadier Guards

As a result of George's warrants and the major reorganisation of cavalry, the senior horse regiment, the Royal Regiment of Horse (Guards) became the Horse Guards (Blue) from its blue livery. The King's (1st Troop of Life Guards of Horse) and Duke's (3rd Troop) merged in 1746 to become the 1st Troop of Life Guards with the Queen's (2nd Troop of Life Guards of Horse) becoming the 2nd Troop of Life Guards. The 4th Troop disbanded. In line with the prestigious title given to the Dragoon Guards, the 1st and 2nd Troop of Horse Grenadiers would be similarly honoured by being designated 1st and 2nd Troop of Horse Grenadier Guards.

Light Dragoons

The Seven Years' War (1756–63), in which Britain, Hanover and Prussia fought against France, saw the raising of one new regiment of light cavalry. Experience at Culloden showed that dragoons were too heavy and cumbersome on soft broken ground and that a lighter form of cavalry horse was required, as foreseen by Hawley. During the Jacobite Rebellion, the Kingston's Light Horse was raised at the colonel's own expense. Mounted on lighter horses, the regiment did well at Culloden but disbanded in 1746 and was re-formed as the Duke of Cumberland's Regiment with smaller horses of 14 hands 2in–15 hands. The regiment was present together with the Scots Greys and

Inniskillings at the Battle of Laufelt in which General Ligonier was unhorsed and taken prisoner. At the peace of 1748 it was disbanded.

In 1756 orders were issued to formally raise experimental light troops with horses of 14 hands 3in high, consisting of seventy-one all ranks attached to three dragoon guards and eight dragoon regiments. It was therefore strange that when formed, the light dragoons were equipped with carbines, and even a 17in bayonet, indicating some doubt as to the nature of their role. Seven full regiments of light dragoons were formed in the period 1759–60 and were numbered 15th to 21st.

Colonel Hale brought news of Wolfe's victory at Quebec and his death to England and was rewarded by being allowed to raise a regiment. He raised the 17th Light Dragoons with the badge a skull and crossbones and motto 'or Glory' as a memorial to the loss of the popular general. The badge and motto remains to the present day with the Royal Lancers, even after amalgamations much later. No heavy cavalry regiments were raised. The role of light dragoon was to fight mounted with a sword, to protect the army on the march, gather intelligence and to harass a defeated enemy. The horses were to be less than 14 hands (as tall as a polo pony) with light saddlery. Six cavalry regiments went to Europe – Blues, 1st and 3rd Dragoon Guards, Scots Greys, 6th Inniskillings and 10th Dragoons.

If Blenheim and Ramillies were considered the British cavalry's finest hour under Marlborough for defeating the cream of the French and Bavarian cavalry, then the Battle of Minden during the Seven Years' War was its lowest point. While the infantry at Minden fought a magnificent battle (reflected in the Battle Honours awarded) when it looked for cavalry support from the cavalry commander Lord George Sackville (later Lord Germain) it was ignored, much to the chagrin of the cavalry rank and file. Four separate orders were given to Sackville to help when the situation was most desperate, and he ignored them all. His second in command, the Marquess of Granby, was not allowed to assist, even with his own regiment. Sackville was relieved of his duties by his superior commander Ferdinand Duke of Brunswick, and later court-martialled. He was relieved of all command forever, but unfortunately appeared later as Secretary of State responsible for North America as Lord Germain, when the American colonies were lost.

The 15th Light Dragoons finally raised the reputation of the cavalry by receiving its first Battle Honour in the British Army at Emsdorff in 1760. They had charged like heavy cavalry defeating five French infantry battalions and capturing an Eagle and nine pieces of cannon. At Warburg in 1760, which was a cavalry success, the Marquess of Granby entered folklore by charging bald headed against the French having lost not only his hat but his wig – hence the expression 'going bald-headed at something'.

Cavalry had by now established itself as heavy cavalry, consisting of the Life Guards, the Royal Horse Guards (Blue), the 1st (Royal Dragoons), the 2nd (Scots Greys) Dragoons and the 6th (Inniskillings) Dragoons. The new dragoon guards and the remaining dragoon regiments up to the 14th were considered mounted infantry, with the 15th to 21st Light Dragoons being the light cavalry. The dragoon guards detested their dismounted role and in the fullness of time would succeed in getting their role changed to heavy cavalry. The dragoons similarly would stay mounted as cavalry. The first manual on military horsemanship was issued on 1761 by Lord Pembroke, Colonel of the Royals.

Light Dragoons: The Rise and Fall of Regiments

After the Seven Years' War in 1763, the light dragoon regiments were reviewed. The 17th, 20th and 21st Light Dragoons were disbanded and the others renumbered. The 18th became the 17th Light Dragoons and the 19th became the 18th Light Dragoons. In 1766 the Light Dragoon regiments were redesignated, with the 15th, 16th, 17th and 18th Light Dragoons becoming the 1st 2nd 3rd and 4th Light Dragoons to parallel the numbered dragoon guard and dragoon titles.

Existing dragoon regiments were to be redesignated light dragoons with the first change being the 12th Dragoons becoming the 12th Light Dragoons in 1768. The 1st, 2nd, 3rd and 4th Light Dragoons reverted to their normal titles as 15th, 16th, 17th and 18th Light Dragoons regiments in 1769, a short-lived experiment. Further dragoon regiments became light dragoons in 1775–76, the 8th and 14th.

The American War of Independence (1776–83) and commitments elsewhere such as the Maratha War in India required the raising of more cavalry regiments. The 19th, 20th, and 21st Light Dragoons were re-formed in 1779 and also the 22nd, known as the Sussex, with the 23rd Light Dragoons in 1781. The 23rd Light Dragoons (later renumbered as the 19th) was the first cavalry regiment to be sent to India, and the 16th and 17th Light Dragoons went to America.

During the American War of Independence, Banastre Tarleton was found to be such a successful cavalry commander that he was given the more important command of the British Legion (Loyalist irregulars) as a captain of 23, commanding both infantry and cavalry. Tarleton had previously gained distinction leading a troop of 16th Light Dragoons and capturing General Lee in his carpet slippers at a brothel at Basking Ridge (Hibbert, p.146). Against General Morgan at Hannah's Cowpens he was thoroughly defeated. The difficulty of sending cavalry – especially heavy cavalry – overseas on long trips was obvious. This would be borne out during the Boer War. In India mounts could be bought, but not in America.

The regiments converted to light dragoons in 1783 were the 7th, 9th, 10th, 11th, and 13th Dragoons. Further disbandment took place with the Treaty of Paris 1783 (Versailles) with the 19th, 20th, 21st and 22nd Light Dragoons being disbanded. The 23rd Light Dragoons were in India and escaped the cuts. In 1786 the 23rd Light Dragoons were renumbered as the 19th Light Dragoons.

Life Guards and Royal Horse Artillery

In 1788 the 1st Troop of Life Guards absorbed the 1st Troop of Horse Grenadier Guards and formed the 1st Life Guards Regiment with the 2nd Troop of Horse Grenadier Guards and 2nd Troop of Life Guards merging to become the 2nd Life Guard Regiment. The ancient title of Horse Grenadier Guards was lost forever. The Royal Horse Artillery was formed in 1793 (mobile artillery) and would wear blue cavalry jackets. The Royal Horse Artillery took precedence over every other unit in the British Army when parading with their guns.

French Revolutionary Wars

The 20th Light Dragoons were re-formed in Jamaica in 1792. Following the French Revolution, France declared war on Britain in 1793. The Duke of York took his army to Flanders in support of Austria. The cavalry, in a smart action by two squadrons of the 15th Light Dragoons, assisted by Austrian hussars, defeated a superior French force and prevented reinforcements at Villers-en-Cauchies. The cavalry were again successful at Beaumont, outflanking the French. A repeat performance took place at Willems where the French infantry were thoroughly routed.

In 1794 the 21st, 22nd, and 23rd Light Dragoons were again re-formed, together with the raising of the 24th and 25th Light Dragoons. The 25th were known as Gwnn's Hussars but 'hussar' was not its official title on the establishment. In the same year eight light dragoon regiments were added to the establishment: the 26th destined for India, the 27th (Duke of York's Own) destined for South Africa, the 28th destined for the West Indies and the 29th in Britain. Four light dragoon regiments raised in the previous year for Ireland were placed on the British strength and numbered 30th to 33rd Light Dragoons, disbanded in 1795. The 33rd was the highest cavalry regimental number raised. The cavalry drill book of 1796 made no distinction between heavy and light cavalry.

The 5th (Royal Irish) Dragoons – who distinguished themselves at Blenheim and Ramillies – was disbanded in 1799 for 'seditious and outrageous proceedings and atrocious acts of disobedience' and lost their seniority (Ascoli, p.51). Hence when the regiment was subsequently re-formed and amalgamated in 1922 with the 16th Dragoons, the new regiment became the 16th/5th and not the 5th/16th as is the normal practice. The unit had apparently allowed Irish insurgents to infiltrate their ranks and bring the reputation of the regiment down. The disbandment was read out to every regiment in the army. The evidence of treachery was flimsy at best.

NINETEENTH CENTURY

The Treaty of Amiens (1802) which ended the hostilities following the French Revolution also led to the disbandment of the 22nd, 23rd, 24th, and 28th Light Dragoons. Renumbering took place again with the 25th, 26th, 27th and 29th Light Dragoons becoming the 22nd, 23rd, 24th and 25th Light Dragoons respectively. The 20th Light Dragoons were re-formed from the Jamaica Light Dragoons after a long absence (from 1783).

Hussars

In 1458 Mathias Corvinus, King of Hungary desperately needed soldiers to protect his border against a Turkish invasion and issued an order for one man in every twenty from every village to serve in an irregular cavalry force. The Magyars were superb horsemen, spending their working life in the saddle. The Magyar word for twenty is *husz* and so '*huszar*' became to mean 'twentieth'. They were light horsemen, without armour and wore a herdsman's fur cap, wolf skin cloak, tight trousers and calf boots. When 3,000 Turks and Tartars besieged Vienna in 1683 for two months, it was the Polish hussars that raised the siege.

The hussar was influencing the organisation of European cavalry. King Frederick had introduced hussars into the Prussian Army, as had other European armies. The King's German Legion was the first in the British Army to be dressed as hussars. The KGL had been raised in England (all arms) in 1803 from escaped refugees of King George's Hanoverian Army fleeing from Napoleon's Europe. It was on the strength of the British Army (just like the Gurkhas of today) and was dressed, disciplined, drilled and armed as the other regiments. The name 'Hussar' had been used previously in the British cavalry, but unofficially. The 10th Light Dragoons were dressed as hussars in 1796 by their colonel, George, Prince of Wales, at his own expense. They were converted officially in the years 1805–06, when the 7th, 15th and 18th Light Dragoons became hussars and a hussar brigade was formed under Major General Lord Paget. The dolman (short jacket), pelisse (over jacket) and sabretache (slung satchel for notes and maps) would soon make their appearance in Spain, Portugal, Belgium and France. While the hussars looked smarter, there was no change in their tactical role.

Wellington's Cavalry

Sir Arthur Wellesley went to Portugal in 1808 with only one cavalry regiment, the 20th Light Dragoons. At Vimiero the 20th made a successful charge against the defeated French infantry but ran out of control and was destroyed by French cavalry, losing half their number. Wellesley took a dim view of the cavalry's lack of discipline. Sir John Moore, in command in Spain, had better luck. At Sahagun, the Light Dragoons under Lord Paget set a standard of behaviour and discipline when charging that other regiments failed to copy. Near Corunna, the 10th and 15th Light Dragoons found the town occupied and Paget led the 400 troopers of the 15th against 600 French dragoons and defeated them. When Wellesley returned in 1809, the Light Cavalry Brigade of 14th Light Dragoons, 16th Light Dragoons and 20th Light Dragoons were under the command of Major General Stapleton-Cotton, with the heavy brigade still in England.

At Talavera, the newly arrived 23rd Light Dragoons made a successful charge late in the battle but over difficult ground – a very deep dry watercourse – and lost over 200 men killed or wounded in the ravine. During the siege of Badajoz, the 13th Light Dragoons was ordered to capture a French siege train at Campo-Mayor but forgot their mission. The 13th Light Dragoons routed the cavalry escort, but concentrated on sabring the drivers and allowed the valuable train to escape. Wellington (after Talavera) was so furious that he issued a 'final warning' to the 13th Light Dragoons.

Some cavalry regiments failed to post vedettes, which resulted on a number of troops being captured. Brigadier Slade at Maguilla came across a French cavalry brigade and with the heavy brigade, put in an immediate charge, but failed to notice that the French general kept half his brigade in reserve. The result was that Slade's blown heavies were destroyed by the fresh French half brigade. The 'Slade Affair' was much talked about and added to the blunders of the cavalry that Wellington severely censured. At Salamanca in July 1812 Wellington had a complete cavalry division. Le Marchant's Heavy Brigade with Anson's Light Brigade charged alongside Major General Pakenham's 3rd Division. Maucunee's two French divisions were completely routed by the British cavalry. Le Marchant was killed, but Salamanca was a cavalry success with 40,000 French defeated in forty minutes. It was Le Marchant who started the military college that came to be Sandhurst, and became its Governor.

Waterloo

The cavalry did not arrive at Quatre Bras until after the battle, although Wellington had the Brunswick cavalry. During the fallback to Waterloo from Quatre Bras, the cavalry delayed the French with the rearguard of the Household Brigade, 23rd Light Dragoons, 7th Hussars, 10th Hussars and 11th Light Dragoons. The 7th Hussars retired in good order keeping the French at bay, but a charge against Polish Lancers packed within the narrow crossing of the River Dyle in Genappe was futile, as the lancers had the better reach. When the French lancers got into the open, the Life Guards saw them off and the French kept their distance. The 10th Hussars dismounted and kept the French cavalry from crossing the river with their fire power.

At Waterloo Wellington's cavalry under Lord Uxbridge was augmented by cavalry from the King's German Legion and totalled seven English brigades with additional

Hanoverian Light, Netherlands Heavy, Netherlands Light (2) and a Brunswick Light Cavalry Brigade. The composition of the brigades was as follows:

1st or Household Brigade: The 1st and 2nd Life Guards, Royal Horse Guards (Blue) and 1st King's Dragoon Guards, commanded by Major General Lord Somerset, stopped Dubois' cuirassiers supporting d'Erlon's Corps.

2nd or Union Brigade: The 1st (Royal) Dragoons, 2nd Royal North British Dragoons (Scots Greys) and 6th (Inniskilling) Dragoons, commanded by Major General Sir William Ponsonby whose brigade broke d'Erlon's Corps, capturing two Eagles. Captain Clarke of the 1st Royal Dragoons captured the Eagle of the 105th Regiment and Sergeant Ewart of the Scots Greys captured the 45th Regiment's Eagle. The 6th Inniskilling Dragoons completely destroyed a brigade of four battalions of infantry from the 54th and 55th regiments.

3rd Brigade: The 23rd Light Dragoons, King's German Legion (KGL) 1st and 2nd Light Dragoons, commanded by Major General Dörnberg. The colonel of the 23rd Light Dragoons was absent without leave the night before the battle and arrived too late and subsequently resigned his commission in disgrace.

4th Brigade: The 11th Light Dragoons, 12th (Prince of Wales's) Light Dragoons and 16th Queen's Light Dragoons, commanded by Major General Vandeleur.

5th Brigade: The 7th (Queen's Own) Hussars, 15th King's Hussars and 2nd Hussars KGL, commanded by Major General Grant.

6th Brigade: The 10th POW's Own Royal Hussars, 18th King's Irish Hussars and KGL 1st Hussars, commanded by Major General Vivian.

7th Brigade: 13th Light Dragoons and KGL 3rd Hussars, commanded by Colonel von Arentschild.

Hanoverian (Light) Brigade: Duke of Cumberland's, Prince Regent's, Bremen & Verden Hussars commanded by Colonel von Estorff.

Netherlands (Heavy) Brigade: 1st Dutch, 3rd Dutch and 2nd Belgian Carbineers commanded by Major General Baron Trip.

1st Netherland (Light) Brigade: 4th Dutch Light Dragoons and 8th Belgian Hussars, commanded by Major General van Ghigny.

2nd Netherland (Light) Brigade: 5th Belgian Light Dragoons and 6th Dutch Hussars, commanded by Major General Baron van Merlen.

Brunswick Cavalry: 2nd Hussars and one squadron of Uhlans.

Lancers

Units of lancers in a set piece were successful and could overreach a square. Napoleon had used lancers successfully at Dresden to break squares. As part of the French cavalry, the Uhlans had caused terrible damage in their only major cavalry success in the Peninsula when they caught Colborne's brigade from behind with lances at Albuhera in 1811. At Waterloo when the heavy brigade smashed d'Erlon's Corps of 16,000 it was the French lancers who picked them off when the Heavy Brigade withdrew, killing Major General Ponsonby. Influenced by Napoleon's lancers at Waterloo, in the following year the 9th, 12th, 16th, 19th and 23rd Light Dragoons were converted to lancers. Two further dragoon regiments, the 3rd and 4th Dragoons, converted to Light Dragoons in 1818. The lance was originally 15ft long, but was reduced to 9ft. In close combat the lance was dropped and the sword used.

The period 1818–22 saw the disbandment of the 18th to 25th regiments. The 21st Light Dragoons had a troop guarding the exiled Napoleon Bonaparte, so this troop disbanded on his death. The 17th Light Dragoons converted to lancers, the 8th (King's Royal Irish) Light Dragoons converted to hussars in 1822.

Sir Robert Stapleton-Cotton – who was passed over as commander of cavalry at Waterloo in favour of Lord Uxbridge – was made Commander-in-Chief India. Problems arose with the East India Company and the successor to the Rajah of Bhurtpore. Now Lord Combermere and his army of 20,000 besieged the fortress at Bhurtpore for two weeks in 1826 and finally stormed it. Cotton would become Field Marshal, 1st Viscount Combermere of Bhurtpore. The 16th Lancers 'washed their spears' at Bhurtpore in 1826.

In 1840 the 11th Light Dragoons became Prince Albert's Own Hussars. The lance was again used effectively in battle at Aliwal in 1846 in the First Sikh War by the 16th Lancers again, who broke Sikh squares in a magnificent charge. During the Second Sikh War at Ramnager in 1849, the 14th King's Light Dragoons charged down a dry riverbed with enemy guns either side, possibly due to confused orders as at Balaclava, and suffered high casualties, including their colonel, William Havelock, eldest brother of Henry Havelock.

The 3rd (King's Own) Light Dragoons won a reputation for consistently charging the fearsome Sikhs, when others would baulk at the task. At Chillianwala, Captain Unett with his squadron of the 3rd King's Own Dragoons prevented a dangerous Sikh threat and was rewarded with an audience with Queen Victoria who congratulated him on his bravery. The 9th Lancers and 14th King's Light Dragoons were not quite so heroic that day when they retreated and had to be rallied by the chaplain.

Balaclava: Two Cavalry Charges and a Thin Red Line

During the Crimean War of 1854–6, the protection of Balaclava and its port was given to Sir Colin Campbell with his 93rd Sutherland Highlanders and a company of the 41st Welsh Regiment and Turks. The area had two main ridges, the Fedioukine Heights with the North Valley in between and the Causeway Heights with the South Valley falling away from it. The Causeway Heights was wide enough to carry the Woronzoff Road. The Heights were fortified with redoubts as they were on a main route. No. 1 Redoubt was on Canrobert Hill, with the remaining five on Causeway Heights with naval guns manned by Turks. On 25 October Raglan received reports before breakfast of Russian infantry preparing to capture the village of Kadicoi and cut off the British at Balaclava. Raglan was slow to respond because previous warnings had proved to be false alarms. He finished breakfast and went to high ground to investigate.

This time the threat was real; the first and second redoubts were being taken and he summoned two divisions from Sevastopol. The other redoubts were falling and the Turks fleeing. The Russians now occupied Causeway Heights and Fedioukine Hills with infantry battalions and the artillery lined up in North Valley. The Russian cavalry of 3,000 men advanced down the North Valley. An advance force of 400 of the Russian cavalry attacked Sir Colin Campbell and his Highlanders guarding the route to Balaclava. Only 550 soldiers stood between Balaclava and the whole Russian Army. The Highlanders – who were lying down – soon stood up and the two thin ranks, bristling with steel, saw off the cavalry with three carefully aimed volleys. The Russians wavered at each volley and finally retired. Balaclava was secure and the event was immortalised as the 'thin red line'.

It was now time for the heavy brigade to show its mettle. The heavy brigade under Scarlett consisted of the Royal Dragoons, the Scots Greys, 6th Inniskilling Dragoons, 5th Dragoon Guards and 4th Dragoon Guards. They were charged by up to 3,000 Russian cavalrymen. Scarlett with half his brigade of 300 troopers slowly and methodically dressed his regiments to face the onslaught and when the Russians apparently stopped, the heavy brigade charged uphill and disappeared amongst them. After a fierce fight with the second half of the brigade joining the melee, the Russians were defeated. Lord Cardigan watching with the light brigade was asked to follow through to rout the cavalry. Cardigan, very much like Sackville at Minden, stayed put waiting for orders, again much to the chagrin of the light cavalry.

Cardigan's infamous Charge of the Light Brigade against the wrong guns was the result of many misfortunes. The Russians had occupied the Causeway Heights which resulted in Lord Raglan issuing his first written order for his cavalry to occupy the Heights and chase the Russians away. When the Russians were subsequently seen by Raglan to be taking away the captured British naval guns from the Heights, Raglan sent his second written order requesting the cavalry to prevent the enemy carrying away the guns and to act immediately. Lord Raglan from his view point high up could see the whole field of battle and reasoned that the Russians were very shaky after the earlier heavy brigade's success. Lord Lucan at ground level could not see anything that appertained to the first order, and considering the Heights to be a formidable task he took nearly an hour to ponder the order.

The second order was delivered by Captain Nolan who had worked himself into a frenzy at the previous inaction by Lucan and the Light Brigade's lack of support earlier that day. When Lucan asked Nolan 'what guns sir?', Nolan's reply – in a tone tantamount to rank insubordination – was to wave his hand in the general direction down the North Valley and not the Causeway Heights, with the repost 'there my lord, is your enemy, there are your guns!' Lord Lucan could only see the Russian guns at the head of the North Valley and gave the order to Cardigan to attack the Russian guns which had now been reinforced with the Russian cavalry and infantry.

Cardigan was not happy with the task, declaring 'here goes the last of the Brudenells'. The animosity that existed between Lucan and Cardigan prevented any reasonable questioning of the order. The 13th Light Dragoons, 11th Hussars, 17th Lancers, 4th Light Dragoons and 8th Hussars went into the history books. 670 troopers charged for 1½ miles into the teeth of the twelve guns of the Russian artillery and additional fire from the heights each side. When they staggered back, the final tally was 118 killed and 127 wounded with 400 horses killed and injured. Nolan was killed as he rode to the front to join Cardigan, almost certainly in a vain effort to prevent the charge on the wrong guns. Cardigan, after bravely leading the charge, apparently disappeared and left his brigade without leadership. He did return a hero in the eyes of the public, but later had to answer to his critics and Parliament. Lord Lucan was recalled when news of the debacle reached London.

The Last of the Light Dragoons

The 18th Light Dragoons were again re-formed in 1858, but were soon to be designated 18th Hussars. The designation 'Light Dragoon' would never be used again until the proposals for the 1991 white paper. Following the Indian Mutiny of 1857, the 19th, 20th, and 21st Hussars were re-formed in 1862 from the former 1st, 2nd and 3rd Bengal European Light Cavalry and the remaining light dragoon regiments converted to hussars becoming the 3rd, 4th, 13th and 14th Hussars in 1861.

The Household Cavalry of Life Guards, Royal Horse Guards (Blue), 1st (Royal) Dragoons, 2nd (Royal Scots) Dragoons, 6th (Inniskillings) Dragoons together with the Dragoon Guards remained heavy cavalry. At the request of the Queen, for the services rendered by Irish regiments in the Indian Mutiny and in Crimea, the 5th Dragoons were reinstated. The 5th (Royal Irish) came out of the cold and were re-formed as lancers in 1858, losing their seniority.

During the Second Afghan War (1878–80), General Roberts sent his cavalry brigade out to look for the Afghan Army. Brigadier Massy found the Afghan Army under Muhammad Jan – all 10,000 of them. Massy with his 500 troopers of the 9th Lancers and four light guns, had a massive task in delaying the Afghans until reinforcements arrived (Roberts was 4 miles away). During the melee the chaplain Reverend Adams gained a Victoria Cross saving the lives of two troopers of the 9th Lancers. The cavalry made an organised withdrawal until the Highlanders from Roberts's force stopped Muhammad Jan.

The Cardwell reforms – which redesignated infantry regiments from numbered regiments into two battalion regiments with county or city titles – bypassed the cavalry who maintained their regimental numbers together with the Royal patronage indicated in their alternative titles. The 21st Hussars converted to lancers in 1897 and still had no Battle Honours and were mockingly referred to as 'non combatants'. The following year at Omburdman (Sudan) they made their cavalry charge wearing khaki drill and excelled themselves with their first Battle Honour. The blue and scarlet were never again seen in battle.

TWENTIETH CENTURY

The Boer War: The Cavalry's Last Hurrah

At Elandslaagte, the infantry had a success under General Hamilton and the Boers were thoroughly routed by the 400 troopers of the 5th Dragoon Guards and 5th Lancers. No mercy was shown, as the Boers had previously abused a flag of truce. The Scots Greys were the first in at the relief of Kimberley and General French's 5,000-strong cavalry division was practically destroyed in the attempt. They were told to ride like the wind by Roberts to relieve Kimberley and they did just that. 1,500 horses were lost, either killed or missing, at the relief of Kimberley.

Roberts was desperate for mounted infantry and wanted 15,000 but could not achieve it. The regular cavalry could not fill this role and stayed on their horses. Some rifle regiments were put onto horses, such was the shortage. Nearly half a million horses were used in the Boer War and approximately 13,000 died on the voyage alone. Nearly every cavalry unit went to South Africa.

Mechanisation

Mechanisation commenced in 1916 with the secret formation of tank detachments, designated for security reasons first as the Armoured Car Section of the Motor Machine Gun Corps, then Heavy Section Machine Gun Corps, then Heavy Branch Machine Gun Corps and finally in 1917 as the Tank Corps. The gestation period was not complete until 1939 when the surviving battalions were redesignated as Royal Tank Regiments. Initially six companies A to F were raised in 1916. Others followed and the units were redesignated as numbered battalions. 1st to 4th Battalions remained on the establishment but the rest disbanded after the war.

During the First World War, many cavalry units stood down from their horses and took up arms, even machine guns, as in the Household Cavalry. The end of the First World War indicated to all but cavalry diehards that tanks and armoured vehicles were the future and would carry out the role cavalry had performed for the last 250 years. Indeed the 20th Hussars made the last regimental cavalry charge against Turkish Nationalists at Ismid in 1920. Prophets like Major General Fuller, a military reformer, and Captain Liddell Hart foresaw the complete mechanisation of warfare (Cooper, p.207).

By 1923 Britain had established a Tank Corps separate from the cavalry and by 1931 tank formations were under the control of lead tanks. Opposition to dismounting the cavalry and becoming mechanised was not peculiar to the British Army. The Americans had problems and Major General Crosby, Chief of US Cavalry 1926–30, recommended to the Secretary of War Dwight Davis that a small number of tanks and anti-tank weapons be added to the existing cavalry divisions. Crosby had been impressed when visiting the UK and had seen a British Experimental Force defeat a mixed infantry and cavalry force three times its size. Crosby energised mechanised policy, 1931–33, with objections from the Chief of Infantry overruled. General Douglas MacArthur, US Chief of Staff, said in 1931, 'Modern firearms had eliminated the horse as a weapon or as a means of transport'.

Even General Guderian who idolised Fuller for his foresight in the development of mechanised warfare, wrote of his struggle to introduce panzers in his earlier years. Guderian proposed Panzer divisions in 1933 with no support from the regular German cavalry who considered him a threat to their existence. It was Hitler who gave Guderian his head to develop tactics for his blitzkrieg with mechanised armour assaulting on a narrow front.

The 11th Hussars were the first cavalry unit to mechanise in 1928. In the early 1930s mechanisation progressed and by 1936 all cavalry except the Life Guards, the Royal Horse Guards and of course the two oldest line cavalry regiments; the (Royal) Dragoons and Royal Scots Greys (2nd Dragoons) had dismounted. The Household Cavalry dismounted in 1939 except for ceremonial duties. The Royal and Scots Greys finally parted with their horses and became mechanised in 1941. Horsepower had finally replaced the power of the horse (Cooper, p.208).

First Amalgamation and Title Changes 1921–22

In 1921, cavalry (and infantry) were allowed to redress their titles. Alternative titles that were in most cases bracketed became the official titles. However, regimental numbers reflecting rank and seniority were maintained, as shown in examples below:

2nd Dragoon Guards (Queen's Bays) became the Queen's Bays (2nd Dragoon Guards)
6th Dragoon Guards became the Carabiniers (6th Dragoon Guards)
4th (Royal Irish) Dragoon Guards became the 4th Royal Irish Dragoon Guards
19th Royal Hussars became the 19th Royal Hussars (Queen Alexandra's Own)

The 2nd Dragoons (Royal Scots Greys) whose title at Waterloo was the 2nd Royal North British Dragoons (Scots Greys) finally decided to dispense with the brackets and recognised the glory of their nickname and restyled themselves the Royal Scots Greys (2nd Dragoons). Similar changes took place with the remainder of the cavalry.

With the establishment of a new Tank Corps, the transition to mechanisation and the introduction of armoured car companies, serious thought had to be given to the future of the cavalry. Sir Eric Geddes proposed the disbandment of eight junior cavalry regiments. After strong opposition, this was modified to selected amalgamations proposed by Sir Charles Harris, Financial Secretary at the War Office. Four regiments actually stood down – the 5th Lancers, 19th, 20th and 21st Hussars – only to be re-formed by Harris, but then amalgamated. The first amalgamations occurred in 1922 with the following mergers:

1st and 2nd Life Guards formed the Life Guards.

3rd (Prince of Wales's) Dragoon Guards and Carabiniers (6th Dragoon Guards) formed the 3rd/6th Dragoon Guards and in 1928 were redesignated the 3rd Carabiniers (Prince of Wales's Dragoon Guards).

4th Royal Irish Dragoon Guards and the 7th Dragoon Guards (Princess Royals) formed the 4th/7th Dragoon Guards.

5th Dragoon Guards (Princess of Wales's) and Inniskilling (6th Dragoons) formed the 5th/6th Dragoons and in 1927 were redesignated the 5th Inniskilling Dragoon Guards. The Inniskilling (6th Dragoons) and its successor the 5th Royal Inniskilling Dragoon Guards are the only regiment to recognise a person (Oates) in place of a Battle Honour on its regimental anniversary on 17 March in commemoration of Captain Oates' selfless death on Scot's expedition to the South Pole.

13th Hussars and the 18th Royal Hussars (Queen Mary's Own) formed the 13th/18th Royal Hussars (Queen Mary's Own).

14th King's Hussars and 20th Hussars formed the 14th/20th Hussars.

15th King's Hussars and 19th Royal Hussars (Queen Alexandra's Own) formed the 15th/19th King's Royal Hussars.

5th Royal Irish Lancers and 16th (Queen's) Lancers formed the 16th/5th Queen's Royal Lancers. The loss of seniority by the 5th due to earlier misdemeanours is reflected in the new title – 16th/5th and not 5th/16th.

17th Lancers (Duke of Cambridge's Own) and the 21st Lancers (Empress of India's Own) formed the 17th/21st Lancers.

In addition to the cavalry, six battalions of the Tank Corps were on the regular establishment. These would be titled Royal Tank Corps in 1923. When George V celebrated his Silver Jubilee in 1935, three cavalry regiments were granted a 'Royal' title:

5th Royal Inniskilling Dragoon Guards
4th/7th Royal Dragoon Guards
14th/20th King's Hussars

Royal Armoured Corps

The Royal Armoured Corps was formed in 1939 to embody the emerging mechanised units, and consisted of the new Royal tank regiments, the mechanised cavalry regiments (except the Household Cavalry) and other associated units. As cavalry regiments mechanised they would join the RAC, as would the thirty-three infantry battalions which became mechanised during the war. When the Royal Armoured Corps was formed, the Royal Tank Corps became the Royal Tank Regiment to avoid the confusion of a corps within a corps. The 5th to 8th Battalions were re-formed and re-designated as regiments. By 1940 the Royal Tank Regiment had increased to twelve regiments and during the war it increased to eighteen regiments.

During the Second World War, six cavalry regiments (now mechanised) were re-formed: the 22nd Dragoons, 23rd Hussars, 24th Lancers, 25th Dragoons, 26th Hussars and 27th Lancers. All were disbanded in 1948. The 9th to 18th Regiments of the Royal Tank Regiment were disbanded in 1945.

Second Amalgamation 1958–71: The Last Dragoons

3rd King's Own Hussars and 7th Queen's Own Hussars formed the Queen's Own Hussars in 1958.

4th Queen's Own Hussars and the 8th King's Royal Irish Hussars formed the Queen's Royal Irish Hussars in 1958.

1st King's Dragoon Guards and Queen's Bays (2nd Dragoon Guards) formed the 1st Queen's Dragoon Guards in 1959.

9th Queen's Royal Lancers and the 12th Royal Lancers (Prince of Wales's) formed the 9th/12th Royal Lancers (Prince of Wales's) in 1960.

The Royal Horse Guards and Royal Dragoons (1st Dragoons) formed the Blues and Royals in 1969. The Royal Dragoons badge of Captain Clarke's 105th French Regiment's Eagle captured at Waterloo has been lost forever.

10th Royal Hussars (Prince of Wales's Own) and the 11th Hussars (Prince Albert's Own) formed the Royal Hussars (Prince of Wales's Own) in 1969.

The Royal Scots Greys (2nd Dragoons) and the 3rd Carabiniers (Prince of Wales's Dragoon Guards) formed the Royal Scots Dragoon Guards (Carabiniers and Greys) in 1971. The badge of the new regiment is taken from the Royal Scots Greys badge depicting Sergeant Ewart's Eagle captured from the French 45th Regiment at Waterloo.

3rd and 6th Royal Tank Regiment merged into the 3rd Royal Tank Regiment.

4th and 7th Royal Tank Regiment merged into the 4th Royal Tank Regiment.

5th and 8th Royal Tank Regiment merged into the 5th Royal Tank Regiment in 1960, only to be disbanded in 1969.

Third Amalgamation: Defence White Paper, July 1991

The proposals in the 1991 Defence White Paper, 'Options for Change', reduced the cavalry regiments from fifteen to nine and the Royal Tank Regiments from four to two.

The Life Guards and the Blues and Royals combined but maintained their identity and cap badges within the new regiment called the Household Cavalry Regiment. This regiment would be identified as a dual regiment with two squadrons of Life Guards and two squadrons of Blues and Royals. Both regiments maintained their traditions and each had an armoured reconnaissance unit and a unit for mounted ceremonial duties.

The 4th/7th Royal Dragoon Guards and 5th Royal Inniskilling Dragoon Guards formed the Royal Dragoon Guards. The Queen's Own Hussars and Queen's Royal Irish Hussars formed the Queen's Royal Hussars. The Royal Hussars and 14th/20th King's Hussars formed the King's Royal Hussars. The 13th/18th Royal Hussars and the 15th/19th King's Royal Hussars formed the Light Dragoons. 16th/5th Queen's Royal Lancers and the 17th/21st Lancers formed the Queen's Royal Lancers. The 1st and 4th Royal Tank Regiment merged into the 1st Royal Tank Regiment, and the 2nd and 3rd Royal Tank Regiment merged into the 2nd Royal Tank Regiment.

Regiments unaffected by the 1991 proposals were the 1st Queen's Dragoon Guards, the Royal Scots Dragoon Guards (Carabiniers and Greys) and the 9th/12th Royal Lancers (Prince of Wales's).

The title of Light Dragoon has finally been resurrected after 130 years. The 1st Queen's Dragoon Guards (which sometimes identify themselves as the Welsh Cavalry) and the 9th/12th Royal Lancers remain the only cavalry regiments with regimental numbers after more than 300 years of history. The infantry changes of 2004 have eliminated all reference to regimental numbers. The regiments now are:

One household cavalry regiment (Life Guards and Blues and Royals)
Three regiments of dragoon guards
Two regiments of hussars
One regiment of light dragoons
Two regiments of lancers
Two Royal tank regiments

TWENTY-FIRST CENTURY

Cavalry Regiments for the Twenty-first Century

The Defence White Paper of 2004 reorganised the infantry into larger regiments, but the cavalry organisation remained untouched. The following is the complete list in order of precedence of all the cavalry regiments to meet the British Army's future needs:

Household Cavalry (Life Guards and Blues and Royals)
1st Queen's Dragoon Guards
Royal Scots Dragoon Guards
Royal Dragoon Guards
Queen's Royal Hussars

9th/12th Royal Lancers
King's Royal Hussars
Light Dragoons
Queen's Royal Lancers
1st Royal Tank Regiment
2nd Royal Tank Regiment

Proposals for the Cavalry (Royal Armoured Corps) as a result of the Strategic Defence and Security Review of 2010:

- Two regiments to go. Amalgamation of two regiments and the 2nd Battalion Royal Tank regiment to go.
- Queen's Royal Lancers to merge with the 9th/12th Royal Lancers (Prince of Wales's).
- The 2nd Royal Tank Regiment to be disbanded.

Cavalry

- Queen's Royal Lancers and 9th/12th Royal Lancers ceremony took place in Richmond, Yorkshire on 30 April 2015 to merge both regiments to form the Royal Lancers.
- Royal Tank Regiment 2nd Battlalion disbanded at Bulfrod Barracks on 4 August 2014.

Current Cavalry Regiments for ARMY 2020

	Regiment	
1	Household Cavalry	Life Guards
		Blues & Royals
2	1st Queen's Dragoon Guards	
3	Royal Scots Dragoon Guards	
4	Royal Dragoon Guards	
5	Queen's Royal Hussars	
6	Royal Lancers	
7	King's Royal Hussars	
8	Light Dragoons	
9	Royal Tank Regiment	

Army Reserve Cavalry

Royal Yeomanry	Royal Wessex Yeomanry	The Scottish & North Irish Yeomanry	Queen's Own Yeomanry

Early Household Regiments, Horse Grenadiers, Regiments of Horse and Dragoon Guards

Rank	*Designation 1661*	*1670*				*1746*	*1788*
1660		*Re-rank*					
1st	His Majesty's Own Troop of Horse Guards	1st	1st Troop (King's Troop)			1st Troop of Life Guards	1st Life Guards
2nd	Duke of York's Troop of Horse Guards	3rd	3rd Troop (Duke's Troop)				
	1678		1680	1684	1693		
	1st Troop of Horse Grenadiers		Disbanded	Re-formed	1st Troop Horse Grenadiers	1st Troop of Horse Grenadier Guards	
	2nd Troop of Horse Grenadiers		Disbanded	Re-formed			
	3rd Troop of Horse Grenadiers		Disbanded	Re-formed			
	1661						
3rd	Monck's or Duke of Albemarle's Troop of of Horse Guards later Queen's Troop	2nd	2nd Troop (Queen's Troop)			2nd Troop of Life Guards	2nd Life Guards
	Scottish Troop of Horse Guards (4th)		1689			Disbanded	
	1686		Disbanded		2nd Troop added 1702	2nd Troop of Horse Grenadier Guards	
4th	Scottish Troop Horse Grenadiers						

Date	*Rank*	*Regiments of Horse*	*Re-rank 1690*	*Re-rank 1694*	*1746*		*1788*	
1661	1st	Royal Regiment of Horse	1st	1st Horse	Royal Regiment of Horse Guards (Blue)			Royal Regiment of Horse Guards
1685	2nd	Queen's	2nd	2nd Horse	1st	(King's) Dragoons Guards	1st	(King's) Dragoon Guards
1685	3rd	Earl of Peterborough's	3rd	3rd Horse	2nd	Queen's Dragoon Guards	2nd	Queen's Dragoon Guards
1685	4th	Earl of Plymouth's	4th	4th Horse	3rd	Dragoon Guards	3rd	Dragoon Guards
1685	5th	Earl of Thanet's	Disbanded 1690					
1685	6th	Earl of Arran's	5th	5th Horse	1st	Horse (Irish or Blue Horse)	4th	(Royal Irish) Dragoon Guards
1685	7th	Earl of Shrewsbury's	6th	6th Horse	2nd	Horse (Irish or Green Horse)	5th	Dragoon Guards
1685	8th	Princess Anne of Denmark's	7th	Disbanded 1694	1st to 4th Horse on the Irish Establishment			

<table>
<tr><td>1685</td><td>9th</td><td>Queen Dowager's</td><td>8th</td><td>7th Horse</td><td>3rd</td><td>Horse (Irish) or Carabiniers</td><td>6th</td><td>Dragoon Guards</td></tr>
<tr><td>1688</td><td>10th</td><td>Earl of Devonshire's</td><td>9th</td><td>8th Horse</td><td>4th</td><td>Horse (Irish or Black Horse)</td><td>7th</td><td>(Princess Royal's) Dragoon Guards</td></tr>
</table>

<table>
<tr><th colspan="9">Household Cavalry, 1st Queen's Dragoon Guards, Royal Scots Dragoon Guards and Royal Dragoon Guards</th></tr>
<tr><th>Current Regiment</th><th colspan="5">Order of Precedence</th><th>By 1815</th><th>Regiment</th><th>Raised</th></tr>
<tr><td rowspan="4">Household Cavalry</td><td rowspan="4">Household Cavalry 1992</td><td colspan="4" rowspan="2">Life Guards 1922</td><td>Life Guards</td><td>1st</td><td>1660</td></tr>
<tr><td>Life Guards</td><td>2nd</td><td></td></tr>
<tr><td colspan="3" rowspan="2">Blues and Royals 1969</td><td>Royal Horse Guards (The Blues) 1819</td><td>Royal Horse Guards (Blue)</td><td></td><td>1661</td></tr>
<tr><td>Royal Dragoons (1st Dragoons) 1961</td><td>(Royal) Dragoons</td><td>1st</td><td>1661</td></tr>
<tr><td rowspan="2">1st Queen's Dragoon Guards</td><td colspan="2" rowspan="2">1st Queen's Dragoon Guards 1959</td><td colspan="3">King's Dragoon Guards</td><td>King's Dragoon Guards</td><td>1st</td><td>1685</td></tr>
<tr><td>Queen's Bays (2nd Dragoon Guards) 1921</td><td colspan="2">2nd Dragoon Guards (Queen's Bays) 1872</td><td>Queen's Dragoon Guards</td><td>2nd</td><td>1685</td></tr>
<tr><td rowspan="3">Royal Scots Dragoon Guards</td><td rowspan="3">Royal Scots Dragoon Guards (Carabiniers and Greys) 1971</td><td colspan="3">Royal Scots Greys (2nd Dragoons) 1921</td><td>2nd Dragoons (Scots Greys) 1877</td><td>Royal North British Dragoons (Scots Greys)</td><td>2nd</td><td>1681</td></tr>
<tr><td rowspan="2">3rd Carabiniers POW's Dragoon Guards 1928</td><td rowspan="2">3/6th Dragoon Guards 1922</td><td colspan="2">Prince of Wales's Dragoon Guards</td><td>Prince of Wales's Dragoon Guards</td><td>3rd</td><td>1685</td></tr>
<tr><td>Carabiniers (6th Dragoon Guards) 1921</td><td>6th Dragoon Guards (Carabiniers) 1826</td><td>Dragoon Guards</td><td>6th</td><td>1685</td></tr>
<tr><td rowspan="4">Royal Dragoon Guards</td><td rowspan="4">Royal Dragoon Guards 1992</td><td colspan="2" rowspan="2">4th/7th Dragoon Guards 1922
4th/7th Royal Dragoon Guards 1935</td><td colspan="2">4th Royal Irish Dragoon Guards 1921</td><td>(Royal Irish) Dragoon Guards</td><td>4th</td><td>1685</td></tr>
<tr><td colspan="2">7th Dragoon Guards (Princess Royal's) 1921</td><td>(Princess Royal's) Dragoon Guards</td><td>7th</td><td>1688</td></tr>
<tr><td rowspan="2">5th Royal Inniskilling Dragoon Guards 1935</td><td rowspan="2">5th Inniskilling Dragoon Guards 1927</td><td rowspan="2">5/6th Dragoons 1922</td><td>5th Dragoon Guards (Princess Charlotte of Wales's) 1921</td><td>(Princess Charlotte of Wales's) Dragoon Guards</td><td>5th</td><td>1685</td></tr>
<tr><td>Inniskillings (6th Dragoons) 1921</td><td>(Inniskilling) Dragoons</td><td>6th</td><td>1689</td></tr>
</table>

<table>
<tr><th colspan="10">Queen's Royal Hussars, Royal Lancers, King's Royal Hussars</th></tr>
<tr><th>Current Regiment</th><th colspan="2">Order of Precedence</th><th colspan="4"></th><th>By 1815</th><th>Regiment</th><th>Raised</th></tr>
<tr><td rowspan="4">Queen's Royal Hussars</td><td rowspan="4">Queen's Royal Hussars 1993</td><td rowspan="2">Queen's Own Hussars 1958</td><td colspan="2">3rd (King's Own) Hussars 1861</td><td colspan="2">3rd (King's Own) Light Dragoons 1818</td><td>(King's Own) Dragoons</td><td>3rd</td><td>1685</td></tr>
<tr><td colspan="4">7th Queen's Own Hussars 1921</td><td>(Queen's Own) Hussars</td><td>7th</td><td>1690</td></tr>
<tr><td rowspan="2">Queen's Royal Irish Hussars 1958</td><td colspan="2">4th (Queen's Own) Hussars 1861</td><td colspan="2">4th Queen's Own Light Dragoons 1818</td><td>Queen's Own Dragoons</td><td>4th</td><td>1685</td></tr>
<tr><td colspan="4">8th (King's Royal Irish) Hussars 1822</td><td>King's Royal Irish Light Dragoons</td><td>8th</td><td>1693</td></tr>
<tr><td rowspan="2">Royal Lancers 2015</td><td colspan="2" rowspan="2">9th/12th Royal Lancers (Prince of Wales's) 1960</td><td colspan="2">9th (Queen's Royal) Lancers 1830</td><td colspan="2">9th Lancers 1816</td><td>Light Dragoons</td><td>9th</td><td>1715</td></tr>
<tr><td colspan="2">12th (Prince of Wales's) Royal Lancers 1817</td><td colspan="2">12th (Prince of Wales's) Lancers1816</td><td>(Prince of Wales's) Light Dragoons</td><td>12th</td><td>1715</td></tr>
<tr><td rowspan="4"></td><td rowspan="4">Queen's Royal Lancers 1993</td><td rowspan="2">16th/5th Queen's Royal Lancers 1922</td><td colspan="4">16th (Queen's) Lancers 1816</td><td>Queen's Light Dragoons</td><td>16th</td><td>1759</td></tr>
<tr><td colspan="2">5th Royal Irish Lancers 1921</td><td colspan="2">Re-formed 5th (Royal Irish) Lancers 1858</td><td>Disbanded</td><td>5th</td><td>1689</td></tr>
<tr><td rowspan="2">17th/21st Lancers 1922</td><td colspan="2">17th Lancers (Duke of Cambridge's Own) 1876</td><td colspan="2">17th Lancers 1822</td><td>Light Dragoons</td><td>17th</td><td>1759</td></tr>
<tr><td>21st (Empress of India's) Lancers 1899</td><td>21st Lancers 1897</td><td>21st Hussars re-formed formally 3rd BELC 1862</td><td>Dis-banded 1819</td><td>Light Dragoons</td><td>21st</td><td>1760</td></tr>
<tr><td rowspan="4">King's Royal Hussars</td><td rowspan="4">King's Royal Hussars 1992</td><td rowspan="2">Royal Hussars (Prince of Wales's Own) 1969</td><td colspan="4">10th Royal Hussars (Prince of Wales's Own) 1921</td><td>Prince of Wales's Own Royal Hussars</td><td>10th</td><td>1715</td></tr>
<tr><td colspan="4">11th Prince Albert's Own Hussars 1840</td><td>Light Dragoons</td><td>11th</td><td>1715</td></tr>
<tr><td rowspan="2">14th/20th Hussars 1922 14th/20th King's Hussars 1935</td><td colspan="2">14th King's Hussars 1861</td><td colspan="2">14th King's Light Dragoons 1830</td><td>Duchess of York's Own Light Dragoons</td><td>14th</td><td>1715</td></tr>
<tr><td colspan="3">1862 20th Hussars formally 2nd Bengal European Light Cavalry</td><td>Disbanded 1819</td><td>Light Dragoons</td><td>20th</td><td>1760</td></tr>
</table>

<table>
<tr><th colspan="12">Light Dragoons and Royal Tank Regiment</th></tr>
<tr><td colspan="2">Current Regiment</td><td colspan="6">Order of Precedence</td><td colspan="2">By 1815</td><td>Regt No</td><td>Raised</td></tr>
<tr><td colspan="2" rowspan="4">Light Dragoons</td><td rowspan="4">Light Dragoons 1992</td><td rowspan="2">13th/18th Royal Hussars (Queen Mary's Own) 1922</td><td colspan="4">13th Hussars 1861</td><td colspan="2">Light Dragoons</td><td>13th</td><td>1715</td></tr>
<tr><td>18th Royal Hussars (Queen Mary's Own) 1919</td><td>18th (Queen Mary's Own) Hussars 1910</td><td>18th Hussars 1858</td><td>Disbanded 1822</td><td colspan="2">King's Irish Hussars</td><td>18th</td><td>1760</td></tr>
<tr><td rowspan="2">15th/19th King's Royal Hussars 1922</td><td colspan="4">15th King's Hussars</td><td colspan="2">King's Hussars</td><td>15th</td><td>1759</td></tr>
<tr><td colspan="2">19th (Queen Alexandra's Own Royal) Hussars 1908</td><td>1862 19th Hussars formerly 1st BELC</td><td>Disbanded 1821</td><td>19th Lancers 1816</td><td>Light Dragoons</td><td>19th</td><td>1781</td></tr>
</table>

<table>
<tr><td colspan="4"></td><td colspan="2">1939</td><td colspan="3">Tank Corps 1917
Royal Tank Corps 1923</td><td colspan="2">Company</td><td>Raised</td></tr>
<tr><td rowspan="3">1st</td><td rowspan="3">Royal Tank Regiment</td><td rowspan="3">1st Royal Tank Regiment 1993</td><td>1st Royal Tank Regiment</td><td colspan="2">1st Royal Tank Regiment</td><td colspan="3">1st Battalion Royal Tank Corps</td><td rowspan="8">For security reasons raised as the Heavy branch of the Machine Gun Corps</td><td>A</td><td>1916</td></tr>
<tr><td rowspan="2">4th Royal Tank Regiment 1959</td><td colspan="2">4th Royal Tank Regiment</td><td colspan="3">4th Battalion Royal Tank Corps</td><td>D</td><td>1916</td></tr>
<tr><td colspan="2">7th Royal Tank Regiment</td><td colspan="3"></td><td></td><td></td></tr>
<tr><td rowspan="3">Disbanded 2014</td><td rowspan="3">Royal Tank Regiment</td><td rowspan="3">2nd Royal Tank Regiment 1992</td><td>2nd Royal Tank Regiment</td><td colspan="2">2nd Royal Tank Regiment</td><td colspan="3">2nd Battalion Royal Tank Corps</td><td>B</td><td>1916</td></tr>
<tr><td rowspan="2">3rd Royal Tank Regiment 1959</td><td colspan="2">3rd Royal Tank Regiment</td><td colspan="3">3rd Battalion Royal Tank Corps</td><td>C</td><td>1916</td></tr>
<tr><td colspan="2">6th Royal Tank Regiment</td><td colspan="3">6th Battalion Royal Tank Corps</td><td>F</td><td>1916</td></tr>
<tr><td colspan="2" rowspan="2"></td><td rowspan="2">Disbanded 1969</td><td rowspan="2">5th Royal Tank Regiment 1960</td><td colspan="2">5th Royal Tank Regiment</td><td colspan="3">5th Battalion Royal Tank Corps</td><td>E</td><td>1916</td></tr>
<tr><td colspan="2">8th Royal Tank Regiment</td><td colspan="3"></td><td></td><td></td></tr>
</table>

Cavalry Regiments and Where Are They Now?

Household Cavalry

Date	*Raised*	*Changes in Title*	*1815 Title*	*Where They Are Now*
1660	Life Guards of Horse	Four troops of Life Guards of Horse and later the addition of four Troops of Horse Grenadier Guards reduced to two troops of each and finally merged 1st and 2nd Regiment of Life Guards 1788	1st Life Guards 2nd Life Guards	Household Cavalry
1661	Royal Regiment of Horse Ranked 1st Horse	Earl of Oxford's Regiment of Horse / Oxford Blues / King's Regiment of Horse Guards / Royal Regiment of Horse Guards	Royal Horse Guards (Blue)	Household Cavalry

Regiments of Horse

Date	*Rank*	*Raised*	*Changes in Title*	*Rank*	*Dragoon Guards*	*Where They Are Now*
1685	2nd	Queen's Regiment	2nd Horse / King's Own Regt of Horse / Re-ranked 1st King's Dragoon Guards	1st	1st King's Dragoon Guard's	1st Queen's Dragoon Guards
1685	3rd	Earl of Peterborough's	3rd Horse / Princess of Wales's Own Regiment of Horse / Queen's Own Regiment of Horse / Re-ranked 2nd Queen's Dragoon Guards	2nd	2nd Queen's Dragoon Guards	1st Queen's Dragoon Guards
1685	4th	Earl of Plymouth's	4th Horse / Re-ranked 3rd Regiment of Dragoon Guards / (Prince of Wales's) Dragoon Guards	3rd	3rd (Prince of Wales's) Dragoon Guards	Royal Scots Dragoon Guards
1685	5th	Earl of Thanets	5th Horse disbanded		Disbanded	Disbanded
1685	6th	Earl of Arran's Cuirassiers	6th Horse / Re-ranked 5th Horse / Prince of Wales's Own Regt of Horse/ 1st Horse (Irish or Blue Horse) / Re-ranked 4th (Royal Irish) Dragoon Guards	4th	4th (Royal Irish) Dragoon Guards	Royal Dragoon Guards
1685	7th	Earl of Shrewsbury's	7th Horse / Re-ranked 6th Horse / 2nd Horse (Irish or Green Horse) / Re-ranked 5th (Princess Charlotte of Wales's) Dragoon Guards	5th	5th (Princess Charlotte of Wales's) Dragoon Guards	Royal Dragoon Guards
1685	8th	Princess of Denmark's	8th Horse Disbanded		Disbanded	Disbanded
1685	9th	Queen Dowager's	9th Horse Re-ranked 8th then 7th Horse / 1st Carabiniers / King's Carabiniers / 3rd Horse (Irish) / Re-ranked 6th Dragoon Guards	6th	6th Dragoon Guards	Royal Scots Dragoon Guards

1688	10th	Earl of Devonshire's	10th Horse / Schomberg's Horse/ Re-ranked 9th then 8th Horse / Ligonier's Horse / 4th Horse (Irish or Black Horse) / Re-ranked 7th (Princess Royal's) Dragoon Guards	7th	7th (Princess Royal's) Dragoon Guards	Royal Dragoon Guards
Dragoons and Light Dragoons						
					1815 Title	*Where They Are Now*
Date	*Rank*	*Raised*	*Changes in Title*	*Rank*	*Dragoons, Light Dragoons and Hussars*	
1661	1st	Tangier Horse	King's Own Royal Regiment of Dragoons / 1st (Royal) Dragoons	1st	(Royal) Dragoons	Household Cavalry
1681	2nd	Royal Regiment of Scots Dragoons	Royal Regiment of North British Dragoons / 2nd Royal North British Dragoons (Scots Greys)	2nd	Royal North British Dragoons (Scots Greys)	Royal Scots Dragoon Guards
1685	3rd	Duke of Somerset's	Queen Consort's Own / King's Own / 3rd (King's Own) Dragoons	3rd	(King's Own) Dragoons	Queen's Royal Hussars
1685	4th	Berkeley's	Princess Anne Of Denmark's Dragoons / 4th Dragoons / 4th Queen's Own Dragoons	4th	Queen's Own Dragoons	Queen's Royal Hussars
1689	5th	Wynne's Enniskillen	Royal Dragoon's of Ireland / 5th Royal Irish Dragoons	5th	Disbanded but re-formed 1858 as Lancers	Queen's Royal Lancers
1689	6th	Conyngham's	Conyngham's Dragoons / Black Dragoons / 6th (Inniskilling) Dragoons	6th	(Inniskilling) Dragoons	Royal Dragoon Guards
1690	7th	Cunningham's	Disbanded 1714, re-formed 1715 / Princess of Wales's Own Royal Dragoons / 7th Queen's Own Dragoons / Queen's Own Light Dragoons / (Queen's Own) Hussars	7th	(Queen's Own) Hussars	Queen's Royal Hussars
1693	8th	Conyngham's	8th Dragoons / 8th King's Royal Irish Light Dragoons	8th	King's Royal Irish Light Dragoons	Queen's Royal Hussars
1715	9th	Wynne's	9th Dragoons / 9th Light Dragoons	9th	Light Dragoons	9th/12th Royal Lancers
1715	10th	Gore's	10th Dragoons / Prince of Wales's Own Light Dragoons / Prince of Wales's Own Hussars	10th	Prince of Wales's Own Royal Hussars	King's Royal Hussars
1715	11th	Honeywood's	11th Dragoons / 11th Light Dragoons	11th	Light Dragoons	King's Royal Hussars
1715	12th	Bowle's	12th Dragoons / 12th (Prince of Wales's) Light Dragoons	12th	(Prince of Wales's) Light Dragoons	9th/12th Royal Lancers

1715	13th	Munden's	13th Dragoons / 13th Light Dragoons	13th	Light Dragoons	Light Dragoons
1715	14th	Dormer's	14th Dragoons / 14th Light Dragoons / Duchess of York's Own Light Dragoons	14th	Duchess of York's Own Light Dragoons	King's Royal Hussars
1745		Kingston's	Disbanded 1746, re-formed as Light Horse or Cumberland's Dragoons, disbanded 1748		Disbanded	Disbanded
1759	15th	Light Dragoons	Elliot's Light Horse / 1st (King's Royal) Light Dragoons / 15th (King's) Light Dragoons / 15th (King's) Light Dragoons Hussars 1807	15th	King's Hussars	Light Dragoons
1759	16th	Light Dragoons	Burgoyne's Light Horse / 2nd Queen's Regiment of Light Dragoons /16th Queen's Light Dragoons	16th	Queen's Light Dragoons	Queen's Royal Lancers
1759	17th	Edinburgh's	Disbanded 1763		Disbanded	Disbanded
1759	18th	Hale's	Renumbered 17th 1763 / 3rd Light Dragoons / 17th Light Dragoons	17th	Light Dragoons	Queen's Royal Lancers
1759	19th	Light Horse	Drogheda's Light Horse / Renumbered 18th Light Horse 1763 / 4th Light Dragoons / 18th Hussars		18th King's Irish Hussars later disbanded 1821	Traditions with Light Dragoons
1760	20th	Light Dragoons (Inniskilling)	Raised three times and disbanded three times		20th Light Dragoons later disbanded 1819	Traditions with King's Royal Hussars
1760	21st	Granby's	Raised three times and disbanded three times		21st Light Dragoons later disbanded 1819	Traditions with Queen's Royal Lancers
1779	22nd	Light Dragoons	Disbanded, re-formed 1794		22nd disbanded 1802	Disbanded
1781	23rd	Light Dragoons	Renumbered 19th Light Dragoons 1786		19th Light Dragoons later disbanded 1821	Traditions with Light Dragoons
1794	23rd	Light Dragoons			23rd disbanded 1802	Disbanded
1794	24th	Light Dragoons			24th disbanded 1802	Disbanded
1794	25th	Light Dragoons	Renumbered 22nd Light Dragoons 1802, disbanded 1821		22nd Light Dragoons	Disbanded
1794	26th	Light Dragoons	Renumbered 23rd Light Dragoons 1802, disbanded 1819		23rd Light Dragoons	Disbanded
1794	27th	Light Dragoons	Renumbered 24th Light Dragoons 1802, disbanded 1819		24th Light Dragoons	Disbanded

1794	28th	Light Dragoons	Disbanded 1802		Disbanded	Disbanded
1794	29th	Light Dragoons	Renumbered 25th Light Dragoons 1802, disbanded 1818		25th Light Dragoons	Disbanded
1794	30th	Light Dragoons	Disbanded 1795		Disbanded	Disbanded
1794	31st	Light Dragoons	Disbanded 1795		Disbanded	Disbanded
1794	32nd	Light Dragoons	Disbanded 1795		Disbanded	Disbanded
1794	33rd	Light Dragoons	Disbanded 1795		Disbanded	Disbanded
1858	18th	Hussars		18th		Light Dragoons
1862	19th	Hussars	Formally 1st Bengal European Light Cavalry	19th		Light Dragoons
1862	20th	Hussars	Formally 2nd Bengal European Light Cavalry	20th		King's Royal Hussars
1862	21st	Hussars	Formally 3rd Bengal European Light Cavalry	21st		Queen's Royal Lancers

Appendix One

Stewardship of the British Army

1483 Office of Master General of Ordnance introduced and responsible for gunners and engineers and for all army equipment and stores, muskets ammunition, cannon etc. Supplying the army in the field would be the responsibility of the Treasury with its commissariat (civilian) departments for rations and transport.

1660 First Secretary at War appointed, Sir William Clarke, who coordinated the various bodies involved in military action.

1660 First Commander-in-Chief appointed. General Monck (later Duke of Albemarle). Titles would vary from Captain General, Generalissimo, General-on-Staff, Field Marshal on the Staff and Commander-in-Chief. Commander-in-Chief commanded troops in Britain but not overseas.

1661 Militia Act – To govern the Militia, as no standing army was supposed to exist.

1661 Articles of War introduced formally by an Act of Parliament.

1662 2nd Militia Act – Authority to the King. Only the King could make war but Parliament maintained the right to control the size and funds of the army during peacetime.

1688 Two Secretaries of State known as 'Their Majesties Principle Secretaries of State for Foreign Affairs' with two departments: Northern Department, dealing with continental powers, and the Southern Department, dealing with the Mediterranean, Ireland, domestic matters, the army and colonies (except America).

1689 Mutiny Act – To govern the discipline of the army in time of peace. Existing Articles of War established Military Law during wartime. It was renewed annually but it excluded the Militia.

1718 Articles of War applied to peacetime.

1741 Royal Military Academy at Woolwich introduced. Formal education for officer cadets of the Royal Artillery and Royal Engineers.

1743 Royal Warrant – Specified only two Colours for each regiment, the Sovereign's Colour and the Regimental Colour.

1747 Royal Warrant – Clothing regulations introduced. Regiments identified in order of precedence with uniform standardised except for facings. Colonel's name eliminated and regimental number introduced.

1751 Royal Warrant – No colonel to have crests or badges on uniform. Recognised badges established for stated regiments.

1755 New Horse Guards building in Whitehall for the Commander-in-Chief.

1756 Mutiny Act to include Militia.

1757 Militia Act defines who is called up.

1782 Territorial titles introduced to those regiments without them.

1782 Northern Department became the Foreign Office. Southern Department became the Home Office controlling Irish and colonial affairs, and Militia.

1792 *The Rules and Regulations for the Movement of His Majesty's Infantry* booklet issued.

1794 War Department created with Secretary of State for War with Cabinet rank, responsible for military policy, granting of commissions, the gazetting of promotions, the allotment and movement of troops on colonial and foreign service, and the general conduct of warlike operations. The Secretary of State at War position still existed; he coordinated the various bodies in time of conflict.

Secretary of State for War
Treasury
- Finance
- Commissariat
- Purveyors Department

Admiralty
Board of Ordnance
- Royal Artillery
- Royal Engineers
- Weapons
- Ammunition
- Stores

Board of Clothing
Paymaster-General
Regimental Agents
Army Medical Department

1794 Act of Parliament authorises the formation of volunteer units.

1794 Militia and Yeomanry taken from Home Office.

1794 Transport and Commissariat transferred from Treasury to Secretary of State for War.

1794 Corps of Artillery Drivers formed.

1795 Commander-in-Chief responsible for the supervision and approval of promotion, discipline and appointments.

1800 Royal Military College founded. It would move to Sandhurst in 1812.

1801 Responsibility for colonial affairs moved from Home Office to the War Department. Minister changed to Secretary of State for War and the Colonies.

1803 The Article of War (and Mutiny Act) extended to include campaigns and active service.

1810 Staff Corps for cavalry raised (disbanded 1814).

1815 Staff Corps for cavalry re-formed, only to be disbanded in 1817.

1816 First campaign medal 'Waterloo Medal' issued to all ranks at Waterloo.

1837 King's Regulations issued.

1847 Limited Service Act – Instead of the previous enlistment of twenty-one years or life the soldier could serve for ten to twelve years with no pension or a further ten to twelve years with a pension.

1853 Corps of Instructors formed at Hythe, Kent. Now the Small Arms School Corps.

1854 The Royal Corps of Musketry Instruction raised in Hythe, Kent. It is now the School of Infantry.

1854 Title changed to Secretary of State for War (the Colonies now omitted) and the minister was responsible for both political and military control of the army. The old office of Master General of Ordnance with its Board of Ordnance was abolished. Its functions were divided between the War Department and Horse Guards (Whitehall headquarters for Commander-in-Chief).

1855 Office of Secretary of State at War merged with Secretary of State for War.

1856 Queen Victoria introduced the Victoria Cross 'For Valour'.

1857 The War Department was renamed the War Office.

1863 Secretary of State at War office abolished with duties going to Secretary of State for War.

1868 The appointment of the reforming Lord Edward Cardwell as Secretary of State for War.

1868 Flogging abolished in Britain but not overseas.

1869 Self-governing colonies were to raise and fund their own defence forces.

1870 War Office Act – The Commander-in-Chief and all his various departments were brought under one roof as the War Office. It had three main offices:

Commander-in-Chief – responsible for the men.

Surveyor-General of Ordnance – responsible for materiel.

Financial Secretary – responsible for finance.

Commander-in-Chief would be principal military adviser to the Secretary for War.

1870 Army Enlistment Act – This was to solve the problem of a lack of reserve forces, which had caused problems during the Indian Mutiny and Crimean War. Men could sign up for a short service engagement for twelve years, six with the Colours and six on the reserve with paid training provided they served the Colours when required. Soldiers could still re-engage up to twenty-one years.

1871 The Regulation of the Forces Act – Single battalions to merge into two-battalion regiments based on defined regimental districts. The 1st Battalion would be for overseas duties, while the 2nd Battalion stayed at home, and the 3rd Battalion to be the Militia. Purchase of commissions was abolished and promotion was to be based on merit. The ranks of cornet (cavalry) and ensign (infantry) were replaced by the rank sub-lieutenant (second lieutenant in 1877). Flogging was abolished in the army except during wartime.

1879 Army Discipline and Regulation Act brought together the Mutiny Act and Articles of War, and introduced a Military Code.

1881 The Army Discipline and Regulation Act had been repealed but reintroduced as the foundation for Military Law.

1883 Commissariat, Ordnance and Pay Department now the responsibility of the Commander-in-Chief.

1887 Surveyor-General's Office abolished with the Commander-in-Chief responsible for clothing, food, equipment, pay, discipline and promotion.

1888 War Office split between a civil and military division, both under the Secretary of State.

1904 Esher Committee, with the following recommendations all accepted:

The establishment of an Army Council.
The abolition of the Office of Commander-in-Chief.
The appointment of a Chief of Staff.

1904 New Army Council arranged as follows:

Secretary of State for War
Chief of the General Staff
Adjutant-General
Quartermaster-General
Master-General of the Ordnance
Parliamentary Under-Secretary of State
Financial Secretary of the War Office
Secretary of the War Office

1906 Secretary of State Richard Haldane's reforms – An expeditionary force to be formed, the Militia to be formed into a special reserve, and the Territorial Force or Territorial Army formed from counties.

1909 Chief of the General Staff becomes Chief of the Imperial General Staff.

1915 The Machine Gun School opens.

1919 Small Arms School replaces Royal School of Musketry.

1923 Amalgamation of the Small Arms and Machine Gun School into a corps.

1929 Small Arms School Corps becomes the new title for training unit.

1947 The Royal Military Academy and Royal Military College amalgamate to become the Royal Military Academy Sandhurst.

1964 The three Service ministries of Army, Navy and Air Force are amalgamated into a single Ministry of Defence (MoD) under a Secretary of State for

Defence with a Chief of Defence Staff, alternating between the three services. There would be an Army Board within the Defence Council under the Chief of the Defence Staff. This replaced the Army Council. The professional head of the British Army is the Chief of the General Staff.

Example of Army Board:

The Secretary of State for Defence
Minister of State for the armed forces
Minister of State for Defence Equipment and Support
Parliamentary Under-Secretary of State for Defence and Minister for Veteran's Affairs
Chief of the General Staff
Second Permanent Under-Secretary of State
Assistant Chief of the Defence Staff
Adjutant-General
Quartermaster-General
Master-General of Ordnance
Commander-in-Chief (Land Command)

2007 Secretary of State for Defence combined with Secretary of State for Scotland. The National armed forces Memorial and Arboretum in Staffordshire was dedicated by Her Majesty Queen Elizabeth II on 12 October.

2009 27 June declared armed forces Day (last Saturday in June). The Elizabeth Cross is introduced. Awarded to next of kin of those who have died on operations or as the result of terrorism. Effective from 1 August and awarded retrospectively from the end of the Second World War. Secretary of State for Defence (no Secretary of State for Scotland).

2016 In July gender restrictions were lifted for front-line close-combat roles (engage with enemy) starting with Royal Armoured Corps in November and then followed by Infantry, Parachute Regiment, Royal Marines and some special forces by the end of 2018.

Appendix Two

Infantry Roles and Weapons

Infantry Roles

Pikemen and Musketeers

A seventeenth-century battalion consisted of a single headquarters company and twelve infantry companies totalling 500–800 men carrying a mixture of pikes and swords, or muskets and swords. The musket had a forked rest (abolished in 1665) and took so long to reload that the musketeers required pikemen to ward off cavalry and to provide a barrier behind which they could retire and reload at a rate of one round every two minutes. Pikemen wore armour and used a 16ft pike to protect the musketeers. When bayonets were introduced in 1673, the musketeers could defend themselves and pikes were phased out and eventually abolished in 1706, except for sergeants. The musketeer carried a heavy leather bandolier with twelve large wooden powder tubes known as the Twelve Apostles, together with his priming horn, flask, bullet bag and slow match.

Grenadiers and Fusiliers

Grenadiers were tall strong soldiers who threw grenades and reinforced the corners of squares. Grenadier companies carrying light muskets, swords, hatchets, a hammer, fuses, a cartouche box and three grenades (no pikes) were introduced in 1678 as an additional company and formed up on the wings. Grenadiers wore a more pointed hat without a brim known as a mitre with a distinctive grenade badge. The unreliable grenade using a slow match soon went out of fashion, but big grenadier companies continued. Grenadier (and light) companies were abolished in 1860 as their role became redundant.

An additional regiment 'Our Ordnance Regiment' also Our Royal Regiment of Fuziliers (later 7th Foot based at the Tower of London where the artillery was situated) was raised in 1685 as a military escort to the Train of Artillery. This was designated a

Fuzileer (now Fusilier) regiment and carried a fusil, a shorter version of the flintlock which was replacing the matchlock. It was considered hazardous for soldiers guarding ammunition trains with barrels of gunpowder and artillery to be using a burning slow match and the new fusil (short musket) with a flint was used by the fusiliers. Grenadiers were soon to be issued with a fusil.

The second early fusilier regiment was the Scots Fusiliers Regiment of Foot (21st Foot) which came onto the English establishment in 1686 having been raised in 1678. With the introduction of the flintlock the title of fusilier became honorary. The Scots Guards became the Scots Fusilier Guards in 1831.

Light Infantrymen

In 1739 the first regiment raised in the north of Scotland was to police the highlands. Previous Scottish regiments were from the lowlands. This highland regiment was so successful that it became the 42nd Royal Highland Regiment (Black Watch), and had more freedom of movement than standard infantry formations. A regiment of light infantry was raised for the Jacobite Rebellion of 1745 but soon disbanded. The Seven Years' War saw the first light troops, with the Highland regiments of the 87th and 88th Foot raised for that purpose. Britain's German allies had Jägers (huntsmen) who were effectively light infantry.

During the French and Indian War Major Rogers raised his irregular Rogers's Rangers. In 1758 all regiments were to have a light company, but the idea did not catch on and both regiments and light companies were disbanded in 1763. In North America the terrain was most suitable for the light infantry concept of concealment and observation. The 77th and 78th Highlanders served as light troops in America, and the Hanoverians brought their light troops, the Jägers, with their hunting horns.

In 1770 light companies were reintroduced into each battalion as the 10th Company and were even banded into whole battalions with great success. The light company soldiers were smaller in stature compared to grenadiers, fitter, more mobile and agile. The bugle horn became the symbol of light infantry and they carried lighter muskets such as the fusil.

After the loss of America, the light companies fell out of favour. It was the Napoleonic period that accelerated the move to light infantry; Bonaparte used his tirailleurs and voltigeurs as skirmishers to great effect. The first light regiment was the 90th (Perthshire Volunteers) – raised in 1794 – but it soon reverted to a standard role. In 1802 under Major General John Moore at Shorncliffe, the first two regiments converted to light infantry. The 43rd and 52nd Regiments were trained together with the 95th (Rifle Regiment) in specialist light-infantry skirmishing tactics such as concealment, fire and movement, and use of ground. Light troops would be used for reconnaissance and outpost duties and were to act as skirmishers to disrupt the main enemy attack and man outposts. If troops were seaborne then light troops would be the first to land.

In a battalion, the light company formed up on the left flank with the grenadier company on the right flank, hence flank companies. Between 1809 and 1815 the 51st, 68th, 71st, 85th and 90th Regiments converted to light infantry. Even the Royal Marines converted in 1855 to the Royal Marine Light Infantry in red jackets and Royal Marine Artillery in blue jackets, hence the reference to Red Marines and Blue Marines (they would revert to 'The Royal Marines' in 1923).

	Left Flank	**Middle**	**Right Flank**
British Line Infantry	Light	Battalion	Grenadiers
British Light Infantry	Light	Light	Light
French Line Infantry	Voltigeurs	Fusiliers	Grenadiers
French Light Infantry	Voltigeurs	Chasseurs	Carabiniers

Napoleon's Old Guard at Waterloo had their light element – the 1st and 2nd Regiment of Chasseurs of the Imperial Guard. The Middle Guard had the 3rd and 4th Regiment of Chasseurs. The apprentice Young Guard were split into the 1st and 2nd Regiment of Tirailleurs – previously known as Tirailleur-Grenadiers – and were tall soldiers. The second half of the Young Guard destined to be Chasseurs, were the 1st and 2nd Regiments of Voltigeurs who were originally Tirailleur-Chasseurs. In 1860, light infantry companies and dress were abolished as the role became redundant, but the light infantry battalions continued the tradition. Some light infantry regiments even adopted a quicker marching pace of 140 paces per minute compared with the traditional 120 paces per minute.

Riflemen

The colonists in America had impressed the British with their use of the rifle, and the 60th (Royal American) Regiment recruited the 5th Battalion in 1797 for service in America. This battalion came from Germany and was the first British Army regiment using German and American rifles; the men were dressed in green jackets. The British Commander-in-Chief decided that a rifle battalion for home use could be raised for selected troops with specialist training and that a suitable rifle had to be found. The Baker Rifle was chosen.

An Experimental Rifle Corps was formed at Horsham in 1800. Manningham's Rifles became the 95th Rifles. Crack shots were soon trained. The 95th became an elite regiment and expanded into three battalions by 1809. The Baker rifle was also used by the two light battalions of the King's German Legion at Waterloo and all the rifle regiments had the advantage over the French. The rifle was also used by the Jäger battalions in the Hanoverian and Netherlands armies in Wellington's order of battle.

The Riflemen wore green that looked black at a distance. The 95th wore white piping and the 60th Rifles wore red piping.

The rifleman in Wellingtons army in both the Peninsula and Waterloo, had a formidable reputation, which was acknowledged by the French. Casualties amongst French officers and senior NCO's were so high in conflicts as warrant investigation at a very high level. A report testifies, from no less than Marshal Soult CIC in Spain to the Minister of War:

> *St Jean de Luz 1 September 1813*
> The loss in prominent and superior officers sustained for some time past by the army is so disproportionate to that of the rank and file that I have been at pains to discover the reason and acquired the following information which of course explains the cause of so extraordinary a circumstance
>
> There is in the English Army a battalion of the 60th consisting of ten companies- the regiment is composed of six battalions ... It is armed with a short rifle, the men are selected for their marksmanship, they perform their duties of scouts and in action are expressly ordered to pick off the officers, especially Field or General Officers.
>
> Thus it has been observed that whenever a superior officer goes to the front in an action ... he is usually shot. This mode of making war and injuring the enemy is very detrimental to us.

Colonel Dumas on Soult's Staff claimed, in support of this that 'Les Riflemen' killed all 500 officers and eight generals between 25 July and 31 August 1813. This report of Marshal Soult refers to the 5th/60th Regiment, but this reputation applied to all riflemen including the 95th Rifles and the King's German Legion light battalions, who were all armed with the Baker Rifle.

Infantry Weapons

Shoulder-held firearms originated in China and Japan, but it was the Europeans in the sixteenth century that developed further the matchlock musket, a gunlock in which powder was ignited by a match. Improvements in metal technology reduced the weight from the original 16½lb and 8 balls to the pound.

The Matchlock Musket

The muskets carried by the musketeers were matchlocks and required a continuous burning slow match, normally wrapped around the priming flask or sometimes the hat or waist. The slow match was a cord soaked in saltpetre and dried. The early matchlocks were heavy and required a fork rest. The cumbersome bandolier with twelve wooden powder tubes was replaced in 1685 by a shoulder belt carrying the cartouche box containing the paper cartridge and ball. The musket issued in 1660 weighed 13½lb with a 42in barrel and fired one shot in two minutes; in 1673 it was fitted with a 12in bayonet which screwed into the barrel. This was replaced by the ring bayonet in 1689.

The Flintlock Musket

Flintlocks were introduced in 1725 at the same time as the steel ramrod, with the Brown Bess (named after the brown stock) having a bore of 0.75in with 14½ balls to the pound. The French ball was twenty to the pound with a bore of 0.69in and in an emergency the British could use French ammunition. The French musket was lighter but the British ball caused more damage. The musket barrel was 46in long when developed, reducing to 39in with a 17in bayonet in 1803. The long bayonet was to fend off cavalry when in square. A square bristling with bayonets and standing firm under the most severe cavalry attack would always carry the day, as the horses would not charge a hedge of steel.

The spark generated by a flint eliminated the tedious slow match process and naturally improved the rate of fire, making volleys possible, at the time a remarkable advance in technology. A round was a charge of gunpowder and a lead ball wrapped in cartridge paper. The gunpowder consisted of saltpetre (potassium nitrate), charcoal and sulphur.

On loading, the cartridge paper was torn or bitten, with a dash of powder poured into the firing pan. The remainder of the powder was poured down the barrel. The cartridge paper was folded or crushed and followed the powder. The ball was dropped into the barrel and then the ramrod pushed ball and paper far down to the firing pan. When cocked the hammer holding the wedge of flint was compressed. When the trigger was pulled the flint held by the hammer struck against the pan lid flicking it open and the spark generated ignited the powder in the pan. This flash passed through the touch hole into the barrel to ignite the main charge.

After ten rounds everything was fouled up and the soldier used a pricker to keep the touch hole clean. The flint had to be constantly adjusted and after thirty to forty rounds had to be replaced. The misfire rate under dry conditions was two in thirteen. A misfire was when the flash in the pan occurred without the main charge exploding and no ball was fired, hence the expression 'flash in the pan'. Flintlocks could not fire in damp conditions.

Light Infantry Fusil

These had a 42in barrel with a 0.66in bore.

Rifles

The sporting rifles used by colonists in America had impressed military thinking and it was decided that there was a place for rifles in the hands of specially trained troops. In 1800 forty different types of rifles were assessed and tested at Woolwich, including models from British, German and American manufacturers. The most suitable was the rifle made by Ezekiel Baker of London. Selected men from a number of regiments were sent to Horsham under Colonel Stuart and Lieutenant Colonel Manningham for training with the new rifle. An Experimental Corps of Riflemen was established in 1800 which in 1802 entered the list as the 95th (Rifle Regiment).

The accuracy of the rifle, due to the rifling in its barrel, was such that at 300yd a man-size target could be hit practically with every shot by a marksman. Indeed, such was the confidence in the accuracy of the Baker rifle that Major Hamlet Wade and Rifleman Spurrey of the 95th used to hold targets for each other at 300yd. This was quite a startling improvement on the musket which could not hit a target with any consistency at 80yd. Napoleon had so much trouble with rifles that he banned them in 1807 but the British persevered with their development.

1800 Baker Rifle

The Baker rifle was a muzzle loader with a bore of 0.625in, weighted 9lb, and was accurate up to 200yd and for a marksman up to 300yd. The barrel was 30in long with a 23in bayonet in order to make the same reach as a musket during defence in squares against cavalry. The seven riflings had half a turn over the barrel length. The initial bayonet was triangular but soon changed to a more useful sword-shape bayonet. Ramming the ball down the muzzle meant a slow rate of fire at one round a minute or two at best. It had the same firing method and was loaded in a similar manner to a musket with the same rate of misfires. The rifle was primed with fine gunpowder carried in the rifleman's powder horn. This was an improvement on the musket, which was primed with powder from the main charge.

1837 Brunswick Rifle – Percussion Cap Replaces Flint

It weighed 9lb 6oz, with a bore of 0.704in, and had a barrel length of 30in with a 22in sword bayonet. A misfire with a flint – especially in damp or wet weather – was a serious handicap for muskets and rifles. It was known that certain forms of explosion could be detonated by a very sharp blow. The Reverend A. Forsyth, a keen wildfowler, devised a compound of fulminate of mercury and chloride of potash, which, when enclosed in a metal tube with a protruding pin could be detonated with a sharp blow of a hammer. The Master of Ordnance took an interest and after some political delays, Forsyth took out a patent for the percussion cap for sportsmen in 1834. The Ordnance Board did trials and found the percussion cap to be twenty-four times more efficient than a flint. Misfires were practically eliminated. The Duke of Wellington took an interest and then all ranks were issued with the Brunswick rifle, which was still muzzle-loaded, in 1837. The percussion cap was inserted against a nipple and when the trigger was pressed a hammer hit the percussion cap against the nipple which caused a small explosion with the flame passing through a hole, to ignite the main charge.

1851 Minié Rifle – Bullet Replaces Ball

The Minié weighed 10lb, had a barrel length of 39in and a 17in socket bayonet. The Frenchman Captain Delvigne developed the conical bullet and Captain Minié of the French School of Musketry developed it further. The shaped bullet still had to be rammed down the rifled barrel with a ramrod, and was made out of soft lead with four greased grooves to assist ramming. The base was hollow and an iron plug or ball was used, which drove forward and splayed out the lead to complete the seal. Later the ball was omitted as gas pressure was sufficient to make the seal. The grooves were reduced to three. The tight fit provided spin with the rifling and made the rifle more accurate and faster loading than previous models. The bore was 0.702in.

At the time of introduction France and Britain were allies, and the Minié rifle was issued to the British in 1851 and was used by both the British and French armies in the Crimean War. The percussion cap was still used and the rifle was considered short-term as a committee was set up to find an effective (British) replacement. It was accurate up to 500yd. It was not generally issued, and soon replaced.

1853 Enfield Rifle

This was 8lb 14oz in weight, with a barrel length of 39in and a 17in socket bayonet. The Enfield was also a muzzle loader and used a greased Minié bullet inside a waxed cartridge, the ammunition that sparked the Indian Mutiny. It had a bore of 0.577in and the rate of fire improved to two rounds a minute. It was used in the Crimean War when available. The Union Army bought nearly half a million Enfields during the American Civil War.

1866 Snider Rifle – Single Shot, Breech Loader

This was 9lb 5oz, with a barrel length of 39in and a 17in socket bayonet. The Snider was the first single shot breech-loaded rifle and the rate of fire rose to ten rounds a minute. It had a bore of 0.577in and used brass cartridges with percussion caps, bullet and propellant all in one. The brass cartridge expanded on firing and effectively sealed the breech.

1874 Martini Henry Rifle – Last of the Black Powder

This was 8lb 10 oz, with a barrel length of 33in and a 22in sword or socket bayonet. Issued in 1874, the Martini Henry Rifle had a bore of 0.45in and was the last of the black powder charge weapons. Henry Peabody of the US invented the action and Friedrich von Martini – a Swiss gunsmith – modified it. Alexander Henry from Britain designed the rifling. The rifle was used during the Zulu Wars. Rate of fire was twelve rounds a minute.

1888 Lee–Metford Rifle – Smokeless, Bolt Action With Magazine

This was 9lb 8oz, with a barrel length of 30in and a 12in sword bayonet. It was the first bolt action rifle. The Mark I issued in 1888 had a 0.303in bore and an eight-round magazine. The Mark II issued in 1892 had a ten-round magazine. It was the first rifle with smokeless propellant based upon cordite, a British development by Sir Frederick Abel and Sir John Dewar from nitro glycerine, gun cotton and vaseline. Gun cotton was a previous development discovered by the German scientist Schönbein in 1845, cotton soaked in nitrocellulose, and was used by the artillery but was considered unsafe and unstable.

The Italian chemist Sobrero discovered the high explosive nitro glycerine, a mixture of glycerine, nitric and sulphuric acids in 1847. This liquid was extremely unstable and the Nobel family, who manufactured explosives, endeavoured to find ways of stabilising it. Alfred Nobel found that by mixing nitro glycerine with kieselghur the material was relatively stable and his dynamite, invented in 1869, made Nobel a household name. The world's first smokeless rifle introduced in 1886 was the French Lebel, which used Poudre B based upon Nobel's developments with nitro glycerine. The Lee–Metford was also the first magazine rifle used by the British Army and was used by Wolseley and Kitchener in Egypt. Rate of fire was twelve rounds a minute.

1895 Lee–Enfield Rifle

9lb 4oz, 30in barrel with a 12in sword bayonet, the Lee–Enfield used a 0.303in round with a ten-round magazine. The rifle was in use during the Boer War and was the same as the Lee–Metford except the barrel had two riflings. Rate of fire was twelve rounds a minute.

1904 SMLE (Short Magazine) Lee–Enfield Rifle Mk 1 – Magazine-loading Charger

8lb 10oz in weight, with a 25.2in barrel and a 17in sword bayonet, the SMLE used a 0.303inch round, with a ten-round magazine and five-round charger. Rate of fire was fifteen rounds a minute.

1939 Lee–Enfield No. 4 Rifle

This was 9lb 1oz in weight, with a 25.2in barrel and an 8in spike (later short sword). It used a 0.303in round and a ten-round magazine. Rate of fire was fifteen rounds a minute. It was the last of the bolt action rifles. First issued in 1939, it was not officially adopted until 1941.

1954 SLR Belgian F.N. – Self-loading Rifle

9.2lb, a 21in barrel and with a short sword bayonet, it was the first automatic gas-operated self-loading rifle. It used a 7.62mm x 51mm rimless round with a twenty-round magazine. Rate of fire was thirty to forty rounds per minute but twenty was practical with controlled aiming. The original development of the rifle was done in Belgium by the Fabrique Nationale (FN) Fusil Automatique Leger, or FAL. The British-made SLR was adapted to fire single shots only.

1980 SA80 Rifle (Small Arms 1980) – Fully Automatic

11lb, 20.4in barrel with a short sword bayonet, this combat rifle came with sights as standard. It used gas-operated self-loading 5.56mm x 45mm rounds with a thirty-round magazine. With the change to a smaller round the weapon could be set to automatic when the recoil was bearable, or self-loading single rounds. A SUSAT (Sight Unit Small Arms Trilux) with a 4x magnification was fitted as standard for the infantry. Reports of its unreliability, especially using continuous fire, led to the SA80 being modified in 2002. The bayonet and scabbard assembly was novel, consisting of a bayonet (doubling as a combat knife), wire cutter (with scabbard), saw blade, bottle opener and sharpening stone. Rate of fire 650–800 rounds a minute cyclic.

Machine Guns

Development

The Gatling gun was developed in 1862, and was four to ten rotating barrels turning a handle, seeing service during the American Civil War. Gatlings manned by sailors were used in the Zulu Wars and Egypt. The British Army took an interest in the Nordenfeldt in 1873 which had four barrels rotating and was fed with a hopper. This was the first true machine gun.

Maxim Gun

The real breakthrough in development came when Maxim (an American turned Briton) invented the mechanism whereby the gasses from the explosive were used to reload the next round. He invented the first water-cooled gas-operated automatic single-barrel machine gun in 1883 and used a 250-round belt. The British did trials using the rifle 0.303 round. This development eliminated the rotation of barrels. Every cavalry and infantry regiment had two Maxim guns by 1914.

Lewis Gun

This was the British Army's first section light machine gun (LMG). It weighed 26lb and was invented by American Colonel Isaac Newton Lewis. Using a 0.303 round it had a distinctive circular magazine that contained forty-seven rounds and was in service 1914–37. It was fitted with a bipod.

Vickers Machine Gun

The platoon/troop's first heavy machine gun was water-cooled, firing a 0.303in round. It entered service in 1915 and stayed for fifty years as a reliable platoon/troop heavy weapon. It was fitted with a tripod and a 250-round belt fed from an ammunition box.

Bren Gun

Weighting 24lb, it was taken from the Brno (Czechoslovakia) and Enfield development. Section LMG from 1937 firing a 0.303in round from a thirty-round magazine. Fitted with a bipod, it became famous for its reliability during the Second World War and the Korean War. Spare barrels were on hand to change when the barrel got too hot.

The Bren eventually changed to a rimless round and in its final years converted to the 7.62mm x 51mm round. Just as the RAF have a special affection for the Spitfire, so the infantryman has a similar attachment to the Bren gun.

General Purpose Machine Gun

The GPMG was developed in the 1960s for two roles: as a section light machine gun with a bipod, and with a tripod for the sustained fire role as a support weapon in the heavy weapons troop/platoon of a battalion. It fired a 7.62mm x 51mm rimless round in a 50–100-round metal-linked belt. Barrels had to be changed when hot. The gun weighed 31lb and the tripod 30lb. The GPMG can be fitted with the SUSAT sight.

Appendix Three

Regimental Identification

Badges, Buttons, Plates and Buckles

In 1751 when George II issued his third warrant to control crests and devices, standardisation within the army occurred except for the seven Royal and 'Six Old Corps' regiments that were allowed to use ancient badges. Later, regiments were given the opportunity to use an identifying emblem or device to commemorate a special event. Name, number and event were placed on badges, buttons, plates and buckles including headdress. In the early eighteenth century these distinctions were embroidered onto the mitre caps of grenadiers.

Near the end of the century metal plates were introduced, first with the regimental number only but they soon became more detailed. The style of headdress denoted size of badge or plate. The stovepipe shako had a large oblong die-stamped metal plate with regimental number. The 1812 model shako had a smaller oval shaped plate with GR inscribed. The smaller 1815 shako had a badge in place of the plate. The badge consisted of a circular dome with the regimental number below a small crown and regimental button. A black leather Hanoverian cockade surmounted the badge, finished off with a plume.

With the bell-topped shako of 1829, a large star pattern badge with a crown was introduced. The smaller 1855 shako required a smaller badge. The introduction of the blue-covered helmet saw the return of the star-shaped badge. In the twentieth century the conventional cap badges we see today were introduced, in brass but with officers's badges in white metal or gilt. White metal was also used for the Scottish badges. Some badges were made from two metals, for example with the scroll in white metal and the emblem in brass. Officers's badges sometimes differ from the men's, for example the Royal Crest (crown and lion) on a Royal Marines officer's cap badge is separate from the main badge, it is in two parts. Officers's cap badges were different for the Coldstream Guards, the Scots Guards, the Royal Hampshire, and the Royal Berkshire Regiments.

When regiments were numbered, a regimental number plate which measured about 2½in x 3½in was attached to the white diagonal shoulder belt. Cross straps disappeared in about 1850 with the introduction of the belt and bayonet frog, but a single shoulder belt or strap with the regimental number continued to carry the ammunition pouch. During Wellington's time the standard redcoat had eighteen large buttons and twelve to fourteen small buttons. The Rifle Corps had twenty-two white metal buttons in three rows. Brass regimental collar badges were introduced in 1874. In some badges the King's crown and Queen's crown differ. At the current time badges are plastic, gold stay-bright or bronze.

Facings and Lace

Even in Cromwell's time, regiments were identified by different lace. Lapels were turned back showing a facing in 1720. The facings were the visible lining at lapels and cuffs and later turnbacks (at coat tails). They were coloured according to regiment and in 1727 the facing Colours were fixed and required a Royal assent to change them. The regulation facing Colours were a Royal regiment blue, English and Welsh white, Scottish yellow and Irish green and were standardised in 1881, although many regiments ignored the command. The 3rd Foot had had buff facing since it was formed and would continue to do so, even changing its name to 'the Buffs' in 1751. The 31st Foot also had buff facings and were incorrectly addressed as the 'old buffs' by George II at Dettingen. When the error was pointed out to him, he corrected himself and called them the 'young buffs'.

In addition to the regulation facing Colours of blue, white, yellow and green, other Colours were used including buff, red, orange, black and purple. The Clothing Warrant of 1751 identified the regiment's facings as follows for regiments up to the 49th Foot:

Blue	1st, 4th, 7th, 8th, 18th, 21st, 23rd and 41st
Buff	3rd, 14th, 27th, 31st, 40th, 42nd and 48th
Pale Buff	22nd
White	32nd, 43rd, 47th and 59th
Greyish White	17th
Yellow	9th, 12th, 15th, 16th, 29th, 37th, 38th, 44th and 46th
Deep Yellow	6th and 25th
Bright Yellow	10th, 28th and 34th
Philemot Yellow	13th
Pale Yellow	20th, 26th and 30th
Green	39th
Sea Green	2nd
Goslin Green	5th
Full Green	11th and 49th
Yellowish Green	19th
Willow Green	24th

Grass Green	36th
Deep Green	45th
Red	33rd and 41st
Orange	35th

The 1802 Clothing Warrant indicated two changes: the 41st Foot changed from blue to red and the 59th changed from purple to white with the following additional regiments's facings up to the 96th Foot (Lawson, Vol. 2, p.102; Barthorp, p.144):

Blue	60th
Buff	52nd, 61st, 71st, 78th, 81st and 96th
Deep Buff	90th
Yellow Buff	62nd
White	65th and 74th
Popinjay Grey	54th
Yellow	57th, 77th, 80th, 85th, 86th, 91st, 92nd and 93rd
Deep Yellow	72nd and 75th
Pale Yellow	67th, 82nd, 83rd, 84th and 88th
Green	87th and 94th
Dark Green	55th, 73rd and 79th
Yellowish Green	66th
Willow Green	69th
Deep Green	51st, 63rd and 68th
Red	53rd and 76th
Purple	56th
Black	50th, 58th, 64th, 70th, 89th and 95th

Regimental lace that reinforced the button holes was as old as the redcoat. Jackets would have the buttons single, or in pairs. The white regimental lace also appeared on cuffs, pockets and turn backs. The lace itself could be plain or have a distinguishing line or lines. The colour of the line, number of lines, straight or worm and which way round would all be specified for each regiment with the Clothing Regulations and suppliers. Lines in the regimental lace could be down the centre, to one side or both sides. For example, the Foot Guards, 1st, 5th and 33rd Foot had plain lace and the lace of the 27th (Inniskillings) had a blue and red stripe.

The lace around the button holes came in a variety of shapes. Straight or square edged, pointed and bastion, which resembled an arrowhead. The bastion pattern came in two styles referred to as Jew's Harp and Flowerpot, the Jew's Harp being the more open design. A basic jacket in Wellington's army would have ten rows of buttonholes in singles or in pairs. If the style was a simple square-edged or pointed regimental lace, then the full ten rows would be completed by the tailor. However, where regiments had the bastion design, the extra space taken up reduced the number of rows to nine for single button holes and only eight for double button holes. If the soldier was very big or very small then this rule would be broken. By 1836 regimental lace went out and plain lace continued. With the new tunic uniform of 1855 the lace was eliminated except for cuffs. The newly formed two-battalion regiments with Territorial titles in 1881 were given the following national facings with regimental titles simplified (Barthorp, p.150):

Foot	**Regiment**	**Facing 1881**	**Corrected**
1st	Royal Scots (Lothian)	Blue	
2nd	Queen's (Royal West Surrey)	Blue	
3rd	Buffs (East Kent)	Buff	
4th	King's Own (Royal Lancaster)	Blue	
5th	Northumberland Fusiliers	White	1899 Gosling Green
6th	Royal Warwickshire	Blue	
7th	Royal Fusiliers	Blue	
8th	King's (Liverpool)	Blue	
9th	Norfolk	White	1925 Yellow
10th	Lincolnshire	White	
11th	Devonshire	White	1905 Green
12th	Suffolk	White	1899 Yellow
13th	Somerset Light Infantry	Blue	
14th	West Yorkshire	White	1900 Buff
15th	East Yorkshire	White	
16th	Bedfordshire	White	
17th	Leicestershire	White	1931 Pearl Grey
18th	Royal Irish	Blue	
19th	Yorkshire	White	1899 Grass Green
20th	Lancashire Fusiliers	White	
21st	Royal Scots Fusiliers	Blue	
22nd	Cheshire	White	1904 Buff
23rd	Royal Welsh Fusiliers	Blue	
24th	South Wales Borderers	White	1905 Green
25th	King's Own Borderers	Blue	
26th/90th	Cameronians (Scottish Rifles)	Green	
27th/108th	Royal Inniskilling Fusiliers	Blue	
28th/61st	Gloucestershire	White	
29th/36th	Worcestershire	White	1920 Green
30th/59th	East Lancashire	White	
31st/70th	East Surrey	White	
32nd/46th	Duke of Cornwall's Light Infantry	White	
33rd/76th	Duke of Wellington's (West Riding)	White	1905 Scarlet

34th/55th	Border	White	1913 Yellow
35th/107th	Royal Sussex	Blue	
37th/67th	Hampshire	White	1904 Yellow
38th/80th	South Staffordshire	White	1936 Yellow
39th/54th	Dorsetshire	White	1904 Grass Green
40th/82nd	South Lancashire	White	1934 Buff
41st/69th	Welsh	White	
42nd/73rd	Black Watch (Royal Highlanders)	Blue	
43rd/52nd	Oxfordshire Light Infantry	White	
44th/56th	Essex	White	1936 Purple
45th/95th	Sherwood Foresters (Derbyshire)	White	1913 Lincoln Green
47th/81st	Loyal North Lancashire	White	
48th/58th	Northamptonshire	White	1926 Buff
49th/66th	Berkshire	White	1885 Blue
50th/97th	Queen's Own (Royal West Kent)	Blue	
51st/105th	King's Own Yorkshire LI	Blue	
53rd/85th	King's Shropshire Light Infantry	Blue	
57th/77th	Middlesex	White	1902 Yellow
60th	King's Royal Rifle Corps	Scarlet	
62nd/99th	Duke of Edinburgh's (Wiltshire)	White	1905 Buff
63rd/96th	Manchester	White	1937 Dark Green
64th/98th	North Staffordshire	White	1937 Black
65th/84th	York and Lancaster	White	
68th/106th	Durham Light Infantry	White	1902 Dark Green
71st/74th	Highland Light Infantry	Yellow	
72nd/78th	Seaforth Highlanders	Yellow	
75th/92nd	Gordon Highlanders	Yellow	
79th	Queen's Own Cameron Highlanders	Blue	
83rd/86th	Royal Irish Rifles	Green	
87th/89th	Royal Irish Fusiliers	Blue	
88th/94th	Connaught Rangers	Green	
91st/93rd	Argyll & Sutherland Highlanders	Yellow	
100th/109th	Prince of Wales's Leinster	Blue	
101st/104th	Royal Munster Fusiliers	Blue	
102nd/103rd	Royal Dublin Fusiliers	Blue	
	Rifle Brigade	Black	

For complete information on uniforms, facings and lace of the British Army 1793–1815, see the incomparable *British Napoleonic Uniforms* by Carl Franklin.

Flashes, Slashes and Sashes

Officers wore a sash around their shoulder initially but changed the position to the waist in 1685. Sergeants wore the sash around their waist in 1745. The officers's sash returned to the shoulder and back to the waist, but was inside the coat in 1768. Sashes for officers and sergeants in 1868 returned to the shoulder, the left shoulder for officers and the right shoulder for sergeants. In the 1850s uniforms became more ornate, with round cuffs with a three-button slash, and slashes at the back of the tunic. These were abolished in 1868 when the cuffs were pointed in white lace. The Guards continue this day to have cuff slashes with buttons.

With Cardwell's amalgamations, regiments now had dedicated titles, and shoulder flashes were introduced with the new regiment's name. These were made of cloth, white on red and then brass in 1908 and cloth again from the Second World War onwards. Line regiments were white on red and Scottish regiments had regimental tartan.

King's Royal Rifle Corps	red on green
Rifle Brigade and Royal Ulster Rifles	black on green
Grenadier and Coldstream Guards	white on red
Scots Guards	yellow on blue
Irish Guards	white on green
Welsh Guards	white on black

Examples of post-war Colours:

Royal Norfolk	black on yellow
Royal Hampshire	yellow on black
South Staffordshire	yellow on maroon
Light Infantry	white/yellow on green
Royal Marines	red on blue

Headwear

From Cromwell's time, hats developed from the buff high crown flat rim through various stages of black felt short crown, and then laced edges with feathers. During Marlborough's time the headwear was a black broad rimmed hat with one or the other sides turned slightly and were soon hemmed with lace. Grenadiers wore a kind of bag which gradually progressed into a mitre hat worn with the front turned up with the Royal cipher.

By 1740, the hats were tricorn with enhanced turn ups. The mitre for grenadiers had the front and rear in the facing colour with the Royal cipher in 1747. The front flap was red with the white horse of Hanover and the motto *Nec Aspera Terrent* was embroidered around the red front flap. In 1751 the regimental number was put on the reverse side.

The end of the century saw a change to the bicorn hat. After 150 years the hat was replaced in 1800 by the lacquered stovepipe shako shape with a peak and the large brass plate. It was made out of felt in 1806. The 1812 pattern shako (as worn at Waterloo) with straight sides and raised front was significant in that all ranks wore them including the Guards regiments. Companies within a battalion were identified with a plume as follows: battalion company – white over red, grenadier – white, and light company – green. Light infantry continued to wear the tapered stovepipe shako and in 1814 had the bugle horn and regimental number on the front together with a central green plume.

The Prussian-styled shako of 1815 had two peaks, was shorter, but with a large crown of 9in diameter and two yellow bands surrounding the shako. The 1st Foot Guards took the title 'Grenadier' after Waterloo and wore a bearskin. A new shorter shako arrived in 1829 with an even bigger crown with an 11in diameter. This had a single peak which was drooped similar to the Guards's caps today. In 1831 the Scots Guards took the honorary title Scots Fusilier Guards and took to wearing a bearskin, as did the Coldstream Guards. In 1843 the Albert shako was introduced and used in the Crimea. The 1855 model arrived and was modified in 1861 and finally the short shako of 1869 was introduced.

The service helmet was used in India in 1860 and for foreign service in 1868. Influenced by Prussia's defeat of France, the helmet with pike appeared in 1878, blue for line infantry and dark green for light infantry. After the Boer War the slouch hat was common and in 1905 the brown peaked cap appeared and was used in the First World War. The Second World War khaki forage field service cap and the general service cap which resembled a tam o'shanter were replaced by the beret after the war. The beret was first used by the Royal Tank Corps in 1924 for its convenience and during the war by motorised rifle regiments. Both the Parachute Regiment with their maroon beret and Commandos with their green beret pioneered its usage. After the war, the blue beret became universal for the infantry, except the Guards (khaki), and the light infantry (dark or rifle green).

Scottish regiments had the Glengarry or tam o'shanter. The Irish regiments adopted the caubeen with a hackle in dark blue for the Royal Irish and Royal Inniskilling Fusiliers, with rifle green for the Royal Ulster Rifles. Fusilier regiments were allowed to wear hackles. Distinctions in headdresses with plumes or feathers were as follows (Barthorp, p.148):

Guards

Grenadier	white plume
Coldstream	red plume
Irish	blue plume
Welsh	white/green plume
Scots	no plume

Scottish Regiments

Royal Scots	blackcock feather
Royal Scots Fusiliers	white plume
King's Own Scottish Borderers	blackcock feather
Cameronians	black plume
Black Watch	scarlet plume
Highland Light Infantry	green black tuft
Seaforth Highlanders	white plume
Gordon Highlanders	white plume
Cameron Highlanders	white plume
Argyll & Sutherland Highlanders	white plume

Fusiliers

Royal Northumberland	scarlet over white
Royal	white
Lancashire	primrose yellow
Royal Scots	white
Royal Welsh	white
Royal Inniskilling	grey
Royal Irish	green
Royal Munster	white and green
Royal Dublin	blue and green

Rifle Regiments

Kings Royal Rifle Corps	scarlet over black
Royal Irish	black and green
Rifle Brigade	black

The current Royal Regiment of Fusiliers wears the red over white hackle, from the tradition of Royal Northumberland Fusiliers who took the white hackle from French dead at St Lucia in 1778. William IV allowed them to tip it with red to distinguish it.

Badges, Symbols and Weapons of Rank

Officers carried a half pike or spontoon (8ft officer's pike) in addition to their shoulder-hung swords, which transferred to the waist by the end of the seventeenth century. Grenadier officers carried fusils in 1768. Sergeants carried a halberd with an axe, which was abolished in 1792 and replaced by a 9ft pike, which was in turn abolished in 1830 and replaced with a fusil. Sergeants of line regiments lost their swords in 1850.

Officers were identified by a metal gorget around their neck that identified their rank (abolished in 1830) and in 1797 wore a right shoulder epaulette in gold or silver to denote rank. Grenadiers and light infantry had epaulettes on both shoulders and chevrons for rank were introduced in 1803, with corporals having two stripes, sergeants three, and four for sergeant majors and quartermaster sergeants. Wellington introduced the rank of colour sergeant in 1813 which was a single stripe on the right with crossed flags and a crown. By 1896 this had simplified to three stripes and a plain crown, which survives.

General Sam Browne introduced a leather belt with a shoulder attachment for supporting the sword or personal arms, and it became official wear in 1899. Officer rank on the collar changed to the shoulder in 1880 in the form of twisted cords with a combination of crowns and stars, then to the cuffs in 1905 with a combination of slashes. The rank badges were too conspicuous on the cuffs during war and moved to the shoulder, where they have remained. In combat dress rank is shown on a a vertical flap on the chest.

Uniforms – Infantry

Red has had a long tradition as the principal colour of the English infantry. Henry VII had red for his Yeoman of the Guard and Henry VIII at the Field of the Cloth of Gold had his army in red coats embroidered with the Tudor Rose. Cromwell's New Model Army had red coats with different lace and facings to distinguish regiments. At Cromwell's funeral in November 1658 all the soldiers were fitted out with new red coats.

Regiments were named after the colonel who raised them and paid them and were fitted out with uniforms that were generally red, a traditional colour more russet in the early days than the scarlet and red of Wellington's army. When the colonel changed so did the name of the regiment and its uniform. As early as 1708 Queen Anne laid down the scale of clothing as 'a full-bodied cloth coat, well lined, a waistcoat, a pair of kersey breeches, a pair of good strong stockings and shoes, two shirts and neck cloths and a hat well laced'. Red uniforms were generally standardised by 1727 except for the facings, with the officers's material of superior quality. Scarlet jackets replaced the red coat for officers in 1797 and for sergeants in 1802.

In 1742, the Clothing Regulation laid down 'A representation of clothing of His Majesty's Household and all forces upon the establishment of Great Britain and Ireland.' George II reinforced this by introducing two Royal Warrants on clothing regulations in 1747, and modified these in 1751 to lay down a regular uniform with regiments numbered according to seniority. These clothing regulations would be issued on a regular basis. When the 5th Battalion 60th Foot (later King's Own Rifle Corps) was raised in 1797 they wore green jackets with red facings with three rows of buttons. In 1820 this became the dress for the whole regiment, hence their nickname 'the Green Jackets'. The 95th (Rifles Regiment), which became the Rifle Brigade, also wore a uniform that was dark (rifle) green with black braid and three rows of buttons and they were also known as 'the Green Jackets'. It is no surprise that when the two regiments amalgamated with the Oxfordshire and Buckinghamshire Light Infantry in 1958 they became the three battalions of the Green Jackets.

With the accuracy of rifles improving, Harry Lumsden of the Queen's Own Corps of Guides introduced khaki-coloured uniforms in 1846. The dye was made from mulberry juice and the uniform was introduced for service on the Indo-Afghan border and for general service in India in 1881 and universally in 1896. The Urdu for mud is *khak*, hence khaki. In 1872 the rank and file tunic changed from red to scarlet as worn by officers and NCOs. The buttons on the tunic were in singles or in pairs. The Guards regiments were unique with the buttons arranged as follows: Grenadiers – singles, Coldstream – pairs, Scots – threes, Irish – fours, Welsh – fives. The red coat was last used at the Battle of Ginniss in 1885. The battledress introduced in 1938 was a universal uniform to be worn by line regiments, guards and Highlanderss.

Uniforms – Cavalry

The Royal Horse Guards wore a blue tunic with red facing, hence their nickname 'the Blues'. The Life Guards wore opposite Colours, a scarlet tunic with blue facings. Heavy cavalry regiments of horse wore red. The dragoons wore red coats (1685) and the 1st Dragoons wore a crimson coat. Cuirasses and back plates were worn by the regiments of horse until 1697/8 except for officers. The early uniforms for the cavalry and horse grenadiers attached were as follows:

Life Guards:

Regiment (1684)	**Coat**	**Lining**	**Facing**	
King's Troop	Scarlet	Blue	Blue	
Horse Grenadiers	Red	Blue	Blue	Blue Loops
Queen's Troop	Scarlet	Blue	Green	
Horse Grenadiers	Red	Blue	Green	Green Loops
Duke's Troop	Scarlet	Blue	Yellow	
Horse Grenadiers	Red	Blue	Yellow	Yellow Loops

Regiments of Horse and Dragoons, 1686:

Regiment	**Coat**	**Lining**
Royal Regiment of Horse	Blue	
Queen's	Red	Yellow
Peterborough's	Red	Red (buff 1694)
Plymouth's	Red	Green
Arran's	Red	White
Shrewsbury's	Red	Buff (White 1689)
Queen Dowager's	Red	Green

Dragoons:		
1st Dragoons	Red	Blue
2nd Dragoons	Grey	

The original uniform of the Scots Greys was grey, but the uniform changed to the family Colours of scarlet bordered by yellow with blue facing in 1687.

Regiments of Horse (later Dragoon Guard title) and Dragoons in 1745:

Regiment	**Coat**	**Facing**	**Waistcoat**
Royal Regiment of Horse Guards	Blue	Red	Red
2nd Horse (1st DG)	Red	Blue	Blue
3rd Horse (2nd DG)	Red	Buff	Buff
4th Horse (3rd DG)	Red	White	White
5th Horse (4th DG)	Red	Blue	Blue
6th Horse (5th DG)	Red	Green	Green
7th Horse (6th DG)	Red	Yellow	Yellow
8th Horse (7th DG)	Red	Black	Buff

The 5th Horse when it went onto the Irish Establishment as the 1st Horse was also known as the Blue Horse, due to its facing colour. The same applied to the 6th Horse (Green Horse) and 8th Horse (Black Horse).

Regiment	**Coat**	**Facing**	**Waistcoat**
1st Dragoons	Red	Blue	Blue
2nd Dragoons	Red	Blue	Blue
3rd Dragoons	Red	Light Blue	Light Blue
4th Dragoons	Red	Green	Green
5th Dragoons	Red	Blue	Blue
6th Dragoons	Red	Yellow	Yellow
7th Dragoons	Red	White	White
8th Dragoons	Red	Orange	Orange
9th Dragoons	Red	Buff	Buff
10th Dragoons	Red	Deep Yellow	Deep Yellow
11th Dragoons	Red	White	White
12th Dragoons	Red	White	White
13th Dragoons	Red	Green	White
14th Dragoons	Red	Pale Yellow	White

By the end of the seventeenth century the cavalry jackets changed from red to crimson or scarlet. The light dragoons in 1785 went from scarlet to blue with regimental facings. The hats of the Life Guards and Royal Horse Guards changed from the cocked hat to the Grecian helmet in 1812, with the flowing horsehair reduced to a tidy blue and red short wool crest in 1814, as they looked too much like the French. The Scots Greys wore their distinctive grenadier cap to celebrate their victory over the French infantry in 1706 capturing their Colours. Royal Regiments wore blue facings with gold lace such as the King's Dragoon Guards and Royals. The Inniskillings had yellow facings and silver lace.

Hussars wore a dolman jacket and a pelisse over jacket, with officers having white fur and men black. When the busbys were worn, they all had a red busby bag, except the 18th Hussars who had blue. The busby (kolbak) hats were soon replaced by shakos, which were more waterproof. The lancer cap was based on the Polish *Czapka* – a square like a mitre board. Dragoons had pointed cuffs and Dragoon Guards had square cuffs. All wore a waist sash. Hussars were barrelled with a vertical coloured stripe and the light dragoons a horizontal coloured stripe. Light dragoons wore a blue tunic with a plastron on the front in a facing colour with a bell-topped shako. Some examples are as follows:

Light Dragoon Regiment	Facing Colour	Officer Lace	Rank Lace
11th Light Dragoons	Buff	Silver	White
12th Light Dragoons	Yellow	Silver	White
13th Light Dragoons	Buff	Gold	Yellow
16th Light Dragoons	Scarlet	Silver	White

Appendix Four

Organisation, Rank and Insignia

Organisation

The basic infantry unit is a battalion, currently about 650 (historically 300–1,000) soldiers commanded by a lieutenant colonel with a major as second in command and captain as adjutant. The adjutant runs the Orderly Room for the battalion and relieves the CO of administrative work. Some regiments such as the Royal Irish Regiment have only one battalion and others such as the Royal Regiment of Scotland and the Rifles have five battalions.

The battalion is normally made up of five companies, subdivided into platoons or troops (Royal Marines) which are again subdivided into sections as follows:

Headquarters Company (HQ Company)
HQ Platoon
  Orderly Room Section
  Intelligence Section
  Provost Section
  Medical Section
Signals Platoon
Quartermasters Platoon – general stores, clothing, munitions, food
Motor Transport Platoon
Catering Platoon
Pay and Records Platoon

Fire Support Company (S Company)
Reconnaissance (Recce) Platoon
Mortar Platoon (Heavy Mortar, 81mm)
Anti-tank Platoon (Milan)
Heavy Weapons Platoon (General Purpose Machine Gun Platoon. GPMG in a sustained fire role mounted on a tripod)

Rifle Company A
No. 1 Platoon/Troop
No. 1 Section
No. 2 Section
No. 3 Section
No. 2 Platoon/Troop, as above
No. 3 Platoon/Troop, as above

Rifle Company B
No. 4 Platoon/Troop, as above
No. 5 Platoon/Troop, as above
No. 6 Platoon/Troop, as above

Rifle Company C
No. 7 Platoon/Troop, as above
No. 8 Platoon/Troop, as above
No. 9 Platoon/Troop, as above

A section consists of nine to ten men which includes a corporal in charge of the section light machine gun (GPMG with a light bipod). A sergeant commands the section.

A platoon has three sections and is commanded by a 2nd lieutenant/lieutenant, and has a Platoon Headquarters. Platoon HQ has a platoon sergeant as the deputy platoon commander, a radio operator, a troop anti-tank weapon, and a troop light 51mm mortar. A total of thirty-two to thirty-five men are in a platoon.

A company normally has five platoons and is commanded by a major or captain. The company sergeant major is responsible for quartermaster duties, supplying weapons and ammunition for each company. The quartermaster's duties relating to rations and general stores can be done by the staff sergeant.

A battalion is commanded by a lieutenant colonel, would normally have five companies and would also have an armourer, sniper, a physical training instructor (PTI), drill instructor (DI) and platoon weapons instructor (PWI) and cyber qualified (Ci). Attachments from the Logistics Corps would provide the catering and supply and service the transport with assault engineers attached to Support Troop or detached from the Royal Engineers. The Regimental Sergeant Major would be the senior Warrant Officer (Class 1) in the battalion, with the regimental quartermaster sergeant (RQMS) as senior Warrant Officer (Class 2) who would be responsible for the battalion stores and ammunition. A battalion would have the use of a chaplain or a honorary regimental chaplain. The Royal Signals would provide signal specialists with a rear link to brigade.

A brigade is commanded by a brigadier general. Operationally it comprises two or more battalions but usually three and supporting units such as artillery, numbering about 2,000–4,000 personnel.

A division is commanded by a major general. Operationally it comprises two or more brigades, but usually three plus supporting units – signals, engineers, medical, and cavalry – numbering 6,000–18,000 personnel.

A corps is commanded by a lieutenant general. Operationally it is comprised of two or more divisions but traditionally three, with supporting units numbering 16,000–70,000 personnel.

An army is commanded by a general. It consists of two or more corps but usually three, with supporting units numbering 40,000–230,000 personnel.

A cavalry regiment originally had ten troops, reduced to eight troops in 1815 with a further reduction in 1822 to six troops of sixty ranks. When squadrons were introduced in 1880 there were two troops to a squadron. The present organisation is five squadrons with a HQ Squadron, Command and Support Squadron and three or four fighting squadrons, A, B, C and D. Certainly four squadrons for a wartime establishment. Each squadron has three or four troops and each troop has three tanks or reconnaissance vehicles depending on the cavalry regiment's role. A squadron would be 100–150 men.

Rank and Insignia – Infantry

Non-commissioned Officers

Role	Rank	Insignia
Part Section	Lance-Corporal	One stripe
Part Section	Corporal	Two stripes
Section	Sergeant	Three stripes
Troop/Platoon	Sergeant	Three stripes
Senior/Company	Staff or Colour Sergeant	Three stripes and crown
Company Sergeant Major (CSM)	Warrant Officer Class 2	Crown
Regimental Quartermaster Sergeant (RQMS)	Warrant Officer Class 2	Crown in wreath
Regimental Sergeant Major (RSM)	Warrant Officer Class 1	Royal coat of arms (small)
Regimental Sergeant Major Household Division	Warrant Officer Class 1	Royal coat of arms (large)
Conductor Royal Logistics Corp		
Royal Artillery Warrant Officer (Master Gunner)		
Academy Sergeant Major, Sandhurst		

Garrison Sergeant Major (GSM) London District	Warrant Officer Class 1	Royal coat of arms (large)

Regimental Sergeant Majors of both Guards and Household Cavalry Regiments of the Household Division are permitted to wear a large Royal coat of arms as insignia. The Garrison Sergeant Major London District, traditionally a Guardsman, is the most senior Warrant Officer in the British Army, whose role since 1952 is wholly ceremonial with responsibilities for military state occasions:

Beating Retreat
Coronations
Garter Ceremony
Remembrance Day Parade Whitehall
Royal British Legion Festival of Remembrance
State Funeral
State Opening of Parliament
Trooping the Colour

For the Royal wedding of Prince William and Miss Catherine Middleton on 29 April 2011 the MoD announced that in recognition of the excellent work carried out by the GSM London District, Her Majesty the Queen had approved the revival of the ancient original insignia of sergeant majors appointed to the court of William IV – a Royal coat of arms over four chevrons.

Commissioned Officers

Unit	Rank	Insignia
Platoon	2nd Lieutenant	One pip
	Lieutenant	Two pips
Company	Captain	Three pips
	Major	One crown
Battalion	Lieutenant Colonel	Crown and one pip
Regiment	Colonel	Crown and two pips
Brigade	Brigadier General	Crown and three pips
Division	Major General	Pip, crossed sabre and scroll case
Corps	Lieutenant General	Crown, crossed sabre and scroll case
Army	Full General	Crown, pip, crossed sabre and scroll case
	Field Marshal	Crown, crossed sabre in a laurel wreath

British generals normally wear British insignia, except on international duty, such as NATO's International Security Assistance Force (ISAF) for peacekeeping, when they wear stars for international recognition, as in the US Army. British colonels and above wear a red collar insignia. Officers's insignia are worn on the shoulder, that for Warrant Officers Class 2 are worn on the lower sleeve, and when in shirt sleeves, as a leather bracelet just like a watch. Senior NCO and junior NCO stripes are worn on the sleeve. In combat dress rank is now shown on a vertical flap on the centre of the chest.

Appendix Five

Battle Honours and Colours

Battle Honours

A Battle Honour is an award granted by the sovereign to a regiment for distinction in a particular battle or campaign, and may be emblazoned on the Regimental Standard, guidon or Colours, and were officially authorised by a Royal Warrant in 1745. The honour may be a town or city where the action took place, such as 'Waterloo' (awarded to fiifteen cavalry and twenty-three infantry regiments), or a country or campaign such as 'Afghanistan 1839' (awarded to two cavalry and four infantry regiments). Awards have been made for sea battles where the infantry have taken an active part, such as 'Copenhagen (1801)' awarded to the Royal Berkshires and Rifle Brigade with the Naval Crown superscribed '2nd April 1801'.

The first Battle Honour (in the sense of a job well done) was awarded by William III, granting the title 'Royal' to the Earl of Granard's Regiment for their bravery at the siege of Namur in 1695. The regiment was redesignated the Royal Regiment of Ireland, which later became the 18th (The Royal Irish Foot) in 1751, and the Royal Irish Regiment during Cardwell's reforms. The regiment was disbanded in 1922. In 1768 a Royal Warrant issued by George III awarded the first Battle Honour (in the modern sense) to the 15th Light Dragoons for distinction in the Seven Years' War at 'Emsdorff' in 1760.

Various committees were set up to make recommendations to the sovereign and the award can be granted at the time of the action or retrospectively going back to the earlier actions such as 'Tangier 1662–1680'. The award may have a date inscribed or may not. In 1882 a committee under General Alison reviewed Battle Honours and its report stated 'The names of such victories only should be retained as either in themselves or by their results have left a mark in history which render their names familiar, not only to the British Army, but also to every educated gentleman.' The term 'victory' was later questioned and corrected and Battle Honours were awarded for actions that were less than victorious, but where gallantry prevailed nonetheless and regiments were rewarded with 'Dunkirk', 'Arnhem', 'Dieppe' and 'Crete'.

In 1909 a similar committee convened to recommend awards for the South African War (1899–1902). It was at this committee that 'Tangier' was recommended after such a long delay. The First World War Battle Honours recognised 163 battles and awards made to 205 regiments. The Second World War granted a total of 633 separate Battle Honours and the Korean War granted sixteen.

Battle Honours may be inscribed on items such as badges or regimental drums, as well as standards (see below). The Border regiment (fourteen), King's Royal Rifle Corps (thirty-six), Rifle Brigade (sixteen), and Royal Green Jackets (sixteen) had selected Battle Honours on their cap badge. Regiments such as Middlesex (Albuhera), Royal Lincolnshire (Egypt), and Northamptonshire (Talavera) all had a single dedicated Battle Honour on their cap badge. Of the cavalry regiments, only the Royal Scots Greys and later the Royal Scots Dragoon Guards continue with Waterloo on their cap badge.

An unusual Battle Honour in the form of music was acquired by the West Yorkshire Regiment when they copied and used very effectively the opposing French regiment's regimental march 'Ça Ira' at the Battle of Famars in 1793. The French heard the music and expecting reinforcements were surprised and beaten when the West Yorkshires marched in. In 1827 the Royal Marines were granted the distinction of a single Battle Honour 'Gibraltar' to appear on their Colours by the Duke of Clarence, together with the cipher GRV in perpetuity, in addition to that of the reigning monarch. The badge of the Globe and Laurel and the motto *Per Mare Per Terram* (By Sea, By Land) was granted at the same time.

Standards, Guidons and Colours

Regiments have always had a flag to represent their unit and act as a rallying point or visual aid in the smoke and chaos of battle. Before the reign of George II, colonels who raised and financed a regiment had their own flags in a multitude of Colours, shapes and sizes. Colonels, lieutenant colonels and even majors carried Colours with the St George Cross in the upper corner. George II in his Royal Warrant of 1743 laid down rules for infantry regiments to carry only two Colours.

The rules stated that the First or King's Colour was to be the great union, and the Second or Regimental Colour was to be the colour of the facing of the regiment, with the great union in the upper canton. In the centre of both Colours was to be the number of the regiment in Roman figures painted in gold within a wreath. The 1743–51 warrants ordered:

> … standards of Horse and Dragoon Guards to be damask embroidered and fringed with gold or silver. The guidons of Dragoons to be of silk, tassels and cords of the whole to be of crimson silk and gold mixed.

Regiments of household cavalry, horse and dragoon guards and the Royal Tank Regiment carried standards which were generally square to oblong, with dragoons, lancers and hussars carrying pointed guidons. The guns act as Colours for the artillery, and the Rifle Brigade by tradition do not have Colours due to their roles as skirmishers who do not wish to advertise their position.

Trooping the Colour is a display of pageantry by troops of the Household Division, held to celebrate the Queen's Official Birthday in June. It involves 1,500 troops of Foot Guards, Household Cavalry and King's Troop Royal Horse Artillery, 500 musicians and 200 horses.

Defending the Colours

The Colours were carried by the most junior officer in a battalion, an ensign (later second lieutenant), who was about 16 years of age, but had a sergeant as an escort as the post was the most dangerous in action. As the Colours represented the regiment, they were a valuable trophy for the enemy. At the Battle of Quatre Bras the 44th Foot's Colours were carried by young Ensign Christie and were under attack:

> A French lancer gallantly charged at the Colours and severely wounded Ensign Christie with his lance which, entering the left eye penetrated to the lower jaw. The Frenchman then endeavoured to seize the standard, but the brave Christie, notwithstanding the agony of his wound, with a presence of mind almost unequalled, flung himself upon it –not to save himself, but to preserve the honour of his regiment.

At Waterloo, Sergeant Lawrence of the 40th Foot was ordered to the Colours in the late afternoon and recorded his experience:

> This was a job I did not at all like; but still I went boldly to work as I could. There had before me that day fourteen sergeants already killed and wounded while in charge of these Colours, with officers in proportion and the staff and Colours were almost cut to pieces.

The infantry were not alone in heroically and defiantly defending their Colours. At Dettingen in 1743, Cornet Richardson was cut with thirty sabre slashes while defending the standard of the 8th Regiment of Horse against the Maison du Roi. The equally damaged standard and lance was presented to Richardson and is now preserved in the Royal United Services Institute. This unique standard is the only preserved example of that era. It is made of crimson damask with a fringe of gold. General Ligonier's crest of a demi lion issuing from a ducal coronet with the motto *Quo Fata Vocant* is on the obverse. The other has his full coat of arms with the regimental Colours worked in gold. A small union three inches square occupies the upper canton.

During the First Aghan War the last stand of the 44th Foot took place at Gandamak with Captain Souter famously standing with the regimental Colours wrapped around him as a waistcoat. The last time the Colours were carried into battle was at Laing's Neck in South Africa in 1881 by the Northamptonshire Regiment.

Amalgamations

In 1922 it was decided that regiments should have no more than twenty-five honours emblazoned on their standard, guidon or Colours, with not more than ten from the Second World War. The recommendation for the Second World War was also ten, with two for the Korean War. However, the amalgamation of regiments meant that the new regiment maintained the honours and traditions of its component regiments. In the 1970s up to forty honours were allowed on each of the Colours.

With the latest amalgamation of regiments finalised in 2008, new Colours were presented to the new regiments. The new regiments held a formation committee to decide on the most appropriate Battle Honours to be emblazoned as representing the honours of the amalgamated regiments. With the latest amalgamation finalising in 2008 new Colours were to be presented to the new regiments. Her Majesty the Queen presented new Colours to the Duke of Lancaster's Regiment on 26 June 2008 and to the Royal Regiment of Scotland on 4 July 2011.

Size

The original 1st Guards Colours in 1684 were 6ft 9in flying and 3in less on the pike. When standardised in 1747 both sovereign's colour and regimental colour for infantry were 6ft 6in by 6ft 2in on a 9ft 10in pike. In 1768 this was reduced to 6ft 6in, in 1855 to 6ft by 5ft 6in, and again in 1858 to 4ft 6in by 4ft. The final size was established in 1868 as 3ft 9in fly by 3ft on the pike.

Exchanging

When the Yorkshire Regiment had to disband its 2nd Battalion (Green Howards) in 2013, as a result of the Strategic Defence and Security Review of 2010, the Regiment decided to merge all three battalions to become two. Thus the 3rd Battalion (Duke of Wellington's) became the 1st Battalion and the 1st Battalion (Prince of Wales's Own) became the new 2nd Battalion with a ceremonial exchanging of Colours at Battlesbury Barracks in Warminster, Wiltshire, on 25 July 2013. The 3rd Battalion laid up their Colours at Halifax Minster on 20 July 2013.

This was possible because all the battalions of the Regiment had the same Colours differentiated only by their battalion number in Roman numerals on the top left corner. The Queen's Colour bears forty-three Battle Honours from both world wars and the same Regimental Colour of the Cross of St George with remaining Battle Honours.

Honorary Colours

The Yorkshire Regiment is unique, in that it carries additional Honorary Colours, both Queen's and Regimental Colours from the 76th Regiment of Foot (Hindoostan) which became the 2nd Battalion The Duke of Wellington's Regiment in 1881 after Cardwell's reforms. The Honorary Colours were awarded to the 76th of Foot for service in India and are now held by the Yorkshire Regiment. The Honorary Colours are rotated between the two regular battalions of the Yorkshire Regiment on a biannual basis. The 76th of Foot was presented the Honorary Colours by the Honourable East India Company in 1809 and the tradition has carried on through the ages and still continues with the Yorkshire Regiment, as the natural heirs and successors.

The Royal Highland Fusiliers, 2nd Battalion Royal Regiment of Scotland also have the distinction of carrying a third Honorary Colour from their antecedent regiment 74th Highland Regiment of Foot, also awarded in India – at Assaye (1803) where every officer was killed and the regiment marched out led by its RSM. The East India Company awarded an third Honorary Colour for its sixteen years in India.

Battle Honours							
From	*To*	*Campaign*	*Battle Honour*	*Cavalry*	*Infantry*	*Where*	*Adversary*
1662	1680	Defence of Tangier	Tangier 1662–80	1	1	North Africa	Moors
1680			Tangier 1680		3	North Africa	Moors
1689	1697	War of the League of Augsburg	Namur 1695 (*with Virtutis Namurcensis Praemium*)		1	Flanders	French
1689	1697		Namur 1695		13	Flanders	French
1702	1715	War of Spanish Succession	Gibraltar 1704–5		8	Gibraltar	Spanish/French
1702	1715		Blenheim (1704)	7	13	Germany	French
1702	1715		Ramillies (1706)	7	15	Flanders	French
1702	1715		Oudenarde (1708)	7	14	Flanders	French
1702	1715		Malplaquet (1709)	7	15	Flanders	French
1740	1748	War of Austrian Succession	Dettingen (1743)	11	15	Germany	French
1751		War in the Carnatic	Arcot		1	India	French
1756	1763	Seven Years' War (India)	Plassey (*with Primus in Indis*)		1	India	French
1756	1763		Plassey (with Royal Tiger) (1757)		2	India	French
1756	1763	Seven Years' War (Canada)	Louisburg (1758)		12	Canada	French
1756	1763		Quebec 1759		7	Canada	French
1756	1763	Seven Years' War (West Indies)	Guadeloupe 1759		8	West Indies	French
1756	1763		Martinique 1762		13	West Indies	French
1756	1763	Seven Years' War (Cuba)	Moro 1762		1	Cuba	Spanish
1756	1763		Havana 1762		15	Cuba	Spanish
1756	1763	Seven Years' War (Europe)	Minden (1759)		6	Germany	French
1756	1763		Emsdorff (1760)	1		Germany	French
1756	1763		Warburg (1760)	12		Germany	French

1756	1763		Belle Isle (1761)		8	Off France	French
1756	1763		Wilhelmstahl (1762)		1	Germany	French
1756	1763	Seven Years' War (India)	Wandiwash (1760)		1	India	French
1756	1763		Pondicherry (1761)		1	India	French
1758		Expedition to Northern Circars	Condore		2	India	French
1759		War in the Carnatic	Masulipatam		1	India	French
1759		Defeat of the Dutch (India)	Badara		1	India	Dutch
1763	1764	Pontiac's Conspiracy	North America 1763–4		2	America	Indians
1764		Against Nawabs of Bengal & Oudh	Buxar		1	India	French
1764			Buxar (with a Royal Tiger)		1	India	French
1767		War in the Carnatic	Amboor		1	India	French
1774		First Rohilla War	Rohilcund 1774		1	India	Indians
1775	1783	War of American Independence	St Lucia 1778		10	West Indies	French
1775	1783		Gibraltar 1779–83 (with Castle & Key and *Montis Insignia Calpe*)		4	Gibraltar	French
1775	1783		Gibraltar 1780–3		1	Gibraltar	French
1776	1782	War in the Carnatic	Guzerat		2	India	Indians
1776	1782		Carnatic		3	India	Indians
1776	1782		Carnatic (with an Elephant)		1	India	Indians
1776	1782		Pondicherry (1778)		1	India	French
1780	1784	Second Mysore War	Sholinghur (1781)		3	India	Indians
1780	1784		Mangalore (1783)		1	India	Indians
1781		Jersey	Jersey 1781 (Militia Honour)		1	Channel Isles	French
1782		Battle of the Saints	Naval Crown '12 April 1782'		1	West Indies	French
1790	1792	Third Mysore War	Nundy Droog (1791)		1	India	Indians

1790	1792		Mysore	1	8	India	Indians
1790	1792		Mysore (with an Elephant)		1	India	Indians
1793	1802	French Revolutionary Wars	Mandora (1801)		2	Egypt	French
1793	1802		Marabout (with Sphinx) (1802)		1	Egypt	French
1793	1802		Egypt (with Sphinx) 1801	2	31	Egypt	French
1793	1802		Pondicherry (1793)		1	India	French
1793	1802		Martinique 1794		10	West Indies	French
1793	1802		St Lucia 1796		2	West Indies	French
1793	1802		Lincelles (1793)		3	France	French
1793	1802		Nieuport (1793)		1	Flanders	French
1793	1802		Villers-en-Cauchies (1794)	1		France	French
1793	1802		Beaumont (1794)	8		Flanders	French
1793	1802		Willems (1794)	11		Flanders	French
1793	1802		Tournai (1794)		3	Flanders	French
1793	1802		Egmont op Zee (1799)	1	8	Holland	French
1793	1802		Naval Crown '1st June 1794'		2	West Indies	French
1793	1802		St Vincent (Naval battle) (1797)		1	West Indies	French
1793	1802		Copenhagen Naval Crown '2nd April 1801'		2	Denmark	Danes
1793	1802	French Revolutionary Wars	Amboyna (1796)		1	Dutch East Indies	Dutch
1793	1802		Banda (1796)		1	Dutch East Indies	Dutch
1793	1802		Ternate (1801)		1	Dutch East Indies	Dutch
1794		Second Rohilla War	Rohilcund		1	India	Indians
1796	1825	India	India		3	India	Indians
1796	1825		India with Royal Tiger		4	India	Indians

1796	1825		Hindoostan	1	4	India	Indians
1796	1825		Hindoostan with Royal Tiger		1	India	Indians
1796	1825		Hindoostan with Elephant		1	India	Indians
1799		Fourth Mysore War	Seringapatam	1	8	India	Indians
1793	1802	French Revolutionary Wars	Fishguard (Militia Honour) (1797)		1	Wales	French
1803	1815	Napoleonic Wars West Indies	St Lucia 1803		2	West Indies	French
1803	1815		Dominica (1805)		1	West Indies	French
1808	1815	Napoleonic Wars Europe	Maida (1806)		7	Italy	French
1803	1815	Napoleonic Wars West Indies	Martinique 1809		9	West Indies	French
1803	1815		Guadeloupe 1810		4	West Indies	French
1803	1805	First Maratha War	Ally Ghur (1803)		1	India	Indians
1803	1805		Delhi 1803		1	India	Indians
1803	1805		Assaye (1803)	1	2	India	Indians
1803	1805		Leswarree (1803)	1	1	India	Indians
1803	1805		Deig (1804)		2	India	Indians
1804		Expedition against the Dutch	Surinam		2	South America	Dutch
1806			Cape of Good Hope		6	South Africa	Dutch
1807		Expedition against the Spanish	Montevideo		4	South America	Spanish
1808	1814	Napoleonic Wars Peninsula	Rolica (1808)		14	Portugal	French
1808	1814		Vimiero (1808)	1	19	Portugal	French
1808	1814		Sahagun (1808)	1		Spain	French
1808	1814		Corunna (1809)		29	Spain	French
1808	1814		Douro (1809)	1	3	Portugal	French
1808	1814		Talavera (1809)	4	17	Spain	French
1808	1814		Busaco (1810)		17	Portugal	French

1808	1814		Barrosa (1811)		7	Spain	French
1808	1814		Fuentes d'Oñoro (1811)	3	17	Spain	French
1808	1814		Albuhera (1811)	3	12	Spain	French
1808	1814		Arroyo dos Molinos (1811)		1	Spain	French
1808	1814		Tarifa (1811)		2	Spain	French
1808	1814		Ciudad Rodrigo (1812)		11	Spain	French
1808	1814		Badajoz (1812)		20	Spain	French
1808	1814		Almaraz (1812)		3	Spain	French
1808	1814		Salamanca (1812)	7	35	Spain	French
1808	1814		Vitoria (1813)	8	41	Spain	French
1808	1814		Pyrenees (1813)	1	38	Spain	French
1808	1814		San Sebastian (1813)		6	Spain	French
1808	1814		Nivelle (1813)		27	Spain	French
1808	1814		Nive (1813)	1	34	Spain	French
1808	1814		Orthez (1814)	3	37	Spain	French
1808	1814		Toulouse (1814)	4	27	France	French
1808	1814		Peninsula	20	66	Spain/Portugal	French
1809		Persian Gulf	Arabia		1	Persian Gulf	Pirates
1810		Napoleonic Wars Asia	Bourbon (now Reunion)		2	Indian Ocean	French
1810			Amboyna		1	Dutch East Indies	Dutch
1810			Banda		1	Dutch East Indies	Dutch
1810			Ternate		1	Dutch East Indies	Dutch
1811			Java		5	Dutch East Indies	Dutch
1812	1815	War of 1812	Detroit (1812)		1	USA	Americans
1812	1815		Queenstown (1812)		2	USA	Americans

1812	1815		Miami (1813)		1	USA	Americans
1812	1815		Niagara (1813)	1	7	USA	Americans
1812	1815		Bladensburg (1814)		4	USA	Americans
1815		Waterloo Campaign	Waterloo	15	23	Belgium	French
1817	1819	Second Maratha and Pindari War	Kirkee (1817)		1	India	Indians
1817	1819		Nagpore (1817)		1	India	Indians
1817	1819		Maharajpore (1817)		2	India	Indians
1819	1821	Against Pirates	Beni Boo Ali (1821)		1	Persian Gulf	Pirates
1824	1826	First Burma War	Ava (1824)		11	Burma	Burmese
1826		Revolt of Rajah of Bhurtpore	Bhurtpore	2	4	India	Indians
1835		Sixth Kaffir War	South Africa 1835		3	South Africa	Kaffirs
1839		Expedition to Aden	Aden		1	Arabia	Arabs
1838	1842	First Afghan War	Ghuznee (1839)	2	4	Afghanistan	Afghans
1838	1842		Khelat (1839)		2	Afghanistan	Afghans
1838	1842		Jalalabad (with Mural Crown)		1	Afghanistan	Afghans
1838	1842		Kandahar 1842	1	5	Afghanistan	Afghans
1838	1842		Ghuznee 1842		2	Afghanistan	Afghans
1838	1842		Kabul 1842		2	Afghanistan	Afghans
1838	1842		Afghanistan 1839	2	4	Afghanistan	Afghans
1839	1842	First Chinese War (Opium War)	China (with Dragon)		5	China	Chinese
1843		Conquest of Scinde	Meeanee		1	India	Indians
1843			Hyderabad		1	India	Indians
1843			Scinde		1	India	Indians
1843		Gwalior Campaign	Maharajpore	1	2	India	Indians

1843			Punniar	1	2	India	Indians
1845	1846	First Sikh War (Punjab)	Moodkee (1845)	1	4	India	Sikhs
1845	1846	First Sikh War	Ferozeshah (1845)	1	7	India	Sikhs
1845	1846		Aliwal (1846)	1	3	India	Sikhs
1845	1846		Sobraon (1846)	3	10	India	Sikhs
1846	1847	Seventh Kaffir War	South Africa 1846–7	1	7	South Africa	Gaikas
1846	1847	First Maori War	New Zealand		3	New Zealand	Maoris
1848	1849	Second Sikh War (Punjab)	Multan (1849)		4	India	Sikhs
1848	1849	Second Sikh War	Chillianwala (1849)	3	9	India	Sikhs
1845	1846		Gujerat (1849)	3	4	India	Sikhs
1848	1849		Punjab	3	10	India	Sikhs
1851	1853	Eight Kaffir War	South Africa 1851–3	1	9	South Africa	Gaikas
1851	1853	Second Burma War	Pegu (1852)		5	Burma	Burmese
1854	1856	Crimean War	Alma (1854)	5	29	Crimea	Russians
1854	1856		Balaclava (1854)	10	1	Crimea	Russians
1854	1856		Inkerman (1854)	5	27	Crimea	Russians
1854	1856		Sevastopol	14	49	Crimea	Russians
1856	1857	Persian War	Reshire (1856)		2	Persia	Persians
1856	1857		Bushire (1856)		2	Persia	Persians
1856	1857		Koosh-ab (1857)		3	Persia	Persians
1856	1857		Persia	1	3	Persia	Persians
1857	1860	Second Chinese War	Canton (1857)		1	China	Chinese
1857	1860		Taku Forts (1860)	1	7	China	Chinese
1857	1860		Peking 1860	1	5	China	Chinese
1857	1858	Indian Mutiny	Delhi 1857	2	7	India	Indians

1857	1858		Lucknow (for Defence) (1857)		7	India	Indians
1857	1858		Lucknow (for Relief) (1857)	1	8	India	Indians
1857	1858		Lucknow (for Capture) (1858)	3	17	India	Indians
1857	1858		Central India	4	9	India	Indians
1860	1861	Second Maori War	New Zealand		5	New Zealand	Maoris
1863	1866	Third Maori War	New Zealand		7	New Zealand	Maoris
1867	1868	Abyssinian War	Abyssinia	1	4	Abyssinia	Abyssinians
1873	1874	Ashantl War	Ashanti		3	Gold Coast	Ashantis
1877	1879	Zulu and Basutu Wars	South Africa 1877–9		3	South Africa	Zulus
1877	1879		South Africa 1878–9		2	South Africa	Zulus
1877	1879		South Africa 1879	2	8	South Africa	Zulus
1878	1880	Second Afghan War	Ali Masjid (1878)	1	4	Afghanistan	Afghans
1878	1880		Peiwar Kotal (1878)		2	Afghanistan	Afghans
1878	1880		Charasiah (1879)	1	3	Afghanistan	Afghans
1878	1880		Kabul 1879	1	5	Afghanistan	Afghans
1878	1880		Ahmed Khel (1880)		2	Afghanistan	Afghans
1878	1880		Kandahar 1880	1	6	Afghanistan	Afghans
1878	1880		Afhanistan 1878–9	1	4	Afghanistan	Afghans
1878	1880		Afghanistan 1878–80	2	11	Afghanistan	Afghans
1878	1880		Afghanistan 1879–80	2	10	Afghanistan	Afghans
1882		Revolt of Arabi Pasha	Tel-el-Kebir	6	13	Egypt	Egyptians
1882	1885	First Sudan War	Egypt 1882	5	16	Egypt	Egyptians
1882	1885		Egypt 1882–4	1	5	Egypt	Egyptians
1882	1885		Egypt 1884	1		Egypt	Egyptians
1885		Egyptian Campaign (Sudan)	Abu Klea	1	1	Sudan	Sudanese

1885			Tofrek		1	Sudan	Sudanese
1885			Kirbekan		2	Sudan	Sudanese
1885			Nile 1884–5	1	9	Sudan	Sudanese
1885			Suakin 1885	2	6	Sudan	Sudanese
1885	1887	Third Burma War	Burma 1885–7		11	Burma	Burmese
1895		Chitral Campaign	Chitral		7	North West Frontier	Indians
1896	1898	Reconquest of the Sudan	Hafir (1896)		1	Sudan	Sudanese
1896	1898		Atbara (1898)		4	Sudan	Sudanese
1896	1898		Khartoum (1898)	1	8	Sudan	Sudanese
1897	1898	Tirah Campaign NW Frontier	Tirah		9	North West Frontier	Afridis
1899	1902	Second Boer War	Modder River (1899)	1	9	South Africa	Boers
1899	1902		Defence of Kimberley (1900)		1	South Africa	Boers
1899	1902		Relief of Kimberley (1900)	8	7	South Africa	Boers
1899	1902		Paardeburg (1900)	8	17	South Africa	Boers
1899	1902		Defence of Ladysmith (1899–1900)	4	8	South Africa	Boers
1899	1902		Relief of Ladysmith (1900)	3	23	South Africa	Boers
1899	1902		South Africa 1899–1902	25	73	South Africa	Boers
1900		Boxer Rebellion	Peking 1900		1	China	Chinese

Dates in parentheses are the dates of the battle. Dates without parentheses are emblazoned on the honour.

Appendix Six

Antecedents of Current Regiments

	Battalions	Antecedent Regiments
Scottish Division		
1. Royal Regiment of Scotland	4	14
Cameronians disbanded		2
Queen's Division		
2. Princess of Wales's Royal Regiment	2	12
3. Royal Regiment of Fusiliers	1	4
4. Royal Anglian	2	9
King's Division		
5. Duke of Lancaster's	2	12
6. Yorkshire	2	5
Yorks and Lancs disbanded		2
Prince of Wales's Division		
7. Mercian	3	9
8. Royal Welsh	2	4
9. Royal Irish	1	6
Disbanded Irish Regiments 1922		9
Light Division		
10. The Rifles	5	21
No Division		
11. Royal Irish	1	6
Disbanded Irish Regiments 1922		9
Total	22	109

Pre-Cardwell (109 regiments of foot and the Rifle Brigade): 110. From Cardwell's 110 regiments with 141 battalions, amalgamations have reduced the number to ten with twenty-two battalions.

	Regiment	Antecedent Regiments
1.	Household Cavalry	4
2.	1st Queen's Dragoon Guards	2
3.	Royal Scots Dragoon Guards	3
4.	Royal Dragoon Guards	4
5.	Queen's Royal Hussars	4
6.	Royal Lancers	6
7.	King's Royal Hussars	4
8.	Light Dragoons	4
	Total	31
	Royal Tank Regiment	8

Appendix Seven

Decline of the Regiments

CAVALRY							
Regiments	1795	1815	1922	1959 to 1962	1969 to 1971	1991 to 1993	2015
Household	3	3	2	2	2	1	1
Dragoon Guards	7	7	5	4	4	3	3
Dragoons	14	6	2	2	Nil	Nil	Nil
Hussars	Nil	4	9	7	6	2	2
Light Dragoons	19	15	Nil	Nil	Nil	1	1
Lancers	Nil	Nil	4	3	3	2	1
Total Cavalry	43	35	22	18	15	9	8
Royal Tank Regiment	Nil	Nil	6	5	4	2	1
Total number of regiments	43	35	28	23	19	11	9

INFANTRY																	
Cardwell 1881					By 1948			1957 to 1962		1962 to 1970		1991 to 1994		2004 to 2007		2014	
	Before		After														
Foot	Regiments	Battalions	Regiments	Battalions		Regiments	Battalions	Regiments	Battalions	Regiments	Battalions	Regiments	Battalions	Regiments	Battalions	Regiments	Battalions
1st to 25th	25	50	25	50	Guards	5	8	5	8	5	8	5	5	5	5	5	5
26th to 109th	82	82	41	82	Line	64	64	49	49	28	39	25	30	10	27	10	22
79th	1	1	1	1	Gurkha	4	8	4	8	4	5	1	2	1	2	1	2
Rifle Bgde	1	4	1	4	Parachute	1	3	1	3	1	3	1	3	1	3	1	3
60th	1	4	1	4													
Total Line	110	141	69	141	Total	74	83	59	68	38	55	32	40	17	37	17	32
	Five Irish Regiments disbanded in 1922 reducing line regiments from sixty-nine to sixty-four				Manpower	330,000		200,000		160,000		118,000		101,000		82,000	
														Army Reserve		30,000	
														ARMY 2020		112,000	

Appendix Eight

Political and Military Control

(Defence Ministers and Defence & Army Chiefs from the Ministry of Defence Formed in 1964)

Chiefs of the Imperial General Staff					
	General or Field Marshal		General or Field Marshal		General or Field Marshal
1909	Gen Sir W. Nicholson	1922	Gen The Earl of Cavan	1940	Gen Sir John Dill
1912	Gen Sir John French	1926	Gen Sir G. Milne	1941	Gen Sir Alan Brooke
1914	Gen Sir C. Douglas	1933	Gen Sir A. Montgomery-Massingberd	1946	F.M. Viscount Montgomery
1914	Gen Sir A. Murray			1948	F.M. Sir William Slim
1915	Gen Sir A. Murray	1936	Gen Sir Cyril Deverell	1952	Gen Sir John Harding
1915	Gen Sir William Robertson	1937	Lt Gen Viscount Gort	1955	Gen Sir Gerald Templer
1918	Gen Sir Henry Wilson	1939	Gen Sir Edmund Ironside	1958	Gen Sir Francis Festing
				1961	Gen Sir Richard Hull

Chiefs of the General Staff (ARMY)					
1964	Gen Sir Richard Hull	1979	Gen Sir Edwin Brammall	1997	Gen Sir Roger Wheeler
1965	Gen Sir James Cassells	1982	Gen Sir John Stannier	2000	Gen Sir Michael Walker
1968	Gen Sir Geoffrey Baker	1985	Gen Sir Nigel Bagnall	2003	Gen Sir Michael Jackson
1971	Gen Sir Michael Carver	1989	Gen Sir John Chapple	2006	Gen Sir Richard Dannatt
1973	Gen Sir Peter Hunt	1992	Gen Sir Peter Inge	2009	Gen Sir David Richards
1976	Gen Sir Roland Gibbs	1994	Gen Sir Charles Guthrie	2010	Gen Sir Peter Wall
				2014	Gen Sir Nick Carter

Secretaries of State for Defence					
1964	Peter Thonycroft	C	1992	Macolm Rifkind	C
1964	Dennis Healey	L	1995	Michael Portillo	C
1970	Lord Carrington	C	1997	George Robinson	L

1974	Ian Gilmore	C	1999	Geoff Hoon	L
1974	Roy Mason	L	2005	John Reid	L
1976	Fred Mullery	L	2006	Des Browne	L
1979	Francis Pym	C	2008	John Hutton	L
1981	John Nott	C	2009	Bob Ainsworth	L
1983	Michael Heseltine	C	2010	Liam Fox	C
1986	Georger Younger	C	2011	Philip Hammond	C
1989	Tom King	C	2014	Michael Fallon	C

L = Labour C = Conservative

On 1 April 1964 the three services were combined into a single Ministry of Defence (MoD) with Chiefs of the Defence Staff rotating from each service.

		Royal Navy	Army	RAF
		Admiral of the Fleet	**Field Marshal**	**Marshal of the RAF**
1	1956			Sir William Dickson
2	1959	Earl Mountbatten		
3	1965		Sir Richard Hull	
4	1967			Sir Charles Elworthy
5	1971	Sir Peter Hill-Norton		
6	1973		Sir Michael Carver	
7	1976			Sir Andrew Humphrey
8	1977	Sir Edward Ashmore		
9	1977			SIr Neil Cameron
10	1979	Sir Terence Lewin		
11	1982		Sir Edwin Brammall	
12	1985	Sir John Fieldhouse		
13	1988			Sir David Craig
14	1991		Sir Richard Vincent	
15	1992			Sir Peter Harding
16	1994		Sir Peter Inge	
		Admiral	**General**	**Air Chief Marshal**
17	1997		Sir Charles Guthrie	
18	2001	Sir Michael Boyce		
19	2003		Sir Michael Walker	
20	2006			Sir Jock Stirrup
21	2010		Sir David Richards	
22	2013		Sir Nick Houghton	
23	2016			Sir Stuart Peach

Appendix Nine

Army Regiments Order of Precedence

	Regiment	Badge	Official Abbreviations	Notes	Badge Description
	Household Cavalry				
1	Life Guards				Royal cipher within a circle bearing the title ensigned with a crown
	Blues & Royals				Royal cipher within a circle bearing the title ensigned with a crown
2	Royal Horse Artillery			1793	Royal cipher within a circle with motto ensigned with a crown
	Royal Armoured Corps (Cavalry)				
3	1st Queen's Dragoon Guards				Double-headed eagle from the arms of the Emperor Franz Joseph I of Austria

4	Royal Scots Dragoon Guards				On crossed carbines, the Eagle of the French 45th Inf Reg upon a tablet Waterloo
5	Royal Dragoon Guards				Upon the star of the Order of St Patrick a circle with the castle of Enniskillen and date of amalgamation
6	Queen's Royal Hussars				The monogram QO reversed and interlaced beneath an angel harp all ensigned with a crown
7	Royal Lancers				Skull and crossbones above the motto 'Or Glory' upon a pair of crossed lancers
8	King's Royal Hussars				A Prussian Eagle in honour of Fredrica Princess Royal of Prussia Letters FR
9	Light Dragoons				A Maltese cross behind a circled wreath ensigned with the Royal Crest
10	Royal Tank Regiment				Within a laurel wreath a tank ensigned with a crown
11	Royal Artillery			1716 separated from Ordnance	A canon with a motto above and below ensigned with a crown
12	Royal Engineers			1716 separated from Ordnance	The Royal cipher within the Garter and motto all enclosed with a laurel and ensigned with a crown

13	Royal Signals			1920	A figure of Mercury holding a caduceus with crown above
	Infantry				
14	Grenadier Guards				A grenade
15	Coldstream Guards				A variant of the Order of the Garter
16	Scots Guards				The star of the Order of the Thistle with motto
17	Irish Guards				The star of the Order of St Patrick with motto and foundation date
18	Welsh Guards				A leek
19	Royal Regiment of Scotland		SCOTS		Saltire & lion rampant with a Scottish crown
20	Princess of Wales's Royal Regiment				Plume and coronet of Prince of Price of Wales, Tuder Dragon, Hampshire Rose within a Garter
21	Duke of Lancasters Regiment		LANCS		Double red rose within a laurel ensigned with a crown

22	Royal Regiment of Fusiliers				A grenade with, on the base St George & dragon within a wreath ensigned with a crown
23	Royal Anglian Regiment				Eight-pointed star upon which is the castle and key of Gibraltar
24	Yorkshire Regiment		YORKS		A double white rose on top of the crest of the Duke of Wellington
25	Mercian regiment		MERCIAN		Taken from the Mercian brigade badge. A Saxon crown above a double headed eagle
26	Royal Welsh Regiment				Plume and crown of the Prince of Wales
27	Royal Irish Regiment				Angel harp ensigned within a crown
28	Parachute Regiment				Within a pair of wings an open parachute ensigned with the Royal Crest
29	Royal Gurkha Rifles				A pair of Kukris ensigned with a crown
	Queen's Gurkha Engineers				
	The Queen's Gurkha Signals				

	Queen's Own Gurkha Logistic Regiment				
	Gurkha Staff and Personnel Support Branch				
30	Rifles Regiment		RIFLES		Stringed bugle-horn ensigned with a crown
31	Army Air Corps			1957 (Wartime disbanded 1950)	A laurel wreath summounted by a crown and within the wreath an eagle
32	Royal Army Chaplain's Department, Christian			1796	A Maltese Cross upon a circle enclosing a quatre foil all within wreath ensigned with a crown
	Royal Army Chaplain's Department, Jewish				The Star of David enclosing a quatrefoil all within a wreath and ensigned with a crown
33	Royal Logistic Corps			1993: From Corps of Transport, Ordnance, Pioneers & Catering	Eight-pointed star ensigned with a crown and upon the star a wreath. Within the star there is a Garter with arms of ordnance and motto
34	Royal Army Medical Corps			1660 Restoration of Standing Army	The rod of aesculopius and serpent within a laurel wreath ensigned with a crown
35	Royal Electrical & Mechanical Engineers			1942	Upon a lightning flash a rearing horse with a coronet collar of Fleur-de-lys a chain over its back standing on a globe

36	Adjutant General's Corps			1992: From the Corps of Pay, Military Police, Military Provost, Educational & Legal	
	Staff & Personnel Support				A laurel wreath with the Royal Crest within and all ensigned with a crown
	Military Provost Staff Corps				A Royal cipher ensigned with a crown above
	Corps of Royal Military Police				The Royal cipher within a laurel wreath ensigned with a crown
	Military Provost Guard Service				Crossed keys behind a Royal Crest
	Educational & Training Services				A fluted flambeau and upon it a crown
	Army Legal Services				Behind crossed swords, a globe and figure of Justice with a Royal Crest
37	Royal Army Veterinary Corps			1796	Figure of Chiron the centaur within a laurel wreath and ensigned with a crown
38	Small Arms School Corps			1854	Crossed rifles and Vickers machine gun surmounted by a crown and surrounded by a laurel wreath

39	Royal Army Dental Corps			Officially 1921	Within a laurel wreath a dragon's head and sword ensigned with a crown below a motto
40	Intelligence Corps			1914	Rose with two laurel leaves ensigned with a crown
41	Royal Army Physical Training Corps			1860	Crossed sabres surmounted by a crown
42	Queen Alexandra's Royal Army Nursing Corps			1866	The cipher of Queen Alexandra upon the Danish Cross all within a laurel wreath and ensigned with a crown
43	Corps of Army Music			Officially 1994	A stringed lyre within a wreath of oak leaves ensigned with a crown
44	77th Brigade (Chindits)				Chinthe the mythical lion that guards Burmese temples
45	Army Reserve (Royal Armoured Corps)				
	Royal Yeomanry				Cipher of Princess Alexandra surmounted by her coronet
	Queen's Own Yeomanry				Vixen
	Scottish and North Irish Yeomanry				Wolf's head in front of crossed lances

	Royal Wessex Yeomanry				Dragon within a garter containing a motto ensigned with Earl of Wessex coronet
46	Army Reserve (Infantry)				
	Honourable Artillery Company			Formed 1537. Oldest military unit in the British Army (possibly the world) of Company strength and has a ceremonial role at Guildhall	Grenade
	London Regiment				St George's shield on a portcullis within a circle
	Royal Marines				The globe (Eastern hemisphere) within a laurel wreath surmounted by the Royal Crest (US Marines have the western hemishere)

Although the Royal Marines (formed in 1664) are administered by the Royal Navy and not formally part of the army structure, their Order of Precedence is after the Princes of Wales's Royal Regiment because the regiment lost its seniority when it disbanded in 1685.

When regiments amalgamate every effort is made to include the cap badges of forebear regiments but the Princess of Wales's Royal Regiment made a particular effort to include the plume (ostrich plume), worn by the Black Prince at the Battle of Crécy (Middlesex) and Tudor dragon (Buffs) all within a Garter (Royal Sussex) from the Queen's Regiment, with the addition of the Hampshire rose (Royal Hampshire), as worn by the trained bands who fought for Henry V at the Battle of Agincourt.

Bibliography

Adams, Henry and Patricia, *History of the British Regular Army 1660–1990* (Chippenham:Rowe, 1990)

Ascoli, D., *Companion to the British Army, 1660–1983* (London: Harrap, 1983)

Asprey, R., *The Rise and Fall of Napoleon Bonaparte*,Vol. II (London: Abacas, 2002)

Barthorp, M., *British Infantry Uniforms Since 1660* (Dorset: Blandford Press, 1982)

Billìere de la, General Sir Peter, *Supreme Courage* (London: Little Brown & Company, 2004)

Caffrey, K., *The Lion and the Union: The Anglo American War, 1812–1815* (London: André Deutsch, 1978)

Castleden, R., *British History* (London: Parragon, 1994)

Chant, C., *Handbook of British Regiments* (Oxford: Routledge, 1988)

Cooper, Leonard, *British Regular Cavalry 1644–1914* (London: Chapman and Hall, 1965)

Crew, Bob, *Gurkhas at War* (London: Metro Publishing Ltd, 2004)

David, Saul, *The Indian Mutiny 1857* (London:Viking/Penguin, 2002)

David, Saul, *Victoria's Wars: The Rise of Empire* (London:Viking, 2006)

Franklin, Carl, *British Napoleonic Uniforms: The First Complete Guide to Uniforms, Facings and Lace* (Stroud: The History Press, 2009)

Gander, T.J., *Infantry of the Line* (Surrey: Ian Allan Ltd, 1988)

Gardner, B., *African Dream* (London: Cassell, 1970

Glover, M., *Warfare from Waterloo to Mons* (London: Book Club, 1980)

Glover, M., *Wellington as Military Commander* (London: Sphere Books, 1973)

Hallows, I., *Regiments and Corps of the British Army* (London: Arms and Armour Press, 1991)

Heathcote, T.A., *The Afghan Wars 1839–1919* (Staplehurst: Spellmount, 2003)

Hibbert, C., *Redcoats and Rebels: The War for America 1770–1781* (London: Grafton, 1990)

Holmes, R., *Wellington: The Iron Duke* (London: Harper Collins, 2002)

Lawrence, James, *Raj* (London: Little Brown & Company, 1997)

Lawson, Cecil C.P., *A History of the Uniforms of the British Army*, Vol. I and II (London: Norman Military Publications, 1962/3)

Liddell, Hart, *The Letters of Private Wheeler 1809–1828* (Gloucester: Windrush Press, 1999)

Keegan, J., *The Face of Battle* (London: Barrie and Jenkins, 1988)

Keegan, J., and Wheatcroft, A., *Who's Who in Military History* (Leicestershire: Bookmart, 1991)

King, M., *History of New Zealand* (London: Penguin, 2003)

Mason, P., *The Men Who Ruled India* (London: Jonathan Cape Ltd, 1985)

Morris, D.R., *The Washing of the Spears* (London: Sphere Books, 1978)

Moulton, J.L., *The Royal Marines* (London: Sphere Books, 1973)

Pakenham, T., *The Boer War* (London: Abacus, Little Brown & Company, 1994)

Parker, J., *The Gurkhas* (London: Headline Book Publishing, 2005)

Perigoli, U., *1815 the Armies at Waterloo* (London: Sphere Books, 1973)

Riehn, R.K., *The French Imperial Army* (Somerset: AA Johnson Military Books, 1984)

Saunders, H., St George, *The Red Beret, The Green Beret* (two volumes) (London: New English Library, 1978)

Schulze, C., 'The Gurkhas', *Europa Militaria No. 31* (Wiltshire: The Crowood Press Ltd, 2003)

Siborne, W., *History of the Waterloo Campaign* (Napoleonic Library) (London: Greenhill Books, 1990)

Smith, E.D., *Valour: A History of the Gurkhas* (Stroud: Spellmount, 2007)

Thompson, J., *Call to Arms: Great Military Speeches* (London: Quercus, 2009)

Thompson, J., *The Royal Marines* (London: Macmillan, 2000)

Travis III, Hanes W. and Sanello F., *The Opium Wars* (London: Robson Books, 2003)

Ulyatt, K., *Hussars of the Napoleonic Wars* (London: Macdonald, 1981)

Westlake, R., *English and Welsh Infantry Regiments* (Kent: Spellmount, 1995)

Wilkinson, F., *Badges of the British Army 1820–1960* (London: Arms and Armour Press, 1972)

Woodham-Smith, C., *The Reason Why* (Middlesex: Penguin Books, 1968)

Index

Note: unfortunately, it is impossible to index regiments individually in the following pages for reasons of space and the author and publishers hope that this does not inconvenience the reader unduly.